What others are saying about this ⌐⌐

"I now know, in the depths of my being, that true spiritual freedom is possible in this lifetime because of the teachings brought to life in this book. Do your Soul the biggest favor imaginable and read THIS book. "
-C.G.B. Wilmington, NC.

"Stirs my Self-Soul with Vistas beyond what I previously could imagine...Thank you for this true road map back to Divine Source!!"
-D.J., Pacific NW, USA

"I have listened to the audio chapters over and over...I loved them! The book is beautifully written and conveyed in a way that is incredibly fantastic, surreal and yet real. Whilst reading the words there was only one thing on my mind: I'm soooooo happy I have found the true path!"
-Shaney, New Zealand

"This book is filled with possibilities to experience the happiness and love I think we all dream of as Souls. Sometimes the Author's experiences are so vivid and colorfully described, it felt like jumping right into a profoundly moving story and participating. I feel blessed, having been guided both to this book and its Authors.
-Randi A.F. Hult, France

THOUSANDS OF VISITS
TO
HEAVEN
AND THE HEART OF
GOD

"THE MOST PROFOUND, VIVIDLY DETAILED OUT OF BODY DISCOVERIES YET!"

THE HURAY GALACTICA

By Heather Giamboi & Allen Feldman

First Edition

An Out of Body Journey into The Heaven Realms of God

The Exciting Story of How Two Individuals Used Out-of-Body Travel to Experience the Pure Positive God Worlds beyond Matter, Energy, Time, Space and Mind; and How You Can Too! One of the most mind blowing books on Spirituality ever written!

iii

DIRECT

PATH   Direct Path Publishing, Roseville, California

Thousands of Visits to Heaven and the Heart of God, "The Most Profound, Vividly Detailed Out of Body Discoveries Yet!" The HURAY Galactica
Copyright © 2014-2015 by Heather Giamboi and Allen Feldman.
All Rights Reserved.
Published in the United States by:
Direct Path Publishing
1911 Douglas Blvd. #85-165
Roseville, CA 95661
www.DirectPathPublishing.com

ISBN-10: 0-9969073-0-0
ISBN-13: 978-0-9969073-0-9

Thousands of Visits to Heaven and The Heart of God, The HURAY Galactica. 1. Out-of-Body Experiences 2. Heaven. 3. Astral Projection 4. Self Realization and God Realization 5. Meditation and Spirituality

DEDICATION

This book is dedicated to . . .

Those who desire Truth above all else and are willing to let go of anything that stands in the way of finding Truth.

Those who desire God more than life itself and know in their heart of hearts that God is here and now and can be experienced here and now!

Those who cry out in the middle of the night to return to the God Head and know that this physical life is but an illusion compared to the splendor of the Pure Positive God Worlds of Heaven.

Those who are not amused by the magic tricks and glitter of Religions, Metaphysics, Psychic Phenomena, Science, Philosophy and Materialism and sincerely cry out for the true Spiritual Traveler to guide them to their own inner answers and experience.

The Order of the Bourchakoun (The true VARDAN Masters) who work tirelessly to help Souls find Self and God Realization in this lifetime.

CONTENTS

I
INTRODUCTION

For over 19 years I have had thousands of near death like out-of-body experiences. My husband Allen who helped write this book has also had thousands of them over the last 30 years. I truly believe with the proper methods almost anyone can do the same.

"I lay as I usually do in bed and closed my eyes. I began a spiritual exercise; as I relaxed more deeply the subtle sensation of numbness flowed through my legs and body until a calm serenity set in. I was drawn up out of my body and appeared in a beautiful world of white light tinged with a subtle purple hue shimmering through the ethers."

"And I heard a sound almost like that of millions of tiny crystal chimes that made a high pitched shimmering sound. This was one of the lower heavens called the Etheric Plane. The sound swept through the bright field of light. And within I saw Lai Tsi, a VARDAN Master from ancient China who had a long white beard and was wearing a long white robe. Lai Tsi seemed to hover about with a silvery white light about him glowing brightly..."

"I then noticed that a great beam of light shown from the top of his head and from the sleeves from his arms, both of which reminded me of a spot light. And then he did something which surprised me, as he moved his arms with these great beams of light in a circular motion. This created a sort of, what seemed to me like a portal of light, an inter-dimensional window he cut into a world that was far brighter.

It was essentially that Lai Tsi the Great Ancient VARDAN Master opened up a doorway and was letting me peer far beyond this lower heaven of the Etheric Plane and into the Pure Positive God Worlds. The light was far brighter and the sound of a higher octave. And then in the next moment I saw a flash of an image of myself in a previous life, in what some people call reincarnation. In this previous life I was a student of Lai Tsi in Ancient China. I had black hair and a long black mustache. I lived in a gorgeous pristine land of green rolling hills and crystal clear waters."

"I watched from a distance as in that life time I went into spiritual contemplation sitting with legs crossed on the wooden floor. The sound shifted in fineness becoming quieter, softer, and of a higher pitch. My body was on Earth but my spirit was in heaven. Through out-of-body travel I suddenly shifted into a state of being surrounded by the most unimaginably intense, brilliant white light, like sitting in the center of a glowing star."

"I had a sense of knowingness that this was deep into the Pure Positive God Worlds. On the inner planes it became my permanent home. So intense was this light that it was beyond any human description. In the midst of this I heard, "One of the false teachings of religions is the idea that we must wait for an afterworld to know the heavenly worlds of God. This is a mistake because it is through these worlds that we can learn of our spiritual purpose and the nature of the vast spiritual worlds.""

This is the extraordinary journey of two individuals who have had countless near death like experiences of indescribable light filled heavens. It had all began when we were both taken under the wing of a Spiritual Traveler: Rebazar Tarzs, an expert in the Science of Out-of- Body Tuza Travel. Tuza meaning Soul.

This book came out of our personal spiritual experiences to heavens and universes, some familiar and some largely unknown. Many people have had near death experiences in spiritual realms and have come back to share them.

We have shared some of our literally thousands of heavenly experiences of what we saw after meeting the Spiritual Travelers of VARDANKAR, the Ancient Science of Out-of-Body Tuza (Soul) Travel. The only purpose of sharing all of this is for the individual to return to HURAY (God).

Not unlike Robert Frost's, *The Road Less Traveled By*, it is not for the masses of people but for the rare, brave individual who wishes to return to God. The path, techniques and experiences contained herein are (not) psychology, religion, new age group, politics, or philosophy of any kind but instead it is an applied Science who's only purpose is for the individual to return to God and become a conscious coworker with IT.

In my late thirties, after two decades of success in out-of-body travel to light filled spiritual planes (heavens) I made a fantastic break through. When my desire for God become much stronger, not so coincidentally Allen and I suddenly met a Spiritual Traveler who is an expert and Master in the ancient science of out-of-body travel to heavenly realms.

Initially my husband and I became his students and as a result made fantastic discoveries of understanding by shifting to experiences at an entirely different level of heavenly worlds and universes, like the many in this book. We then experienced what the Spiritual Travelers call the Pure Positive God Worlds of total awareness.

What is a little known understanding and even a great and

13

ancient secret is that there are two very different, distinct levels of heavens or universes. In the lower levels of heaven called the lower worlds, the mesmerizing and blazing light of the mid to upper Astral Plane is so incredible and heavenly that most who have near death experiences mistake this region for the ultimate.

Near death experiences that almost always occur in the lower heavens (Astral, Causal, Mental and Etheric Planes) of time and space are illusionary mirages compared to the indescribable Pure Positive God Worlds that lay beyond them. *(See God Worlds Chart in Appendix I) These worlds have no duality of dark and light, good and evil (like the Astral and Mental heavens do). They contain no matter but instead are composed of pure Spirit and incredible light and sound that make the lower worlds look like dark caves. It is necessary to explain this so that the reader has insight more clear like glass in visiting the various universes touched upon in this book.

The divine love that is experienced in these higher worlds is indescribable beyond the comprehension of the mind. The Love, Wisdom, Power and incredible Freedom experienced in these Pure Positive God Worlds is much, much greater then what is described in the many popular books on near death experiences such as *"Embraced by the Light"* by Betty Eadie. Unlike the beautiful heavens described in this and many other books, the Pure Positive God Worlds are the heavens far beyond duality and M.E.S.T (Matter, Energy, Space and Time). The mind is simply too dense and limited to enter these worlds. They begin from the fifth plane (not to be confused with what some groups call the 5th dimension). The 5th plane, also called the Soul Plane, is the plane of Self Realization. Then we move on up through various heavens until we reach the 10th plane, called the Anami Lok, which is truly beyond description and is the plane where Soul finds

14

true God Realization. There are countless levels above this.

Many of those experiences chronicled in near death experience books center on the 2nd through 4th planes (Astral, Causal and Mental Planes). Perhaps you can see how easy it would be for a Soul to falsely think it has reached a high, high level upon coming in contact with such heavenly worlds of apparent splendor?

Unknown to some we are not our physical bodies but a spiritual essence or spark of God and our true God self-Soul takes on various bodies in these lower worlds of time, space and duality. In these lower worlds we cannot have light without darkness, love without hate and Soul must take on a mind or mental body to act as a thin sheath in order to interact with the course vibrations of these worlds of duality.

This is much like a Deep Sea Diver must wear a diving suite to protect him from the enormous pressures of the ocean above him.

Without these bodies Soul simply cannot interact with the gross vibrations of the lower worlds of time and space. But these worlds were never intended to be Soul's permanent home; only a school ground to train Souls to become conscious coworkers with God.

Soul also must take on an astral or emotional body and of course a physical body. In the Pure Positive God Worlds Soul finds itself unencumbered and free of all negativity and bodies!

Continuing with our story beyond this world…Allen and I began an unexpected quest and to our great surprise and shock we found ourselves stepping away from preconceptions of reality within our old new-age religion.

This was the very change which allowed the VARDAN, Divine Spirit, to steer the ship of Soul more fully so that finally my husband and I shifted from feeling like prisoners in the lower Worlds, which are again lower worlds of M.E.S.T. matter, energy, time, space and reincarnation, to instead becoming established in indescribable universes of Total Awareness: the Pure Positive God Worlds of indescribable light, sound and pure Spirit.

Initially you come to these pure heavens as a visitor but with the proper instruction you become a permanent resident in the God Worlds and hence you become perhaps for the first time in eons spiritually free! Except of course to serve; you no longer have to reincarnate in the worlds of time and space! You become a free agent, a conscious awakened coworker with the HURAY, God throughout eternity.

The excitement of those lower heavens that many experience is, for the adventurous at heart, just the exciting beginning! With practice and instruction from a true VARDAN Spiritual Traveler in Out-of-Body Tuza Travel we can reach higher states like Self Realization (Awakening on the Soul Plane to one's true nature and mission) and God Realization (The experience of HURAY or God of ITSELF).

We each are not merely a physical body, personality, emotions, memories and mind but our true essence is that we are each Soul, a radiant particle of God with a body of light capable of moving far beyond the physical world and all its problems to travel into vast spiritual worlds far greater.

My husband and I share how we learned to accelerate this movement as the spark of light and sound we are to these amazing spiritual realms. This was only possible because the pull to be centered in the currents of the God force as a coworker was stronger than the pull of social currents that tried to pull us away from it.

For those who long to return to God the road may have been a long one. But then, when you reach a point that you are ready to return, an invisible force compels you to move in a new direction. The direction may even seem counter to the mind and the opinions of others because it comes from the world of spirit.

There are many theories, myths, techniques and rituals that individuals practice in the hopes of moving towards God and the ultimate heaven. But eventually in your journeying when you have tried everything else for five, twenty or even forty years and you find that it just didn't bring you as close to God as you long for in your heart but instead fills you with exciting but limited spiritual experiences or theories; and you still may feel trapped in the lower heavens and desire greater freedom and adventure, then this book is for you. Both my husband and I sensed something important felt missing until we came across the true Spiritual Traveler.

Some people who have had this experience stumble upon the ancient practice of Out-of-Body Tuza Travel of the VARDAN Spiritual Travelers and they learn to explore the spiritual planes and beyond to the pure universes of God that are vast beyond words and unlimited in scope.

It is only through this method and this method alone (of leaving one's body as Soul, not Astral Projection, but as Soul) under the guidance and protection of the VARDAN Spiritual Travelers that the God seeker can return to IT, by having the experience of HURAY (God) while still living in this world.

Thus in a way you could say one has his feet on Earth and his consciousness in heaven. Soon he or she will learn the art of balancing the two worlds and finds that they can be in heaven while serving here on Earth…for time and space are an illusion and there is no real separation. But this realization takes time doing the spiritual exercises of VARDANKAR for spiritual travel to occur on a conscious basis.

Some believe that one can wait until the "afterlife" to return to heaven but this keeps the individual stuck in what are called the lower heavens and endless M.E.S.T. (Matter, Energy, Space and Time) universes where Soul is not truly free but has to return to this, the physical world again and again until it learns of it's true nature.

Through countless ages the Spiritual Travelers have given the Ancient Science of Tuza Travel into heavenly worlds to their students so they can escape these lower world prisons.

Some people will read the fantastic experiences in this book and say it is fantastical, whimsical science fiction but who can say if something is real until we take a brave leap and explore the other realms ourselves!

In science fiction they may show a space ship where an individual can teleport from one location to another location on another world. And so it is with Out-of-Body Tuza Travel. The Spiritual Travelers teach the individual that it is his vital purpose to learn this ancient science of out-of-body travel because it will help him to have the only sort of experience that will return him to God.

We will also share in these pages spiritual techniques so those of you who desire them can have these journeys as well. My husband and I will also share deep and profound experiences of these Pure Positive God Worlds to help open doors that are beyond Energy, Matter, Time and Space in this book like the many countless students and spiritual travelers have done before us.

VARDANKAR is the Ancient Science of Out-of-Body Soul or Tuza Travel to heavens. Its only purpose is to return to God.

VARDANKAR is not a religion, new age group, philosophy, metaphysics or politics of any kind nor does it identify with any lower bodies or planetary races of any kind but rather it is only a path and a Science of pure Soul movement to heaven. In the past and today, less than one percent of people practice VARDANKAR. It is not for the masses but for the rare individual who desires God more than the things of this world.

In our former spiritual teaching, Self and God Realization and to become a permanent resident of the Pure Positive God Worlds to be one of God's conscious coworkers seemed like an impossible dream or at least this is what we were persuaded to believe. We were encouraged to feel we would never be good enough, never be worthy enough or perfect enough. I am here to say through this book that it is not an impossible dream in some distant, never to known future, but possible in this lifetime NOW! With the help of the Spiritual Traveler, the Living VARDAN Master it is entirely and fully possible!

Heather Giamboi, October 2014

1
THE ASTRAL PLANE
Part 1- The Mountain of Light

One morning upon rising the sun looked like a glowing ball of light that streamed into my room through a shade in long white rays. My husband, a witty bright livewire with crystal blue eyes and sense of humor that has me roaring with laughter and I, a witty, wildly creative spirit have over a period of decades had thousands of fantastic near death like out-of-body experiences to the realms people call "heaven."

Believe it or not there are many heavens or what are also known as planes of existence, and some are more filled with Love, Wisdom, Power and Freedom than others.

On one occasion when I was twenty-one and only just beginning, I sat in a chair in a crowd in a large hotel conference room, with crystal chandeliers glittering in light over our heads.

I closed my eyes to do a spiritual exercise while tuning out the soft whispering voices. In my contemplation I saw a gloomy house in a dismal, foggy, dark woods. The woodlands were thick and the interior of the house was also thick with a dreary fog.

And then in this spiritual exercise, I took before me a vacuum to suck out the darkness of smog. The nozzle like a trunk of an elephant pulled the thick darkness out of the

20

room. More and more of the room cleared and then suddenly, it was no longer I that directed the spiritual exercise, but suddenly the VARDAN (Divine Spirit) took over the visualization and the scene shifted from imagination into an out-of-body experience far beyond this mortal world.

My attention was no longer on my physical body which was sitting peacefully in a chair. The dark house in my visualization, the very walls of this house suddenly vanished and became crystal clear glass from floor to ceiling!

The gray smog and dark woods were suddenly replaced with the most pure, brilliant light. And out the panoramic window in their place I saw to my astonishment a vast breathtaking landscape composed of light and sound. This spectacular heaven filled with misty, white light and a high pitched other worldly sound went on and on in all directions for thousands of miles.

It was literally like a whole new world was revealed and appeared to me. A world I once didn't know existed until the VARDAN (Holy Spirit) unveiled it.

I had felt like a refugee in a dark underground cave, suddenly set free into the cool open air of a bright sun lit meadow filled with singing birds. There was a fantastic feeling of freedom and adventure, joy and pure elation and discovering that heaven is real! That God is real!

That I was like a child on a fantastic adventure to discover the great spiritual mysteries!

Prayer, meditation, reading of books, or the words of Earth bound Gurus; none of these things can free Soul from the bounds and shackles of its human shell which binds Soul from its ability to soar through the heavens to return to the essences of the universe (God).

In all his 29 years of practice in out-of-body travel, my husband Allen at one point had an incredible experience, which shattered his most pervasive spiritual illusion like glass. From that point onward he would truly become the cliff hanger who looks above at the social and religious consciousness from afar, like dangling off a cliff looking down; high above, but too high to dare let go!

Allen and I were sitting among fellow students in a packed class of about 45 people in what was at that time our former new age religion. The classroom was inside of a pyramid shaped church. The walls were beige white with sparse artwork on the walls. In spite of the fact that we both did out-of-body travel successfully for decades and literally had thousands of experiences during that time period, we both still felt like our quest to return to God was far, far away and by our peers standards impossible.

Everyone present was seated in rows shoulder to shoulder and were discussing the topic of spiritual exercises. The Instructor who was a high standing leader and had been in the group for over 43 years announced the whole class would do a spiritual exercise.

This excited Allen for he had noticed the class had accelerated the number of times and intensity of his out-of-body travels!

Everyone closed their eyes and Allen left his body. But, this was not the part that was surprising. What surprised him was what happened next! Allen unexpectedly was shown by the VARDAN (Holy Spirit) what was happening in the same class but from an inner level on the inner planes (heavens). This experience would prove later to be only the second plane or what is known as the Astral Plane.

In this out-of-body experience Allen felt himself pulled out of his body and then brought to soar like a bird. He then hovered, floating as one suspended midair above a gigantic mountain that made Mount Everest look small by comparison. This mountain was located on an island that was lush and green with waterfalls everywhere and surrounded by a deep blue ocean. Allen could see all of this as Soul as if a bird with a 360 degree viewpoint seeing in all directions simultaneously.

Although the size of this mountain was most impressive, that was just the beginning. This huge mountain that was perhaps 10 to 12 miles in height produced a sound and like a volcano beams of multi colored lights spewed out of the top in all directions. There were hundreds upon hundreds of colors of these lights and the power that emanated from this mountain was most impressive.

Each color was breaking the light into different pieces like laser beams, as each was a different ray designed to sustain the lower universes. This mountain ironically was spoken of in *"The Tigers Fang,"* a book by Paul Twitchell who was a true Spiritual Traveler and VARDAN Master when VARDANKAR was briefly known as "Eckankar" from 1965 to 1971. [1]

The huge multi-colored lights poured from the top and with it was also a sound almost like thunder only much more pleasant and enchanting. Within this sound one could also hear the mighty roar of the sea.

It made some go into ecstasy and desire to listen to this sound as it sustained them. It was the audible life force

1. Paul Twitchell, *The Tigers Fang* (New York, NY: Lancer Books. 1969)

stepped down to the vibrations of this world.

The sound carried down and gave one the feeling it was eternal, unchanging and life sustaining, perhaps some sort of fountain of youth?

This mountain again was so incredibly huge it made the tallest mountains on Earth look pale by comparison. The mountain itself was on this island, a beautiful paradise like Hawaii only 100 times more beautiful and enchanting with waterfalls, trees, especially colored flowers, forest, and beautiful life sustaining water.

The powerful mountain itself was a huge transformer of the spiritual energies that flow into the lower worlds from the Astral down into all the physical universes of time, space, matter and energy. Its power sustained all below it, much like a power station might sustain all the electricity for a city.

On this inner plane or heaven, Allen was startled to see all of our classmates gathered around this mountain, many of them we knew by name. This is because at the time we all shared the same new age religion and were actually sitting together in class as this occurred on the inner plane.

After Paul Twitchell translated in 1971 there was no true Master to replace him and so the outer group became an offshoot path. In 2013 the Ancient VARDAN Masters made the path public under the new name of VARDANKAR.

He saw most of our class mates but also many people who were not present in class. There were thousands of people and the vast majority of them were gathered at the mountain's base.

The very Instructor who had begun the exercise in the

physical was now explaining to the class that this was the mountain of God and offered instruction as if his words were the gospel. He explained in reverence that one must climb this mountain to the very top and then surrender to it and jump into the top where the light was streaming out. In doing so one would fall into the center of this great light and gain God Realization!

Allen's reaction to his words was one of disbelief. Although it appeared that everyone around the Teacher was most impressed and believed his every word. To Allen his words did not ring true. This mountain had an eerie resemblance to the Astral Mountain mentioned in Paul Twitchell's *"The Tigers Fang."*[1] Although Allen was not 100% entirely sure of his impressions at the time, due to the fact he was surrounded by his peers.

This plane had the look and feel of the Astral Plane or what would be the first plane above the physical. God Realization begins at the 10th plane far, far from this Hawaiian like paradise and impressive mountain of light. It just did not make sense to Allen that one would get God Realization from jumping into an Astral mountain, no matter how much light and sound streamed out of it.

But Allen remained quiet as he watched and listened. He was curious what would happen next! Remember he was still a member of this new age church so he was trying to give the Instructor the benefit of the doubt.

A tiny number of individuals, roughly 12 people had trekked far up to reach the middle. Those rare few chosen individuals who reached the middle were considered spiritual celebrities of the group. And then even fewer rare birds were nearing the top. The vast majority of people who gathered at the base were chattering and commenting with excitement in their voices in conversations like, "Do you think so and so is going to make it to the top?" "Yeah, he is doing really well. Look he's getting much higher." "I think he'll make it!" Many were excitedly conversing with admiration and excited expectation wondering who will be the lucky few to reach the top of the glowing mountain of light.

This seemed to be the norm in this group, which is of personality worship rather than sincerely aspiring to reach the God head. But Allen did not yet understand what was going on, he was still trying to sort through this whole mess.

The ones near the top of the mountain where supposed to reach the top where this light and sound streamed out into the worlds here and below and then simply jump into this light and gain God Realization. How lucky they were, or so the conversational chatter went.

But as I mentioned before, Allen was not buying it. It did not feel right. It appeared this was the distribution center of power that sustained the Astral and Physical worlds. Sounds emanated from this mountain and the light was impressive. The light and sound issuing from this mountain as said before had to be impressive for it was this mountain of light that acted as a sort of transformer or distribution center for all worlds below including lower regions of the Astral Plane. But it did not feel like the pure positive light of God…only the dull streams of the lower worlds where opposites exist: Light and dark, good and evil; time, space, matter and energy.

But it appeared that everyone in the class was convinced this mountain was the key and gateway to God Realization.

Ironically again it was only on the second plane, not even reaching the Causal or Mental Planes, the 3rd and 4th Planes respectively. One does not reach even Self Realization until they reach the 5th region known in VARDANKAR as the Soul Plane.

He knew from his studies that the Astral Plane was a lower heaven, a heaven like a dark cave when compared to the true Pure Positive God Worlds. The Astral Plane is filled with just enough light to fool those who don't understand and that by all appearances looks dazzling and spiritual by comparison to the physical world but traps Soul.

Allen wondered what was Divine Spirit or the VARDAN telling him by bringing him here?

Could he be wrong in his feelings? Something did not feel right. But was he the one who was off? Could all his fellow members be wrong and he right? Or was he just missing the truth of what they were saying?

The vast majority of those he knew were conversing near the base in the valley and were gathered by the thousands. Some individuals left the valleys and actually pitched tents near the base a few miles up where they would camp out.

The Teacher with graying blond hair and pale blue eyes began a treatise to encourage the others to advance on the journey that he called, "The journey to God Realization." As he continues his discourse on exercises to get to this summit, one individual off in the distance finally reaches the top peak where he can see from vast distances the heaven below. And suddenly he hurls himself in the core where he experiences a spiritual ecstasy, a state of Cosmic Consciousness.

To bring a little clarification here, Cosmic Consciousness is a much misunderstood spiritual state. It is commonly mistaken for God Realization or Self Realization. Those who reach this state of Cosmic Consciousness are almost always worshiped on Earth because of their impressive M.E.S.T. (matter, energy, space and time) abilities. If they are a Guru they can in out-of-body travel meet their students in lower heavens. Those in Cosmic Consciousness may have special abilities that are impressive such as foreseeing the future, seeing all life with universal love, or performing miracles.

Although from a human state of consciousness this looks very lofty and spiritually impressive, it is from my experience only one of many stepping stones on the journey to God. Many who have this experience mistake Cosmic Consciousness for Self or God Realization.

But often unknown to most, Cosmic Consciousness is only a spiritual experience in the lower heavens of time, space and duality (light and dark, good and evil). The regions far beyond this Astral zone and beyond the Causal and Mental heavens rests a vast dark void and far beyond that void is the brilliant light and sound filled Pure Positive God Worlds which contain no duality but only pure spirit. Even though one who achieves Cosmic Consciousness appears quite spiritually or psychically advanced, until he finds the true VARDAN Spiritual Traveler he is still a prisoner of the lower worlds.

The man who jumped into the mountain of light and experienced this cosmic bliss soon moves on to the lower Mental Plane. The others look on in awe wondering who will be next.

The unsettling feeling that Allen had about this supposed, "Mountain of God" that supposedly gave one God Realization caused him to pull back and view more of this island beyond focusing on the mountain where the man had jumped.

Allen then felt a knowingness rise within him and his attention went in a completely different direction as his vision was brought to rest on an Ocean off in another direction.

He noticed that very few individuals were moving toward the Ocean that sparkled in the distance.

At first his lower bodies and social opinion from his peers caused a slight hesitation. Perhaps it was the human urge or herd instinct to safely do what everybody else was doing pulling at him.

He could hear people trying to convince him: "This is the mountain of God." Here he was surrounded by people he had been spiritual peers with for nearly thirty years. Perhaps so many people mesmerized by the mountain of light was proof enough that there might be something to it?

But then again Allen gazed at the Ocean that sparkled in the light.
So few individuals were going by that route. He only counted 4 or 5 as he hovered in the Soul Body above the island.

Allen knew of the different levels of heaven. This Astral heaven with the mountain was in the lower worlds. But he knew that the Ocean of Love and Mercy, the home of the HURAY or God is far, far beyond the lower heavens of Matter, Energy, Time and Space and deep into the light and sound filled Pure Positive God Worlds. At that moment a deep feeling of knowingness pulled him to completely change directions, breaking free from the pack to go instead to the shining magnificent Ocean.

At this moment he remembered then the words of Rebazar Tarzs to Paul Twitchell, as written in the book, *"The*

Tiger's Fang," "Only the courageous and the adventurous, daring and enterprising, can have God."[1] (Twitchell, 59)

After this shocking inner experience given to him by the VARDAN, he abruptly found himself drawn back to his physical body and then became more aware of his surroundings sitting physically among classmates again.

The Instructor was talking and Allen became aware that he was speaking from a mental perspective and not from the Seeing, Knowing and Beingness of Soul. Still, he felt puzzled as to why his peers were enamored by the mountain on the Astral Plane and wondered about the full meaning of this experience from spirit.

Two months later he discovered why. After making God and God Realization a priority in our lives, both Allen and I were drawn like a powerful magnet to a VARDAN Spiritual Traveler who was capable of going far beyond these lower heavens of reincarnation and matter, energy, space and time.

Our preconceptions were shattered like the film "The Matrix." We realized that the VARDAN, Divine Spirit had shown to us that the mountain of light on the Astral Plane was not the road to the higher worlds.

The Astral Mountain of light was also not the route to God Realization as everyone tried to convince us. But instead it was by route of taking up spiritual exercises for out-of-body travel under the wing of the true spiritual traveler who would help us to our destination, the Ocean of Love and Mercy.

The illusion of the mountain of light and the religion's Guru was shattered on the inner planes for us and

1. Paul Twitchell, *Tigers Fang*, Illuminated Way Press. (Las Vegas Nevada. 1967.)

symbolically glass was shattered in the outer world on our car; as we both received a realization that a vital element within what we had built our lives upon in the spiritual religion had an element of illusion: Spiritual experiences of themselves and the blazing light and sound of the lower worlds under those that claim to be enlightened or God Realized but aren't, do not lead to liberation from the lower worlds.

Our prior new age religion appeared to go to the highest heaven and God Realization and everyone on that path said it did, but suddenly this illusion quite unexpectedly, to our utter shock was shattered like glass by the VARDAN, Divine Spirit. It was able to do this for us because our urge for God Realization had become much stronger than our urge for social approval.

We had both reached the Mental Plane. Although the Mental Plane and more commonly the Astral Plane was the glass ceiling of our former religion and ironically the consciousness of the paths Guru and leader. In spite of all the promises few if any passed this glass ceiling.

Reflecting back, it was strange for Allen to see that what was a mountain of the Astral heaven was clearly mistaken for the gateway to the Pure Positive God Worlds, heavens beyond time and space and for returning to God ITSELF.

It was a blazingly bright beautiful Astral Plane for which many Souls see as the ultimate, the supreme. Many were enamored by the presence of the majestic light beings, the radiant heavenly sights, the brilliance of the light, the glowing enormous mountain, the divine wisdom, and the spiritual heavenly wonders that surrounded them. But this was not the Pure Positive God Worlds but only the heights of a light filled Astral Plane Heaven. Not even remotely comparable to even the 5th or Soul Plane…the first of the Pure Positive

God Worlds or heavens of VARDAN.

Everyone present was convinced that this mountain of light was the doorway into God Realization. But Allen in spite of all his training, instead of being blown by the winds of social tides, bravely charted a new direction... to the Ocean.

His assurance became more and more clear as an inner Knowingness from Spirit compelled him to continue towards this Ocean. He saw others moving that way but they were few in number.

He wondered at first, should he dare to be so bold as to venture where so few were going? He wondered if his judgment was off. Somehow he knew that not only the leadership and followers of his religion were behind this ideal of the mountain, but Allen somehow knew this ideal came from the Spiritual Leader and Guru himself and was passed down deep into the roots of the organization.

It was shortly after this inner out-of-body experience that weeks later Allen had another even more profound near death like out-of-body experience of a completely different sort in a moment of despair.

Just prior to finding the spiritual traveler, Allen had felt hopeless that whenever he asked to be of spiritual service in his old religion his requests and pleas were met with disinterest and so often ignored, put down or denied or if he was lucky he was given the most menial tasks.

For that reason he felt completely useless to God. It felt as though he were dying a physical and spiritual death and he suffered and over the years had become quite ill.

And here he was going off in a different direction to the

Ocean, unlike his classmates and instead of reading the books of his religion he was suddenly instead reading the books of the religions predecessor Paul Twitchell. In his sadness he began his spiritual exercise where he left his body....soon he confided his woes to an ancient VARDAN Master who was surrounded by a beautiful white light: Yaubl Sacabi. He explained to Yaubl very sadly that he felt useless to God.

Feeling useless and deeply sad Allen said to Yaubl Sacabi, "I have nothing to give to God...Nothing of use to give." Yaubl in turn warmly comforted him, "You can give yourself." Allen realized that Yaubl meant surrender. In that moment Allen surrendered and gave himself to Spirit and God as Yaubl advised.

Unexpectedly, Allen then suddenly was drawn quickly like a flash of light to the most spectacular, incredible, indescribable sound and intense burning, white light filled breathtaking heaven. It made the mountain of light and the Astral Heavens light look like dark caves, as this heaven was filled with the most intense, magnificent, searing white light and sound.

The light was so strong that Allen could barely stand that tremendous incredible intensity which was beyond all description. Its intensity was so strong he could barely withstand to be there. It was a Pure Positive heaven far beyond the mountain of light of the Astral Plane.

It was a heaven in the Pure Positive God Worlds whose searing light burned away impurities. Unlike any other experience he had ever had, the light and sound seemed to go through him and move down through all his lower bodies. With this he could barely stand the vibration and a part of him wanted it to stop and another part to continue on. When it was finally over Allen felt a change had come over him.

He had a sense that the presence of God had entered his life in a new and different way. What he did not understand completely was that he had simply unfolded to become more aware of what was there all along.

The same is true of you. We are all God beings in various disguises. Like the prince who is begging for a crust of bread because he has forgotten who he really is. We have forgotten who we are. And no amount of mental understanding or emotional fulfillment can make up for Soul's experience in the higher Pure Positive God Worlds of VARDAN or Spirit.

After this experience Allen realized that we don't need to have amazing talents or doings to be worthy of God. We simply need to give ourselves, to let go of all attachments and surrender to God in these Pure Positive God Worlds. It was immediately after this incredible breathtaking experience that he met a true Spiritual Traveler and his life changed completely.

Like Allen I also had reached the glass ceiling and went from feeling trapped in the lower worlds of reincarnation to shifting into having a much deeper relationship with HURAY (God) through many out-of-body experiences. The Pure Positive God Worlds that have become and always were our true home...and yours as well!

I reflected back, "We are all riding the same wave home to God; or more accurately our conscious awareness of God in the Pure Positive God Worlds. Some may appear to be a little further along or a little further behind but in actuality we ride on the same wave together. There is no separation, no time, no space. Time is an illusion and all Souls are loved by HURAY (God) and return to IT on this returning wave in eternity."

In spite of guidance from the VARDAN, Divine Spirit and the travelers it is very easy for the human self to attach itself to one particular reality; to clutch and not let go because it is the familiar.

Likewise we both at first clutched to dogma and social opinion but then broke away and went by the route to the shining Ocean.

What is familiar is safe and swimming off in a new direction was at first scary, especially since we were no longer swimming with the currents of the crowd. Instead we swam with the currents of HURAY, God.

This is why Paul Twitchell recommended to the individual randominity, to flow like the wind with the will of God and not be caught in the talons of dogma, personality worship, idolatry, vanity, religion, materialism, lust, anger, greed, attachment, vanity and a thousand other things that the human self would put between itself and God.

This is why the VARDAN Masters say that only the brave venture towards God because many prefer the safety of the familiar and the safety of the crowd.

If the love of God over-powers what is attaching individuals, whether it be personality worship, dogma, vanity, etc., the curtain will lift and the fog will clear either in this life or the next and they will like a magnet be drawn back to HURAY (God) when it is their time.

In another moment I found myself on yet another area of this heavenly inner realm in the "afterworld" with a different group of people gathered. Many were accompanied by what looked like light beings of ethereal bodies composed of light.

These radiant Souls hovered near offering spiritual guidance. In the distance a women who apparently had just passed on from her earthly life appeared in the light of this beautiful heaven.

She has a happy expression on her continence as she was met by a light being, who like a tour guide or orientation guide, began a telepathic discourse to explain just where she was. And then he brought her to mingle among others in a small gathering, which was her family who had passed on before. She embraced the loved ones warmly. Shortly after the homecoming the light being gave her a grand tour of the Astral paradise afterworld. There were numerous Souls welcomed to their new heavenly home after passing over to this light filled heaven.

She was not aware that she was only on the second plane. She also had no idea that she would only be allowed to stay for a limited time here and then would have to move on. She was not actually spiritually free and would have to incarnate back on Earth. The worlds below the Soul Plane are not Soul's true home but most are fooled into believing they are.

1
THE ASTRAL PLANE
Part 2- Deeper Insights into the Astral Plane

After death many Souls who travel out-of-body and come to "heaven," come to what is called the Astral Plane. There are many regions in the Astral Plane that correspond to shared beliefs such as angels playing harps or the Astral mountain of light. Many who come to the Astral Plane are moved with great awe by the dazzling heavenly sights before them, the beings of light who share a divine wisdom. At that, they conclude that they have reached the afterworld, the ultimate, the end in eternity.

Within the Astral World are many sub-planes, much like on Earth, where we have various places ranging from the blissful Hawaiian Islands to blisteringly hot war torn deserts and everything in between. The physical universe with its countless suns, planets, galaxies and universes is incredibly huge and then by comparison the Astral Plane is much larger. For this reason it is easy to see why so many get lost or so easily mistake a lower heaven for a higher dimension or heaven. For as we ascend or experience illumination into higher vibrational regions like the mid Astral Plane to high Astral Plane there is so much less matter and it is so much more heavenly that Soul is often falsely convinced it has found great spiritual advancement, when it has only just begun.

Often unknown to most, this heaven rests only within the

gates. Visitors often become blissfully contented to stay in some region within the Astral Plane for a day or for hundreds or even thousands of years which can seem like eternity, until the day comes that the individual is sometimes surprised to learn that he is required to reincarnate again, as this is actually not the heaven of spiritual freedom. Although the beings living here tend to live longer than on Earth, the Astral Body has a finite life span and is not eternal. This is true of all of the lower worlds, including the Physical, Astral, Causal, Mental and Etheric.

All are mixtures of spirit and matter, time and space; and opposites of good and evil, light and dark, happiness and sadness, mountains and valleys.

Many who come upon the lower heavens may also meet the mighty Lord of one of these lower heavens which can have human like attributes but is not God. These Lords or Rulers may appear like God and are extremely powerful within their own world and the worlds below them. Depending on the lower plane they may go by different names such as Jehovah, The Brahm, Brahmanda, Ramkar, Omkar, the Kal Niranjan and so on.

When individuals come across this powerful, huge glowing being they are often immediately convinced it is the Lord. They believe that they have found God, a powerful creator being. This being however is a distributor and controller in the lower worlds and its duty is to keep Soul a prisoner. Its impressive features dazzle many individuals and it will claim to be God itself to trap Souls in these lower worlds. And it has two faces: a face of love and light and a face of darkness and cruelty. These lower world rulers may appear as a man or they may appear as a blinding light or in some other form. Because of their enormous power, without a true Spiritual Traveler by our sides we are generally fooled into thinking we have met God and experienced the ultimate and there is no further need to advance.

There was once a man from India who shared his inner experience that all of his family and those he knew worshiped one of these Lords, a lower world God as their God. He, believing he had found the ultimate, surrendered himself to this powerful glowing being who claimed to be God, and to his shock and horror it seized him and was throwing people into some strange gruesome volcano. And as this happened in horror he screamed out to be saved by God.

The moment he did so he awoke from this inner experience and was guided by Divine Spirit, where upon he found the very name of the deity his family worshiped as God listed on the spiritual travelers God Worlds chart. He was shocked to see that what he thought was the ultimate God was a powerful negative Ruler of a lower plane. It was in fact not God but the negative force itself. The lower rulers such as the Kal or Jot Niranjan, or the Brahm or Brahmanda are in fact a mixture of the positive and negative or spirit and matter. They often have two faces: one of good, love and light and one of evil, destruction and anger.

Given that most people are not trained in Out-of-Body Tuza Travel they usually have not been shown the detours and tricks of the lower heavens that are meant to trap Souls. Had they practiced Out-of-Body Tuza Travel under a true VARDAN Spiritual Traveler while living they would be able to read these worlds like a map and know where they are.

They would give to themselves grace, the grace of receiving the divine God knowledge, not through hearsay of humans whose motives can be questionable but through directly visiting the heavens while living.

Out-of-Body Tuza Travel is the method by which the Spiritual Travelers help the individual remove the veil of spiritual ignorance and become Self Realized and eventually God Realized within their lifetime and not at some future promised date or after the death of their physical body.

If those who entered the Astral Heaven had practiced Tuza Travel while living and stocked themselves with greater bravery and a greater adventurous spirit they might be compelled to continue the journey and venture on.

This is much more likely if they were with a true Spiritual Traveler who would guide them and show them the way back home to God and guide them away from the rocks and shoals that can stop their true spiritual progress.

Without the help of a Spiritual Traveler they might still discover yet another level of heaven that contains even less matter and even more Spirit. But then again, of those who journey to the next heaven most immediately conclude, given the much greater light and much greater concentration of spirit and even greater heavenly beauty, that this next heaven (the Causal Plane) is much, much greater than the Astral Plane heaven and therefore of course this must be the ultimate heaven or heavens. And of course the entities and spiritual forces there will falsely confirm this. All of the lower worlds contain illusion, are not permanent and are not the true home of Soul our God self and are only temporary. Soul's goal is always to escape and return back to the God head.

Most who venture in this way are certain they have found the very highest, the most brilliant, the most spiritual, the most intelligent, most evolved expression; with a rock hard certainty that leaves them frozen in a fixated state of consciousness that corresponds to whichever inner plane they cling most often for their entire lifetime or lifetimes.

Then again this captivating contentedness keeps the individual a captive audience, literally. The negative power who rules over all the lower heavens and the physical world wants Soul to be dazzled, awestruck, and a captive audience in the prisons of the lower worlds which dazzle the senses; the physical, psychic, and mental worlds.

In addition to keeping Souls awestruck and contented, the negative also traps Souls to introvert themselves in being distracted by a barrage of lower world problems and crisis's. This is often why it takes Souls millions of incarnations to complete its training.

The Kal or negative power uses the five passions or perversions of the mind: Anger, Lust, Vanity, Attachment and Greed to keep Souls in an almost constant state of entrapment and identification with the lower worlds, problems, and mesmerizing and hypnotic fixations on one or more of the five passions.

For example one individual may become obsessed with gathering wealth and power (greed, attachment, vanity), another prestige and social approval; still another may desire people looking up to him. (Vanity, attachment). Others may strive to find human love, sex, (lust, attachment) or get involved in the punishment of others calling it justice (anger), or become attached to their particular brand of religion to the point of looking down at others (vanity).

There is nothing wrong in desiring love, a relationship or money…it is when we become attached to these goals and raise them above God and Divine Spirit or the VARDAN that we lose sight of truth and can become entrapped. Often the Kal's traps are subtle and not easy for us to spot, such as a person who performs volunteer work but does so partly because it makes him feel special, superior and above others in stature.

After many ages of having gone through every imaginable experience in the lower worlds, a Soul's desire to return increases more strongly than its desire for opinion, dogma and engaging in the five passions of the mind. Soul's desire becomes so strong it will accept nothing less than to find the VARDAN Spiritual Traveler and to return to the essences of the universes, God itself.

You cannot judge who is ready and who is not by outer circumstances. There are Kings and great thinkers who are not ready and there are Homeless drunkards who are ready. This is because one cannot judge a Soul's spiritual enfoldment by outer appearances.

This idea flings in the face of conventional thinking and religion which for the most part says a man must be righteous, good and exhibit all the socially acceptable positive traits before he is worthy of God and of being an advanced spiritual being. This is one of the great lies that holds Souls in the lower worlds, since as alluded to earlier, time and space are an illusion and God or the HURAY desires Soul to return to IT.

Soul is a happy entity and exists only in the present moment within eternity, never in the past or future therefore God is here and now! Not to be projected into the future like some science fiction ideal or antiquated into the past like some old museum relic. To put God off into the past or future is to hate God!

At that point when Soul has had enough experiences in the lower worlds and desires God more than the lower experiences of life, its desire for God brings it to the Spiritual Traveler.

The individual then can finally realize that the Astral Plane is not the plane of God nor is it the plane of God Realization as many religions falsely teach, but only a way station on the long road home to God.

At that moment the spell is broken, for the individual discovers he cannot rely on the outer appearances or the spiritual flock or the spiritual entities that dazzle him with Astral wisdom but all of which chain him to the lower heavens with a beautiful golden chain.

It is then that he instead learns to become as a spiritual adult with the help of the Margatma (an expert and spiritual Master of Out-of-Body Tuza Travel) he learns to stand on his own feet spiritually and gather his own spiritual awareness directly from the source of all sources, the Spirit of God of the Pure Positive God Worlds.

The lower worlds or heavens have wisdom but also unknown to most they are also filled with illusions. And even our trusted forms of spiritual guidance such as one's inner voice, dreams, miracles, healings, waking dreams, visions, visitations of gurus, and spiritual experiences; all of these can be from Spirit or they can equally be from the negative power itself, lulling us into feeling contented to stay forever where we are, in one of the lower heavens that claims to be the heaven of all heavens.

However once the spell is broken, for belief is a form of brainwashing, the individual will go out of his way to confirm and reconfirm that his spiritual guidance and spiritual direction in life shall only come from the Pure Positive heavens alone least he awaken one day to realize it wasn't. In the pure positive heavens he has total awareness in Pure Positive God Worlds of pure spirit, light and sound; the Knowingness, Seeingness, and Beingness of HURAY (God). He now operates beyond the mind and uses the mind as a tool rather than letting the mind and Negative power control him like a marionette or puppet.

The Astral heaven is a vast region that most Souls go to after death. They tend to gravitate to the region of the Astral Plane which corresponds to shared beliefs. This place, like the mountain of light was just one of many countless regions unnumbered like tiny cities contained within a large country but it rested within the Astral Plane heaven.

Within our former new age religion I had thought for certain we had reached a spiritual pinnacle that would bring us to the heights of Self and God Realization. It was not until through out-of-body travel we consulted the ancient VARDAN Masters and focused more deeply on God that the illusion shattered into a million pieces like glass.

In closing this chapter on the mountain of light, Allen came to consult with an ancient VARDAN Master of great spiritual wisdom, "It was during contemplation while laying in bed one evening that I found myself transported into another dimension, another world where stood a muscular man perhaps five foot ten or eleven with short cropped jet black hair and beard. He had flashing dark eyes and a maroon robe. I immediately recognized him as the great VARDAN Master Rebazar Tarzs."

"He began to speak to me as if every word was urgent. For Rebazar was a great messenger; a voice of reason in a world of insanity. For Rebazar knew the very secrets of the universe and how to return to God here and now."

Allen continued, "I asked Rebazar why there was confusion after the passing of Peddar Zask, also known as Paul Twitchell on Earth." And he responded, "People became confused at the idea of a new spiritual Living VARDAN Master. They attach themselves to the personality of the Master. When the new one comes along they don't recognize him because their love for God isn't strong enough to break the spell of what they've attached themselves to or worshiping personality because they are not ready for more."

"Most men are like children who play petty games that have no purpose in order to amuse themselves. They are the immature Souls who flounder around from life time to life time. I do not speak to them for they do not have the ears to hear or the eyes to see the great universal truths that set Soul free from the M.E.S.T. worlds (matter, energy, space, and time). No I say. I address those Souls who are starving for truth, who are tired of playing games and who wish to find God here and now!"

"Man's primitive religions, primitive philosophies, and other pseudo sciences pretend that man is bound to his lower bodies and must wait patiently until the death of his physical body before knowing truth."

"This is the great lie that the negative power tries to grow like a fungus inside the immature Soul. It is a terrible illness for it causes man endless hardship as he reincarnates on the various lower planes including the Physical, Astral, Causal, and Mental Planes (the lower heavens)."

"The Soul who desires truth will meet a true VARDAN Master, VARDAN meaning Spirit, who will teach him the art and science of Out-of-Body Tuza Travel. The Tuza or Soul in its natural state may leave the lower bodies and travel at will into all the worlds including the very heart of God on the

10th Plane, the Anami Lok and above into the 11th and 12th planes where the light and sound is beyond description and Soul is free. Spiritual freedom is never possible for the lazy or fearful."

"Therefore I tell man to discard his fear. Like a caterpillar discards its cocoon. There is no need to be trapped in the worlds of matter, energy, space, and time. The true God Worlds are filled with the pure light and sound emanating from the true God: HURAY, located in the very Ocean of Love and Mercy."

"Here Soul experiences pure Beingness, Seeing and Knowing without the hindrance of the mind. So far beyond the Physical, Astral as well as Mental Planes are the higher worlds, that the difference is indescribable and can only be experienced through Out-of-Body Tuza Travel."

"The VARDAN Masters are grateful that this book has been printed for although it is made out of nothing but paper it holds the key to truth, not the truth of the religionist, nor the philosophers, nor the metaphysicians, nor the world reformers, but the eternal truth, the living reality of HURAY, God."

Allen continued, "And with that I awoke inspired to finish writing this book for I knew that Rebazar Tarzs was a Master of the highest order. Far more advanced than any guru, religionist, or philosopher that most men look to for wisdom."

2
PLANETS, GALAXIES, & UNIVERSES

There are many who thrill in the revel of the Sciences and films which explore the far reaches of dark outer space speckled with bright stars. In some books and films we travel through dark outer space in futuristic high tech spaceships to as they say in "*Star Trek*", "...to explore new worlds"[2] as well as universes, galaxies and planets and meet mysterious beings. Many people find these things amusing or exciting but later on after we have a glimmer of memory flashed in our awareness of having been the Space Traveler ourselves for countless lifetimes, the sparkling veneer of wonder wears off and we realize these space experiences are just another enthralling, larger prison. It is the prison of the lower worlds of reincarnation. Just like the lower heavens of the Astral Plane dazzle the emotional and spiritual senses, the black heavens of outer space dazzle the Scientist Space Traveler on his insatiable thirst for adventure and for physical realm knowledge.

In an out-of-body experience Allen sat with his eyes open to view these things. Allen experienced such a past life millions of years ago on a planet called Eltron. But before we delve into life on this distant ancient planet it is important to explain the basic cycles of the lower universes and how this understanding sheds light on hidden understandings of this past life in a galaxy far away.

2. Roddenberry, Gene, The Original Star Trek Series. Paramount Television, 1967- 1969.

47

In the Physical Plane of the lower worlds which include all planets, there are cycles that all existence goes through contained in cyclic delineations called Yugas.

The first cycle of experience called the Satya Yuga, which is otherwise known as the Golden Age lasts 1,728,000 years. It is the age where life is joyful, easy and heavenly; all people are spiritual and follow spiritual law in this age. People do not have to work or toil in a golden age. It is what some would associate with living in a utopia, like a heaven on Earth with perpetual spring. Many mistake utopia on Earth as the ultimate goal without realizing that creating heaven on Earth is still being trapped in the lower worlds of matter, energy, time and space.

This is why many individuals of different faiths often speak of the coming of a heavenly utopia on Earth. Deep in our unconscious are memories of past lives in such incredible utopias in the physical realm on this and other worlds which occurred during the golden age, however these are not the heavens of freedom but a prison in a more beautiful package.

Then after the Golden Age comes the cycle called the Silver age or Tretya Yuga, which runs for 1,296,000 years. In the Tretya Yuga a small amount of discord is introduced into our lives. Challenges and discomforts are introduced. Then following this cycle comes the Copper age, also called the Dwapara Yuga that lasts for 864,000 years. The Dwapara Yuga is half positive and half negative.

In the Copper Age violence and crime may appear. Eternal spring divides into four seasons and Soul must toil and work to survive. Then lastly the current cycle we are in now is called the Kali Yuga, meaning Dark Age. The Kali Yuga lasts 432,000 years. In the Dark Age people must work harder for their wares and there is more ignorance, darkness, suffering, and spiritual unawareness. Then within each of these cycles are still smaller cycles such as now we are in: the Golden Cycle within the Dark Age.

In dark ages otherwise called the Iron Age there is much anger, war and karma created through revenge, war, depression, in which individuals can become trapped in negativity. In Golden Ages there are no wars and people are not killing or harming life. They are pursuing things like Art, Science, Human love, Philosophy, and Spirituality. They treat the planet like a living being with love. Although more positive, in the golden age we unknowingly become dazzled by a utopic heaven on Earth and the lower planes and don't lose any sleep over not finding God since we assume God is already here now. And we are happily contented with illusions of spiritual attainment. The Soul then often translates with a smile on its face to reincarnate into a darker age.

The other trap of a dark age is the notion that we can create the once lost golden age utopia on Earth. That we can end war, famine, discord, and create the lost golden age once again. There is nothing wrong with improving conditions, that is until it becomes nearly the driving goal for the individual. This reduces religions into something of a lower state than religion, as attention is shifted away from God itself and onto "everyday life" and social do-gooding. The focus on social reform is social rather than spiritual and the individual ends up in do-gooding and perfecting the lower world which becomes a distraction instead of returning oneself to God through out-of-body travel where he can give back as a conscious coworker with God.

The purpose of these ages is the unfoldment of Soul that goes through many types of experience. By facing challenges within a dark age or facing illusions within a golden age we develop different abilities in our future as Spiritual Travelers in spiritual partnership with God.

There are many people who think of life as living only one lifetime and other people who believe that we only live a few hundred years. In my opinion this is because before coming to these lower worlds God through its grace and compassion, in giving the Soul a new body and a new brain closes the curtain to its vast past that it may not be excessively distracted by the past to better do its spiritual mission in the present.

The Soul passes through each of the twelve signs of the zodiac seven times each and reincarnates very often for millions of lifetimes in countless worlds, planets and planes for spiritual evolution until the day comes that it grows tired of the lower world prizes through the different cycles and instead seeks to return to become a coworker with HURAY, God.

In an out-of-body experience Allen sat with his eyes open to view a past life on a planet that occurred during the Tretya Yuga, or Silver age. Allen experienced this past life of millions of years ago on the planet called Eltron. Out in deep dark space a glowing Eltron shimmered before Allen's vision. On its surface were the beauties of pristine nature, oceans, fields, and forest.

Advanced silvery space vessels would rise off the planet's surface and zoom through space at incredible speeds to other worlds and galaxies.

In this past life Allen was one such Scientist who regularly left the planet on long extended trips to study other life forms from other worlds far throughout the galaxies.

As he saw these space vessels soaring through space he recalled in his current life time that he was much less enamored by these space wonders since he remembered many lives as a Space Scientist were he felt his time was wasted entertaining himself with lower world phenomena and knowledge. On Eltron this was much the same.

Allen re-experienced life on Eltron: "The people of Eltron were a tall race: Women roughly six feet and men roughly six and a half to seven feet in height. Every living person was highly physically attractive and everyone was in perfect physical health. All of the people looked like attractive models.

No one was overweight and disease and illness was very rare as this was a silver age and such challenges didn't yet exist. Because this was a silver age and therefore illness generally was extremely rare, people lived long, for several thousand years. These people were overly developed in intellect and less developed emotionally and spiritually. However, they were more emotionally and spiritually developed then Earth as a whole. The people of Eltron had a philosophy that people should freely pursue their life's calling whether it be Sciences or Arts."

In that life being a Scientist, Allen took space travels on an "Observation Space Ship." The crew would board the shiny ship in white silver shiny suits and launch into space to some distant planet. Since the ship itself was specifically designed for observation to study other worlds they had special features such as the deck could holographically disappear so that it appeared as though he were hovering in space for a full panoramic, unobstructed view.

It was almost as if one were standing on a plane of glass and could see everything in all directions. And then just as easily it could shape shift back into a space ship and all could view the planet from a smaller visual screen.

He could likewise glide the ship close to the planet's surface and record his observations of viewing beings with devices that could see through them like enhanced X-ray clear vision. All of these things contributed to his studies of endless, countless planets and life forms.

At that time Earth wasn't notable to them as a destination, as it was populated with dinosaurs and mammoths. They explored through outer space many other countless worlds.

After thousands of years of studying planets in different galaxies, given that these people of Eltron lived for roughly three thousand four hundred years, eventually Allen came to feel his life felt empty. This experience which could much be like an Earth Scientists wildest dreams became to him rather boring.

In fact most of the Eltron people became at some point in their lives very bored. Because they lacked more emotional development and spiritual development they were obsessed with mental acrobatics and their "field of study." Books had absurd titles of excess complexity. Their whole life's purpose was their "field of study." Because of the high level of technology, money was not used and people didn't have to have a job to eat, so people pursued different Arts and Sciences as though it were the very core of life.

In this out-of-body experience Allen watched as some people pursued with gusto Music and others Dance and Painting. Both Scientists and Artists displayed their findings and accomplishments because they equated self-worth with perfection in these studies. He likewise saw that in that lifetime we were married. It was very unusual that two people in different fields were married (his in Science and mine in Dance and Art) and therefore given obsessions with work and being as a people less emotionally developed we seldom saw each other. People would live to do their field of study so if they stopped, work was optional. They didn't have to do anything; they didn't have anything else to live for but their field of study.

Life had no other purpose then this and therefore eventually many came to realize that their lives felt empty. Many of the people of Eltron would suddenly create a time to stop their art or science to do what they labeled a lofty word of going into "Reflection" which was really only that they would see the people working and then suddenly they would stop and do absolutely nothing like stare at a wall because they were so bored. People sometimes did "Reflection" for ten or more years. During these periods they would sometimes consult with Counselors who would throw out ideas of other fun life hobbies they could pursue to busy themselves within life.

During reflection, since this was a silver age, when they stopped working they would still have a home and still receive food so there was nothing to work for. The hidden issue behind their boredom was that they were living their lives connecting only to the Astral Plane. They were aware of the nature of reincarnation, that you lived this life and then returned, however it's nature and purpose didn't interest them much. Without spiritual understanding people felt themselves like ships drifting off towards nothing.

In his many space travels in this and other lives he came to realize that even though he traveled the universes that spanned endless miles he realized he felt like he went nowhere.

He would make trivial physical discoveries and then in their place many more endless questions would arise. And in his accomplishment of making scientific discoveries he would then have to return to darker ages in a new lifetime to repeat the cycles.

In addition to planets explored in the far reaches of space there were also many planets that didn't have much technological development. In some of these worlds people dabbled in magic which instead of helping them became a scourge to their worlds.

On one occasion of shifting into Tuza Travel I saw myself in a former lifetime living out in the beauties of nature on a pristine blue planet. I had long straight white hair that blew in the wind and wore a long white robe. In that lifetime I looked a lot like one of the Wizard characters from "Lord of The Rings." I stood upon a breathtaking mountain top with my arms outstretched overlooking the vast beauty of nature moving the winds and weather to help the planet.

In this particular life time my name was Khara Neshani. Khara was a VARDAN Master and lived alone in the wilds. However this type of life contrary to all appearances was not a life of magic but a life of spirituality. I will explain this later.

The people of this world lived in simple villages. Allen who also knew me in that lifetime was also a member of VARDANKAR. But he kept his spiritual interests secret among only four trusted friends. It was for him necessary to keep it secret as the people of this planet all really believed in magic and many common people greatly feared it. For this reason anyone who was found to practice such things was quickly executed because of the abuses of both the black magicians and white magicians. This created a paranoia and an intolerance for these things in a way that was much like the Salem Witch incidents of Earth.

For this reason Allen kept his spiritual interest in VARDANKAR secret among his friends even though it had nothing to do with such practices. And likewise Khara was forced to live in the wilds alone for whenever she entered Allen's fishing village or any town she would be approached by mean spirited people suspiciously asking questions. Some White or Dark Magicians of this world had in the past caused people trouble that scared them so the wizards were executed. There was a reward system for people to spot wizards. And unscrupulous people in very suspicious tones would ask people questions. When Khara Neshani visited the villages she was asked questions about her personal life in a nosy, mean spirited way: "Why are you here?" "How long have you been here?" "Do you have a family?" "Where do you live?" After several bad experiences and realizing that they were hoping to make her out to be a problem, she instead often lived in isolation in the beauties of nature to be of service to God in other ways. During bad weather she took shelter in caves.

At this time there was a transition taking place in which the serenity of the Silver age was shifting into a Copper age. People were confused as to why over the past fifty years people were suddenly beginning to do strange things like stealing and killing and crime. They didn't know how to handle these things and were suspicious and made life unpleasant for everyone by over reacting.

Allen lived with his wife and two children in a peaceful small village lined with small one or two story homes that much resembled the 14th century of Earth. He met secretly with four other friends to study the teachings of VARDANKAR together to deepen their spiritual understandings. His village was a small fishing village and during the day he shared a crude little wooden boat with other fishermen to seek their daily catch.

On one occasion they brought their simple little boat out into the ocean. As they got much further out Allen realized that the weather was suddenly getting too rough and he felt a sudden feeling of danger for the little boat. As things got rougher and scarier, quietly in his mind he called out to the VARDAN (Holy Spirit).

He knew he would be doomed to sinking so he asked the VARDAN (Divine Spirit) for help. At that moment the VARDAN (Holy Spirit) directed Khara Neshani to come to the water's edge a far distance from them. She lifted her arms and divine spirit moved the storm away from their ship. Then she walked off disappearing into the forest. They never knew she was there. Allen and the fishing crew returned to shore with a sense of great relief at having survived.

Later after this incident Khara met Allen on the inner planes in dreams where he saw Khara meeting with him. He didn't understand the reason for these dreams and he didn't know who it was he saw.

Even though by all appearances Khara's behavior appeared to be magic it was not. In that life Khara Neshani was a VARDAN Master so she was aware of spiritual law. Black Magic or white magic which the magicians of that world practiced is a violation of spiritual law. Something is black magic or white magic when what is done, is done because the person (their ego) wants something done. Or the individual assumes incorrectly that it is God's will for them to use phychic and or spiritual forces to interfere, rescue, or heal someone, even though it may not be God's will at all, for reasons unknown to the human mind.

It is very common for example that people who pray commit white magic and break spiritual law by assuming something is God's will and thereby bending the spiritual forces in a way that interferes with the Holy Spirits plan.

If for example there was a women who in past lives deeply needed to learn surrender to God. Perhaps the Holy Spirit set up conditions that took thousands of years to arrange the proper conditions for her to learn surrender to God. Before this lifetime, as strange as it seems to the human mind, on the Soul level this women agrees to develop cancer because conditions are finally right that she will through this experience learn to surrender to God by having such a challenging experience.

If her friends quickly guess that God's will is the cancer be gone and they interfere without consulting Divine Spirit and pray for her that the cancer is gone, now they are practicing white magic and breaking spiritual law. They interfere with the conditions of the women learning surrender to God and as a result the women has to reincarnate for another 200 years until the conditions are right again for her to learn to surrender to God in the same way. Her friends then on spiritual levels become responsible for the two hundred years of the living and suffering the women must endure.

And as a result because these friends unknowingly broke the spiritual law, the law of non-interference they may take on her karma in some way such as developing cancer in this life or another life themselves. On the other hand if a healing is God's will and the ill individual gives permission this is not magic but Divine Spirit.

Both appear to be miracles but one is magic and one is not. This is why it is vital to know with certainty and not guess what is God's will and what is not. When we manipulate any forces in a way that is not God's will, white magic or black magic we cause ourselves great harm and we unknowingly take on serious problems or other people's karma.

When we try using our own will rather than God's will the forces we are using are psychic and not spiritual. And psychic forces will turn against the user at some point.

Even if we use the psychic powers for our own benefit this can often be dangerous because the psychic forces are a two edged sword and are cyclical in nature meaning they may work for a period of time and then abandon us. It is the wise Soul who utterly and completely surrenders to Gods will and who humbly declares "Thy will be done and not mine."

Our ultimate goal is to become a conscious coworker with God. Emphasis on the word "conscious." This means TOTAL AWARENESS and total responsibility but in order to do this we must practice Soul or Tuza Travel. God Consciousness cannot descend into the human state of consciousness, it is far too negative and dense. And its vibratory rate too low.

Through Soul or Tuza Travel we move into those ecstatic states of the Pure Positive God Worlds. And eventually to the Ocean of Love and Mercy where dwells the HURAY or God ITSELF. When we reach God Realization we have reached a new zenith in our life. And are now a fully conscious God being who acts as a conscious coworker in the divine scheme of creation.

Returning to the topic of the dangers of bending the spiritual forces. If we practice these magical things we may be setting up conditions to, in this life or another life, live in mental asylums, be possessed by entities, or undergo hardships to learn spiritual law. And in this case, spiritual law being that if we wish to pray for someone, the person has to give permission and we also need to be granted permission by the VARDAN or divine Spirit, for the act not to be practicing magic.

From my view point we don't need magic when we have a much better alternative which is we can lead an adventurous life exploring the far reaches of Tuza Travel to heaven. Instead of white magic or black magic we will be taught by the VARDAN or Divine Spirit itself (God's voice) the proper way to work with people and life that is in harmony with the will of God.

When we seek to play with spiritual forces without proper training we become a danger to ourselves and to others.

It is very similar to the "prime directive" in Star Trek where the protocol is that we do not interfere with the free will of others by trying to force, change or convert uninterested people to our opinions or ways or interfere in the lives of others. From out-of-body divine instruction in heavens I have learned that we can only assist people who give us permission and that Holy Spirit gives permission.

If you are walking around asleep spiritually going around healing people and interfering in social things and people's lives you become dangerous because you are not conscious of what you are doing and the consequences to yourself or others. Instead of this we can more deeply learn who we are as a Soul spark of God and learn to live in harmony with the will of God. We instead can become a conscious coworker with God with Self and God Realization instead of being a channel for negativity or only a channel for social reform.

These are both an expression of negative nature itself. The negative force which some call Satan, Lucifer, or Kal is said to have two heads. One head has an expression of wrath, hatred,

59

and viciousness and the other head is sweet, kind, helpful, and smiling. In a dark age one head is more dominating and in a golden age the other head is more dominating. In its kind form the negative force speaks of saving the world, social reform and things that seem very noble like helping people but both heads ironically lead the individual to the same place, the prison of the lower worlds. The person lives out their lives entertaining themselves in distractions and inevitably become trapped in the Astral Plane prepared to reincarnate yet again. Hence the right hand path of white magic and the left hand path of black magic don't lead to spiritual liberation. It is rather the VARDAN or middle path that does.

Doing kindnesses and good works can be loving and positive however an excessive focus of social reform that is used to replace spirituality or replace a focus on God is falling into this negative trap. The person prioritizes social do-gooding and then doesn't seek to return to God and as a result continues to reincarnate. They are serving man and humans instead of serving God and that is the problem. It is like giving aid and comfort to an unjustly prisoned prisoner by giving them better food rather than aiding them to be free.

In one individual's past life long ago he was a Wizard. He wore a long robe and carried a large staff he called his "magical scepter." He threw pyrotechnics into the air to impress others and spent a great deal of time reading metaphysical books. On one occasion a suffering man came to him with a gangrene leg to work his magic. The Wizard desiring more money made exaggerated claims of his healing powers. He went about healing the man's leg and yet months later the ailment returned causing great suffering and the loss of the man's leg.

On another occasion the Wizard also for others performed love spells. He coerced a women to fall in love against her will which is a violation of the law of non-interference. He found pleasure in parties and magic. After this life the Wizard was utterly shocked in the afterworld when he learned he had created a tremendous amount of karma in only one life.

In the next incarnation he returned and went through a similar suffering and pain of the man with the gangrene leg, losing his own leg and living crippled and in pain for decades. Then in yet another life he was born mentally less developed and felt alone all his life as he could never find love. The karma for doing love spells against the will of others led to a painful life of endless isolation.

Upon viewing these causes and effects he realized that the lower worlds are reflective and like a mirror bring back to Soul not as a punishment but spiritual education awareness of God's divine laws such as, the law of love and the law of non-interference. He realized he could transcend the road of karma and reincarnation, the duality of magic, transcend pleasure and pain and the long, slow, and difficult road by learning the direct path to God.

A friend once shared that in a past life he worked with technology and flew a space ship. He unwittingly blew up nearly half a planet. Following this to his shock and horror he then went through millions of lifetimes of strife balancing out the karma of each life he disturbed. We are often not told there is a much easier road to travel then the long road of pleasure and pain, illusion and magic that is karma.

Practicing magic and interference gives the illusion of power and control. But most Souls eventually have the realization from studying their past lives that it only brings the loss of power and the loss of control, suffering to ourselves and others and a longer stay in the lower worlds prisons. For powers or that which we abuse we inevitably lose.

Power of itself is not bad. When we surrender to the Holy Spirit or VARDAN in true humility then we find that we have an endless wellspring of Love, Wisdom, Power and Freedom.

Magic, controlling prayer and breaking the law of non-interference of course does not lead to spiritual liberation. It is when we let go of our ugly and beautiful past and focus on returning to God that things take an entirely different direction beyond frontiers that we ever imagined. When we do this we gain more control then we have ever had because we become co-creators with HURAY (God) and the Holy Spirit. We earn the right to go to any world, and choose our form of spiritual service with God, such as planetary spirit, guide, elemental, angel, or Spiritual VARDAN Master.

White and black magic often cause hidden harm to everyone involved. In that lifetime Khara avoided white and black magic at all cost. The VARDAN Masters avoid white or black magic but only do the will of the VARDAN, the will of God. And therefore in this instance since the VARDAN (spirit) directed Khara to let it save the ship of four people, it did so through the individual. If Spirit did not direct Khara to let it move the storm, the ship would have sunk into the Ocean because she had no interest in breaking spiritual law.

The universes of the Physical Plane with its many galaxies and planets can feel endless. For the space traveler in his vessel it seems to go on and on forever.

When we practice Tuza Travel we eventually can see we have been inhabitants to these many worlds and planets throughout the universe; but no amount of worldly knowledge, technology, magic, social reform, or golden age spirituality will bring us to a truly worthwhile destination. Instead we, like a space traveler venture off for millions of endless miles yet getting nowhere.

In these out-of-body journeys for both Allen and I, seeing these other worlds showed us how vital it is to seek out our true spiritual destination: the Ocean of Love and Mercy where dwells God of ITSELF. What we call the HURAY. This is not the god of positive and negative, nor male nor female but is beyond all duality, beyond mind and beyond description and must be experienced via out-of-body travel.

No amount of worldly knowledge, philosophy, religion, adventure nor power will take the place of God Realization and Soul's return to the God head. We must reach first the state of Self Realization and then that state known as Total Awareness or God Realization. To aspire for any less is to shirk our spiritual responsibility and miss the great Love, Wisdom, Power and Freedom of Soul's true home in the Pure Positive God Worlds.

3
THE CAUSAL PLANE AKASHIC RECORDS

In his early adventures in visiting the various heavens, at one point Allen developed a fascination in exploring past lives. Allen shared upon traveling to the Causal Plane Heaven that after death many feel the Causal Plane is so much more heavenly and beautiful then the Astral Plane Heaven and then they instantly feel it is the ultimate heaven. As a result they stay in this heaven of white, golden orange light for hundreds of years. And because it is nicer than the Astral Plane and it contains even less matter and even more spirit a lot of people are fooled into thinking they've reached a very high state of consciousness.

"You feel you have reached this very lofty state. People feel as they evolve to higher levels of this plane, later on, that they have developed powers and have a lot of power and control over their own past, present and future. They also feel a sense of Mastery over cause and effect and may have developed psychic abilities or can perform small miracles which give them a feeling of spiritual evolution."

"To an extent they are developed, however this is also illusion in that the individual evolved to the Causal Plane is still in the lower worlds of time and space. Although it appears they have reached the ultimate heaven in eternity, in reality they are still prisoners in the realms of reincarnation."

"Many of the Gurus from India and China wear orange

robes often indicating their establishment in the Causal Plane which has orange white light.   People are often very impressed when they see Gurus that express powers that come from Causal Plane realization such as performing miracles, manifesting things, seeing into the past, psychic powers, reading people's past lives and revealing why they are here or their purpose in life. This gives the illusion that they are the highest Guru or even a master when in reality they are drawing upon this Causal Plane, the 3rd heaven."

"The Margatma, The Living VARDAN Master is working from a much higher state of consciousness."

"So a Guru working from the Causal Plane can't bring the individual to spiritual freedom. They can only bring them to the Causal Plane where they still have to reincarnate. It is a beautiful heaven but they are not free of Maya (illusion); even though it appears a much nicer place because there is less negativity. As you go higher there is more spirit and less matter, so it gives the illusion that you're in the ultimate heaven. But the lower heavens are still controlled by the Kal (the negative power)."

As we mentioned before the Kal has two faces: the positive face and the negative face. Since Kal's job is to keep Soul in the lower worlds as long as possible, Souls are constantly alternating between extremely negative lifetimes where things are very difficult and more positive lifetimes where things seem like they are almost heavenly.

Since the Kal is constantly presenting different sides of life ranging from extremely negative to the positive, it allows the Kal to trap Soul for extremely long periods of time. If the Kal were to hit Soul with nothing but negativity Soul's desire to escape from the lower worlds would be increased to the point where Souls would surrender everything to the Living

VARDAN Master and to God in order to escape, therefore the Kal in its cleverness gives Soul temporary relief to try and delay Soul from seeking a true Master and going back to HURAY, God."

Allen had an expansive view of the inner planes and he shifted through Out-of-Body Tuza Travel to explore a realm in the lower heavens called the Causal Plane.

This plane is a realm of wisdom mixed with illusion and is a place where like a radio, Psychics tune in to see the future or explore the past. Unlike the Atma Lok (Soul Plane) these Akashic records are not nearly as complete as the Soul Records of the Pure Positive God Worlds in the realms beyond. In his out-of-body travel he had an interest in exploring the Causal Plane to gain a deeper understanding of his past lives.

In the late evening he surrounded himself with images on his wall of the Ancient VARDAN Masters and would gaze at them as he closed his eyes and do a spiritual exercise shifting to explore the Causal World.

In his out-of-body travel to the Causal World Allen entered an ethereal spacious room with muted, soft light containing what looked like large holographic cards running four feet high by six feet wide. These holographic cards were multi-dimensional and he could telepathically make them hover closer if he wished. Allen knew that the Akashic records can appear as holographic cards or any form we choose. These cards or picture files contained many pieces of information, including visual, auditory, smells, emotions and even thoughts that occurred during this past time period. He noticed he could find answers and search the records with ease moving the holographic pictures around like floating windows and peer into other lives.

This was essential given the vast nature of these. For example, he could waste time and enter a life in ancient Greece to watch himself laboring for nine hours if not for the ability to control their direction and use. It much resembled when one uses a VCR recorder however he could zero in on an image, pulling in close, or pull back or fast forward, freeze frame or reverse and direct these according to what he wished to better understand for his spiritual growth.

Next he explored a more dangerous spiritual exercise. It is actually very dangerous if not done with the permission and under the protection of a true VARDAN Spiritual Traveler. After practicing out-of-body travel for several years he decided to view with permission from the Master a tremendous amount of past life records from the Soul Plane and Casual plane simultaneously and at great speed. There are complete records of all past lives on the Soul Plane, These are known as the Soul Records, and then there are the Akashic records on the Casual Plane. These Akashic records are not complete and are from a much lower state of consciousness. To try and bring that much awareness into the lower bodies of our past lives too quickly would run the danger of throwing one completely out of balance or worse.

Allen knew that if he viewed them fast and avoided stopping at any particular image it was less risky that he could be harmed by seeing any traumatic material. In the past there were occasions where Allen failed to ask permission of the traveler as to what is spiritually appropriate to view and as a result he saw a past life of such pain that he was traumatized for days. Under the Spiritual Travelers protection he viewed the Akashic records flipping through several million lifetimes. He later realized he had viewed both the Soul Records and the Akashic records at the same time. But mostly the Akashic records. Allen was not yet a VARDAN Master and was still learning how to navigate the lower worlds.

Please remember Soul is a unit of Awareness and there is nothing that Soul is not capable of doing. It is only in our lower M.E.S.T. (matter, energy, space and time) bodies that we have severe limitations and even these can to a certain extent be overcome as we learn to use the lower bodies: Physical, Astral, Casual, Mental and Etheric as springboards and most important, as servants to our true Self Soul and to the VARDAN or audible life stream.

Allen viewed these eons of lives from a distant and detached position making sure not to look too closely or for too long at any one.

In Allen's own words:
"I realized during this expanded viewpoint that I was like all of life on the entire Earth planet."

"I witnessed myself in endless lifetimes of every imaginable experience on the planet. I had lifetimes where I had been: a Farmer, a Warrior, a Homeless Person, a Composer, a Musician, a King, a Queen, a Servant, University Professor, a Retarded Person, a Serial Killer, a Deformed Child, a Prostitute, a Nun, a Priest, a Con Man, a Thief, a Murderer, a Lawyer, a Dictator, a Slave, an Assassin, a Politician, a Judge, a House Wife, a Business Man, an Elderly Sage, anything and everything you can think of or imagine I had done on Earth of other planets. And this sort of reincarnation past I knew wasn't only common to myself but a universal experience among all Souls who come to the physical realm."

"I realized that we are all ancient beings not limited to what we look like at the very surface of our being. So many people see themselves and define themselves by what character or role they play or what they look like such as elderly or youth or defined by the name of their profession. They believe these attributes define them but deeper down we are none of these shallow things. It is like looking through a vast sea of lifetimes of every type and pulling out one as a clown and making that our whole reality, self-worth, and self-definition."

"After viewing this vast montage I got a strange feeling that it didn't really matter what a person appeared to be at a given moment because at some point we were everything. In this way we step back for a bigger picture. I more deeply realized that we are not our past lives. We are not the things we have done or the profession we have had. We are not what we look like or our accomplishments. Sometimes individuals search for past lives where they were famous or in some important role or position but this becomes a way of becoming tied to the past and traps the individual from making a much improved present."

"I also noticed that on many occasions I was in long almost endless feuds. On many occasions when someone did me wrong in one past life at first I would immediately assume that they were the bad guy. But then it was almost always the case that in a previous life time or previous lives I had done the same hurtful thing to them. I learned that we can be quick to judge other people without seeing the big picture. Eventually we learn to stop lashing out at others and instead start to identify less with our ego self and become more and more spiritually mature in ways that free us."

"We realize that our past does not have to bind us and that we may seek a true Spiritual Master or Traveler who can guide us beyond illusion."

"I realized that we need to learn to die daily and be reborn in consciousness. This means letting go of dead old images or picture files from the past so that we can embrace truth which is only found in the Audible Life Stream or VARDAN also known as the Holy Spirit."

When Allen became more spiritually mature and saw a bigger picture, he started to focus more on his relationship with the Spiritual Traveler who is the Inner Master, the light and sound and Self Realization and God Realization.

Instead of just toying around with past lives he felt that when we become ready enough the Spiritual Travelers will show us past lifetimes when the information is actually most highly useful to us spiritually.

Exploring past lives sheerly for entertainment or for selfish motives from his experience felt like playing with fire. Playing with psychic forces for any other reason than to return to God is dangerous. He found it was easy to get burned. He eventually came to the conclusion that everyone does really wonderful things and everyone does really terrible things and everything in the middle. He realized it is an illusion to magnify the flaws in others and be upset by them instead of taking responsibility for ourselves.

He felt that this vast reincarnation overview gave him a greater lesson in tolerance and compassion. One of God's important principles is to not harm or hurt ITS creatures. His out-of-body experiences in the Causal heaven showed him the vital importance of that.

Both Allen and I have had many lifetimes in both Golden ages and Iron Ages. Even though we have described what may be to some interesting or exciting lifetimes, life in the lower worlds is not always so interesting or joyful. In fact a vast number of lifetimes are monotonous and painful.

Creating a heaven on Earth so that we can stay in this endless cycle longer is a trick of the Kal or negative power for soon every positive cycle shifts to the darker or negative cycle. The lower worlds are places of learning but they are still prisons for Soul's education.

During the black plague of the middle ages I recall a life as a very ill small child. My parents lovingly spoon fed me soup because I was too weak. And then they gave me spoons of herbs like medicines. There were garlic bulbs throughout in the house. Everywhere in the town large numbers of people were falling horribly ill and dying. There was much suffering among the people. And sometimes bodies laid in the streets and were pushed away in carts. In dark ages the physical bodies we wear can undergo much suffering and illness. Although like an old shell when it becomes too sick we slip out of it like an over coat, only to put on another one in another life.

Although we enjoy some lives of relative comfort and advantage there were also equally many lifetimes of enduring great challenges like living in a dark cold dungeon with thick medieval castle walls or fighting in senseless brutal wars with the clash of metal, or laboring as a metal worker for endless hours. And then moving as gypsy entertainers with theater and song bundled up in coats and blankets moving town to town surviving the bitter cold winters that went through us with little food. It is important to see some of these more toilsome experiences because it is important to understand that the lower worlds are not the magnificent heaven we are told they are or embody the pleasant experience we may have in a single lifetime or cycle.

Promises that the lower worlds can become a utopia of themselves or that the lower heavens are the ultimate, lead to more reincarnations of both painful suffering and worldly pleasure without returning to our ultimate destination as a coworker with HURAY (God).

The following past life experience from a Utopian like planet illustrates clearly how a heaven on Earth, utopia or golden ages, appear to give us the satisfaction with our special spiritual talents, evolved mental apparatus, and lofty psychic awareness, but this illusion creates a contentedness that prevents us from being freed of the lower worlds of matter, energy, time and space and finding God in the Pure Positive God Worlds.

In recent times to the bewilderment of many Archeologists they had discovered what looked like human skeletons, except these skeletons were like an anomaly, incredible in size ranging from 15 feet in height to much taller. The Archeologists who made these shocking findings such as an entire grouping of eleven of such skeletons resting beside each other, plus other such finds sought for repressing this knowledge since it was in contradiction to the history as modern man knows and that they would not want to explain or choose to know themselves.

Upon being shown by the VARDAN past life records I saw myself in a previous life millions of years ago on a distant planet called Seres. This planet from long ago had two suns, pristine waterfalls and forests flourishing with vibrancy. The suns shown upon a beautiful, pristine forest world.

Pure crystal like bodies of water rested between beautiful land masses protected and thriving. The name of these people were the Seres. They were the fathering race of many humanoid races throughout the universe. They were humanoid in form but by human standard quite tall. The Seres were a tall race, well over 17 feet in height. Roughly 24 to be more exact.

In this incarnation on Seres I was well over 17 feet tall and wore a white robe. I went by my spiritual name Gah-Shy-Zah.[3] Gah had white hair and was several thousand years old. Gah's facial features were loving and warm. In that lifetime Gah Shy-Zah did not practice any of the assigned religions as he was the Living VARDAN Master on Seres whose job it was to educate Souls to travel through the Pure Positive God Worlds to return to God.

In this lifetime Gah-Shy-Zah had found it frustrating how individuals became fixated at one level of heaven with a sort of golden age form of apathy.

The Seres people had profound golden age psychic advancements and technology to travel the universes. But simultaneously they were not aware that they were still prisoners of the heavens of reincarnation.

Gah-Shy-Zah felt that one of the greatest stumbling blocks among the Seres was most had such a strong sense of spiritual advancement and in that way other doors became closed.

Then when the next door was presented by divine spirit itself, the Soul in its confidence does not step through.

On Seres the individuals who often stepped through were called "Seekers" because they longed for God so strongly and therefore took up divine training to learn out-of-body travel to return home.

In this lifetime my husband Allen was a close friend. He was at that time 800 years old and had a youthful brown hair. In Earth years that would be 24 years old.

3. Heathers spiritual name is Gah-Shy-Zah while Allen's is Nye-Dah-Zah.

Because there was such a great harmony among people and a great harmony of people to the planet their vitality was greatly increased because we fed divine love energy to the planet and in return the planet sustained us and fed divine love energy back to them which vitalized them physically. For that reason and being that it was a golden age, people lived for several thousand years.

People had a very deep appreciation of nature on Seres. All life forms were seen as pure spirit. One of the most striking things about the Seres people as a whole was how gentle and loving the people were.

There wasn't competitiveness as there is on Earth. There wasn't jealousy or resentment. Being a golden age, a lot of the negative emotions that humans have on Earth like anger, insecurity, fear, mistrust, agitation and judgmentalness; there was much less of that.

Overall there was a feeling of genuine love. Instead of behaving like strangers, people were helping each other like an extended global family. Instead of having thoughts like, "I wonder if this guy is a jerk", instead they felt a universal trust and harmony such as, "This man before me is Spirit." Being that this was a golden age there was no crime, violence, war, cheating people of money, polluting the environment or harm to any of God's creatures. The general understanding that everyone had on Seres is that everyone is Spirit.

And since everyone is Spirit if you help anything or anyone you are helping yourself. They didn't look at it like, "What's in it for me." They saw God in everything. However, in spite of how exalted this serene state of consciousness appears, on a more psychically evolved planet when compared to a lower state planet, it is still only Cosmic Consciousness which appears very lofty but is of the lower worlds of reincarnation.

The Seres people used telepathic communications that as a whole we could send picture images, knowingness, and whole ideas to other people. They were much more intelligent than humans. If one were to take a College Professor of Earth and a child of Series, a small child would be much more intelligent. And being a golden age there was no pollution or poisonous thought energies or substances so their bodies were more resilient with stronger organs. Education was prized and better, being more accurate, important, relevant, and truthful so learning was a pleasure for everyone.

Given the law of cause and effect we knew that what we gave out returned to us. We lived in a beautiful, peaceful world. Some would call the Seres People's world a majestic heaven or a utopia but this is an illusion as it was only a golden age within the bowls of the lower worlds. And being in the lower worlds it was not the ultimate.

One of the great problems Gah-Shy-Zah faced as a Master was that the population as a whole agreed that the mid to high Astral Plane was the ultimate heaven. The high Astral Plane is a beautiful place and although it may appear as containing the highest dimensional heavenly realms it is only cosmic consciousness on the Astral Plane.

One of the ways in which the Kal or negative force trapped Souls in this golden age was at an early age people would always pick a religion for good. It usually matched that of their family and it was considered quite out of order to not identify with it as strongly as those of the seventeen hundreds felt that marriage to one person was absolute. They were so married to their religion of philosophy, upon attending any events they were often closed minded and would say upon attending a VARDANKAR talk, "Oh That was wonderful, beautiful, can I give you a hug? Well nice seeing you... bye!" For Gah as a Master this was frustrating because things went in one ear and out the other.

Being that people saw God in everything they had no animosity but they also felt no need to ever change. It was like a highly developed form of golden age apathy.

All of the Seres religions and philosophies believed in reincarnation, divine love, and knew of the universal spiritual laws. And yet they weren't overly concerned as to where reincarnation led them.

Religions with long standing traditions were even more popular. People could change religions but it was considered a very serious matter that required an excess of contemplation. Then there were the more rare individuals and they changed religions a number of times searching for what fit them best. They were called "Seekers." They were not satisfied or happy with their spiritual progress or the Astral Plane heaven, feeling something was missing. They desired God.

Many of them were not satisfied with the popular golden age idea that God is just there and higher consciousness just happens and nothing further is required. They felt something was missing. Those were often ones who would find the VARDAN Spiritual Traveler.

VARDANists often attended local gatherings. Most people on Seres committed to dogmas and did not attend these events, as they were communicating with the spirit of trees, spirits of the air or the Great Spirit.

On one occasion Gah-Shy-Zah coordinated a class. Those who attended were serious students of VARDANKAR, the Ancient Science of Out-of-Body Tuza Travel.

Everyone listened as beautiful otherworldly sounds and flute filled the air. They were seated in chairs as two musicians played ethereal otherworldly melodies with instruments unknown to Earth. One instrument resembled a flute and the enchanting sound echoed through the room.

There were huge soft curtains, long tapestries with intricate beautiful patterns hung from floor to ceiling giving the room a feeling of warmth and security.

The experience sort of felt like being by the ocean because the air was electric, like the air was enlivening and had a high vibration feeling that filled the entire room.

On a large podium rested an enormous Shariyat-Ki-HURAY (the spiritual book of the VARDAN Spiritual Travelers located in each Temple of Golden Wisdom in each heavenly plane) that spanned roughly three feet high and two feet wide and was covered with leather and gold leaf lining the pages.

These were large because the people themselves were large. The tremendous book was extremely thick since people in golden ages lived longer and therefore we had a lot more time to write. Gah-Shy-Zah opened the Shariyat which is the book of the VARDAN Masters and began to speak about VARDANKAR.

Gah-Shy-Zah spoke telepathically, "It is important to listen really carefully, minutely to the sound current. And letting yourself vibrate like a rocking, like being on a lake where waves are going up and down and you are flowing with it rather than against it. The wave goes up and down. When you don't have patience you interrupt the cycle and create problems like you are fighting spirit. It creates a bumpy, choppy agitation on the water."

"Sometimes we need that to undergo purification but it's important to not let it go on to long. If we are not carful the agitation can grow stronger and lead to bigger problems."

"The answer is to let go and stop fighting it, going back to the wave of the natural rhythm of the sound. Patience is very important in flowing with and riding on the light and sound current."

"The misuse of power is like throwing a rock in the lake it creates a blast wave. The wave travels and returns rippling back to us. This has nothing to do with God not loving the individual but is simply the spiritual law where the individual is creating disharmony and the wave returns to the sender."

"Most people do not know what power is. Power is not throwing a big rock in the lake. Power is harmony and vibration. When you are really in harmony with the VARDAN you are letting the power flow through you in greater concentration."

"When you are of a higher vibration you are letting the power of the VARDAN more fully flow through you."

"Picture a lake and how the wind is like spirit moving over the lake creating wave vibrations. Just like the waves are vibrating, each molecule of water is vibrating at a much higher rate than the waves. So its vibrations, inside vibrations, inside vibrations. Each one has a greater harmony than the next and you are traveling inwardly and getting closer and closer to the source."

"The microcosm and the macrocosm; the world of molecules is a reflection of the God Worlds and the spiraling galaxies are also a reflection of the God Worlds. You see the same principle, whether you are looking though a microscope or looking through a telescope, the theme is these vibrations that are moving higher and higher."

"There is the importance of being in harmony with it and not fighting it which is being in disharmony with it. However, this by itself doesn't bring you spiritual freedom. You have to follow the path of VARDANKAR and become active otherwise you stagnate at a particular vibratory level. So VARDANKAR allows you to shift with the help of the Master so that you are not stuck at a particular vibration. You avoid getting trapped and can move toward God Realization."

"The natural order of the Kal world is to get you stuck, trapped at a particular vibration for thousands of years, so harmony by itself is not necessarily a good thing…because it can be a trap."

"But when you combine harmony with Out-of-Body Tuza Travel you have a very powerful combination, because you are able to dwell in any of these states of consciousness whenever you want and you have full control of where you go and how long you remain there…because you are in balance. And balance comes from detachment and patience and harmony. Your mind has to be in harmony in order to ride the sound and light."

"It is like riding on a horse. You are able to ride the horse because you are in harmony with it. If you are not in sink you separate and you fall off. The idea is to join forces and flow with it."

While Gah-Shy-Zah discussed this he soon referred to a large chart of the God Worlds very similar to the one in this book that was hung nearby which we all used in discussion of our journeys in Out-of-Body Tuza Travel to the various planes of HURAY. It was Gah-Shy-Zah's wish to see that all of his students become God Realized Masters themselves and therefore they focused on the learning and Mastering of Tuza Travel.

In their free moments in that lifetime Allen and Gah being close friends on occasion went on excursions in nature. They took out hover boards which much resemble today's snow boards or even skate boards but were not. The hover boards would levitate 6 to 12 feet off the ground floating mid-air.

These boards which were curved in shape and were capable of moving really fast and in a sense felt like standing on a rocket. Gah and Allen took their hover boards to a pristine snowcapped mountain. They would roar with laugher and smile as they raced each other, hair blowing in the sharp winds.

The air was invigorating, enlivening, filled with spirit so much so that it made one feel more alive.

As they were riding down the mountain it made a sudden fast drop and they both went fast with it, moving with great speed like falling from a skyscraper.

The hover boards had a special feature that they protected the rider from all collisions by redirecting itself. If either of us started to go into a tree the hover board would swiftly swerve around the tree gracefully. If a branch was too close the hover board would shift out of harm's way. They went fast roughly 60 to 80 miles per hour down the mountain laughing, expressing telepathically feelings of fun and exhilaration in a feeling that was like flying as trees flashed by.

Gah raced gleefully beside Allen. They had a lot of exhilarating joy in the rushing momentum like the sensation of flying down the slope racing each other.

At another time Gah would float hovering over the stillness of a peaceful lake as though frozen. Some found peace in seeking rest from hammocks in tree tops of huge towering trees that seemed immense like skyscrapers.

These sports were fun, however their greatest joy was their practices in VARDANKAR to move deeper into the heavenly spheres of the vast God universes beyond time and space and to share those blessings with others.

Beyond that distant ancient planet and returning to the Causal heaven, Allen over the years grew proficient in this area of reading the Akashic records of the Causal Plane and the Soul Plane in which he was able to view many of his previous lives such as those we shared here.

One of the realities revealed in this holographic world of records is how the law of karma plays out in each of the lower heavens including Earth itself.

He learned how on spiritually evolved planets or in golden ages Soul becomes lulled into not pursuing God because of being contented in our utopic surrounding.

It was also revealed to him how for countless reincarnated lives in one way or another, people by habit lash out at others not realizing that the universe operates much like the laws of physics: every action has an equal and opposite reaction. The universe is like a gigantic mirror, it is reflective in nature and therefore we are harming ourselves. Karma is an automated exacting system of the lower universes that like a mega computer is constantly sending out the return of our words and deeds that come back to us over the course of many, many lifetimes.

This Causal Plane heaven is like the visionary Warehouse of our recorded millions of endless reincarnations on the wheel of eighty four. The number of lives or reincarnations far exceeds what most Past Life Regressionists or psychics would care to know.

This is daunting or even horrifying to the human mind but for each new lifetime the individual's memory is often erased like a clean slate so he can, with less distraction, carry out his spiritual mission or learn in the present moment his lessons and advance spiritually in the moment without being overwhelmed. Soul receives a hands-on spiritual education that in these worlds of experience, it eventually learns to appreciate that all of the monotonous endless experiences, pleasure and suffering were all worth it, now that it has reached becoming a conscious coworker with God.

When we reach this spiritual state we are released from the wheel of eighty-four in a state of spiritual liberation. This state of liberation that is sometimes referred to as Jivan Mukti is possible under the guidance of the VARDAN Spiritual Traveler, as he will teach the individual through Out-of-Body Tuza Travel how to return to God.

Through experiences such as this we have learned that the VARDAN Spiritual traveler teaches the science of out-of-body travel which will free the individual from this wheel of reincarnations. Through this process we learned to read our records and understand the hidden karmic conditions that affect us in our lives now.

However it is not necessary to view many past lives to become spiritually free, only by learning Tuza Travel to the worlds beyond time and space of total awareness do we find Jivan Mukti.

In this exploration of an overview of the mistakes and illusions we have repeated in many reincarnations on Earth, other planets, and in other heavens; by having a deeper understanding of these we can all put ourselves back on track spiritually.

4
THE ETHERIC PLANE

In a reverie I began a contemplation while chanting names for God and peering into the inner realms. I lay as I usually do in bed, closed my eyes and began my next journey into the far country, those places that some call heaven.

As I relaxed more deeply, the subtle sensation of numbness flowed through my legs and body until a calm serenity set in. I was drawn up out of my body and appeared in a beautiful world of white light tinged with a subtle purple hue shimmering in the ethers. And I heard an indescribable sound, almost like that of millions of tiny crystal chimes that made a high pitched shimmering sound.

This was one of the lower heavens called the Etheric plane. The Etheric plane is the top of the Mental Plane, the area of the intuition that lies directly below the Pure Positive God Worlds.

The sound swept through a bright field of light. And within I saw Lai Tsi, a VARDAN Master from ancient China who had a long white beard and was wearing a long white robe.

Lai Tsi seemed to hover about with a silvery white light about him, glowing brightly.

I then noticed a bright beam of light that shown from the

top of his head and from the sleeves of his arms. Both of which reminded me of an intense search light.

And then he did something which surprised me; as he moved his arms with these great beams of light in a circular motion.

This created what appeared to be like a portal of light, an inter-dimensional window he cut out into a world that was far brighter.

It felt as if Lai Tsi opened a doorway and was letting me peer far beyond this magnificent but lower heaven of the Etheric plane and into the Pure Positive God Worlds.

The Pure Positive God Worlds are a series of heavens or planes beyond matter, energy, time and space, far beyond the mind and the twin currents of positive and negative. They are Soul's true home.

Drawn into this doorway into the pure positive God Worlds or higher worlds, the light was far brighter and more refined and the sound was more uplifting and finer with a pure, higher octave.

Then in the next moment I had a knowing flash of myself in a previous life. I was in a state of Seeing, Knowing and Being.

In this previous life my name was Changji and I was a student of Lai Tsi in ancient China. I had black hair and a long black mustache.

I lived in a gorgeous, pristine land of green rolling hills and crystal clear waters. I watched from a distance as in that life time I went into spiritual contemplation sitting with legs crossed on the wooden floor.

The sound shifted in fineness and became quieter, softer and of a higher pitch. My body was on Earth but my spirit was in heaven.

Through out-of-body travel I suddenly shifted into a state of being surrounded by the most unimaginable, intense, brilliant, white light... like sitting in the center of a glowing star.

I had a sense of knowingness that this was deep into the Pure Positive God Worlds.

I felt blissfully centered in HURAY, God. I felt a knowing that HURAY is the only reality. God is the one true reality. And I was in the center of IT. There was a knowing and experiencing IT.

I had a feeling beyond serenity that IT is indescribable. For God is my universe, my air, my spirit, being present in spirit. And all present. It was silent and yet simultaneously I heard again the endless shimmering of millions of tiny crystal chimes in a high pitched sound current that flowed through all things, in all worlds and is omnipresent.

It is the deepest peace of knowing that I am home, not partly home or almost home but actually home; home in the presence of the essences of the universe; the HURAY, God, the majestic, the wondrous.

On the inner planes it became my permanent home.

And yet simultaneously we live, move more fully in partnership with HURAY as God's coworker in these lower universes of matter, energy, time, and space while dwelling in the higher worlds of magnificent, pure spirit.

We have our feet on Earth and our consciousness in heaven. For we truly know the meaning of the words, "in God I live, move and have my being."

From then on we never leave the higher worlds of God but dwell in two places simultaneously.

So intense, was this light of the higher worlds that it was beyond any human description.

In the midst of this I heard the words, "One of the false teachings of religions is the idea that we must wait for an afterworld to know the heavenly worlds of God. This is a mistake because it is through these worlds that we can learn of our spiritual purpose and the nature of the vast spiritual worlds."

I expressed gratitude to Lai Tsi for this moment and for his past love, training and guidance with me as a spiritual VARDAN Master in ancient China.

I perceived through a window Etheric plane cities of light spread out in the distance glowing.

I was reminded again of the portal which Lai Tsi drew that opened like a window into a spectacular brilliant white light shining from the Pure Positive God heavens.

"When the individual is ready the door opens. Attachment is the thing which often stands between us and this door that keeps the student from stepping through. We cannot step through while simultaneously clinging tightly to all the things of the lower worlds. We fail to see the doorway shimmering in the distance because we may be frightened of what we may have to give up to approach it."

Under the Spiritual Travelers guiding hand the student learns to surrender all things to the VARDAN Master. He learns to surrender his true self Soul, his concerns, his sadness, his hopes, and all that encompasses him to the Living VARDAN Master. And you might ask why would he do this?

It is because when we surrender all to the Margatma, the Living VARDAN Master whose very consciousness is in the heart of the Ocean of Love and Mercy, we are surrendering all to God (the HURAY). And in doing so we are freed of these stresses because our lives are in the hands of the VARDAN (Holy Spirit)."

Then instead of swimming against the current of God we are swimming with the current of God, back to IT.

It is every Soul's destiny to become a conscious coworker of the infinite one, the HURAY, God. In ancient China it was moving to see Changji, like his Spiritual Master, could help others go from feeling lost in the lower world prisons to feeling truly spiritually free!

It is the movement towards God Realization on the returning wave. I saw Changji journey out-of-body to help students learn out-of-body travel too. This sort of experience of conscious coworkership with God throughout eternity is not limited to perfect sages or so-called special people but we learn it by practicing this science ourselves. The HURAY or God wants us to drop our self-deprecation of spiritual low self-esteem and drop our vanity of self-importance and become conscious coworkers with IT, not according to ego but according to God's will. The HURAY or God wants us to return to IT.

You can return to God which is the state called God Realization and have such experiences of the pure spirit heavens if you have the patience, discipline and perseverance to study with the Spiritual Traveler, The Living VARDAN Master whose role it is to help Soul reach Self and God Realization. The path has been called by many names and taught by many different Masters for eternities but in its essence it remains the same, to bring the individual home to God ITSELF.

5
THE SOUL PLANE

Since ancient times such as the times of the Ancient Greeks, people were advised by the sages of their day through time immortal, "Man know thyself." In ancient Egypt at the entrance of each place of learning and each spiritual temple these words were seen. Above the entrance of the Temple of Delphi of Ancient Greece were the words, "Know thyself."

The Soul absorbed in his new incarnation is often instead swept up in the strong spiritual social tides of his day. For him the hidden nature of himself remains forever hidden until he one day awakens perhaps by being struck by lightning, or sees a bit of heaven and notices that maybe there is more to his life than his house and his worldly position; that there are vast spiritual riches unknown to him. This knowing, when deepened is really the striving for Self Realization.

From my perspective people have often looked in all the wrong places to solve the riddle of the self.

Self Realization has nothing to do with the lower bodies of man which are only temporal in nature but with our eternal God Self: Soul. Self Realization occurs when Soul becomes completely conscious of the Atma Lok or 5th plane also known as the Soul Plane. The Soul Plane is the first of the Pure Positive God Worlds. The vibratory rate here is so high that it cannot descend into the human state of consciousness but Soul must leave its body and travel into this exalted plane of pure positive light and sound.

Many who are not too tightly bound in belief grapple to find and define themselves, but too often are swept in the currents of the mind forces and define life and selfhood as a mind thing that exists within the parameters of the astral, mental or material spheres. Others interested in or enamored with Science define man as a material object composed of chemical processes as his entire being and purpose of existence. His spiritual experiences of heaven are to him a chemical reaction in his brain.

Others define the self with philosophy, religion, or metaphysics. And others define themselves according to their talents, profession, wealth, assets, physical appearance or social spiritual role. These things that can be strongly identified with are helpful in life but are not the self, but the most superficial level of one's being, like the exposed tip of an iceberg.

The important part is hidden deep beneath the surface, beneath consciousness awareness. This is like being born in the physical universe and having nearby a galactic manual that reveals how it all works but instead of reading it Soul lets it collect dust on a shelf while having a party. Without the inner manual that comes with Self Realization the person can go through their entire life not remembering who they truly are and the entirely different level of their spiritual mission; or not remembering why before they were born, they chose to return to this world; or perhaps only learning a spiritual mission given in the Astral or Mental Plane states of consciousness which can only bring them so far.

Out-of-Body Tuza Travel to heavens is the fantastic journey which opens up spiritual instruction with the Spiritual Travelers so that the individual can work his way through deeper understandings of the heavens until he reaches the Self Realization state.

The various VARDAN Temples of Golden Wisdom located on each plane give students divine instruction in the God knowledge.

Many who have near death experiences speak of feeling as though they were asleep and had suddenly woken up. Usually this is because they have woken up on one level of heaven.

Yet they may not realize that they can likewise wake up on higher levels of heaven yet again. In out-of-body travel we realize and have a firsthand experience that we ourselves are not our human costume but instead a pure Soul, a pure God spark with a body of light and sound, a selfhood beyond human bounds. This is the self we awaken to in a profound experience of Self Realization which awakens us beyond our contrived nature to our true nature.

After experiencing looking through the spectacular window Lai Tsi had cut for me to view the higher Pure Positive God World or heaven, a window to see past the worlds of duality, time and space; I journeyed through out-of-body travel through the dark void that lays between one plane to the next; the in between world. Following this world is a world far greater.

The world of the Atma Lok is a Heaven that is a pure positive heavenly plane of God.

It is the first plane of true spiritual freedom. Before entering the Soul plane I tuned into the higher vibrations. The spiritual travelers who reach the state called Self Realization can pass through the endless region of darkness the separates the lower worlds or heavens from the first of the Pure

Positive God Worlds or pure spirit heavens beyond.

In the distance was a vast shimmering light spread out in a glow. I could hear layers of sound simultaneously; one like a soft high pitched breath and a singing bowl shimmering. And one like that of a flute flowing without pause on and on. There is a vast emptiness of pure light and sound with spiritual palaces in the distance composed of sound and light.

And then like a lake that is white liquid light in substance. There is a placid stillness as time does not exist here. And everywhere I see Godly Souls in many directions that appear like globes of light and sound and other times they appear in a radiance with slightly human like attributes, the Light filled beings each one brighter than many suns. All of Soul's lower bodies are left behind in the lower worlds. Instead we exist in our pure self Soul.

Each Soul here radiates an internal light which appears to come from the core of Soul. They no longer contain material substance but are instead composed of pure light and sound, the substance of spirit. The dualistic fragmentation of the individual in the lower planes is healed and made whole here as the Soul once fragmented into pieces of male and female, good and evil and so on, are healed. The individual is put back together again like the fragmented puzzle or shards of glass reformed, made complete, we become whole, a complete atom of God in radiance and fuller realization.

I felt again a pull to move further within this first beautiful light and sound filled heaven of the Pure Positive God Worlds called the Atma Lok, which is otherwise known as the Soul Plane, fifth plane or house of Soul. This is the world where spiritual wisdom reigns. This realm of Sach Kand, the Soul Plane is the first realm of true spiritual freedom or spiritual liberation, where Soul in its long quest is once fully established here, finally freed from the wheel of reincarnation, the wheel of 84.

The Soul Plane is the spiritual heaven where Soul finally reaches the long awaited state called "Self Realization." Here Soul's long awaited questions of various lives, "Who am I?" "Why am I here?" "What is the purpose of life?" ...all of which are answered. Then Soul knows and experiences first hand its true identity, nature, purpose, as it realizes itself, who it is. Soul discovers it is divine and composed of the same fabric as God. We find we are a drop of water from the breathtaking Ocean of God. A Soul composed of pure spirit of a body of pure light and sound.

Nearby I sensed the presence of Rebazar Tarzs, who at the time of writing this book was the Margatma, the Living VARDAN Master.

Within this world I hovered and my vision rested on a bright glowing vast light that emanated from a great spiritual being off in the distance.

Within the center of this sparkling brilliant whiteness and shimmering sound was a greater concentration of brilliance, a brilliant presence of all-encompassing magnitude. This brilliant presence was that of Sat Nam, a divine reflector of God.

The 5th Plane refers to the Soul Plane, that region beyond energy, matter, time and space in the Pure Positive God Worlds. Not to be confused with what some call the 5th dimension in the lower worlds.

There was an appearance of almost hovering and glowing with a vast internal light. He was not God itself but the first true manifestation or pure reflector of the HURAY of the

God Worlds: Sat Nam meaning true identity.

The light that flowed from Sat Nam flowed out like a cosmic shock wave throughout this infinite universe. He existed in the core like being in a brilliant cloud of light which to me resembled light vapors like that from a frozen explosion of brilliant particles that appear in a flash of pure spirit radiance.

He was in a sense like a youth yet composed entirely of a brilliant light or pure spirit substance. While doing a loving spiritual exercise waves of light rolled from him echoing out in all directions like a cosmic wave of brilliant white particles.

I inwardly smiled and telepathically expressed my love for Sat Nam and thanked him for helping me when I was a youth. Sat Nam centered in this shining glow and continued focusing on contemplation. I continued, "What of the lovable Souls who want to return to you and your heavenly universe?"

He did not speak in words but instead projected for me to see a bird's eye, panoramic view of the vast cosmic planes. It was an expanded view that included far vast reaches through planes and worlds and this world of countless Souls like trillions of glowing particles of light in an Ocean of light. Within these worlds many of the Souls were busy and enamored or preoccupied by various things within their minute microcosmic universe.

There on the mountain of light again in the lower worlds were spiritual peoples enthralled by their various Spiritual Leaders, Guides or Gurus. I saw large numbers of individuals in towns and cities, countless people in offices taken up in business. I saw others engaged in a myriad of human pursuits, arts, learning and interests all busily preoccupied moving to and fro like busy honey bees swarming in human and astral affairs. I saw beings in the lower heavens after death. The individuals were having experiences in these lower worlds of energy, matter, time, and space. Seeing these lower worlds from the Soul Plane which is the first Pure Positive God Realm heaven brings a higher perspective of stepping back to see a bigger picture.

Then in a flash the scene suddenly expanded and pulled back even further for a wider panoramic view of layers upon layers of cosmic existence that fanned out endlessly. Everywhere Souls in these worlds upon worlds of existence appeared. I again look with reverence to Sat Nam and telepathically spoke: "What of your world?" As though a curtain opened I saw with that a vast pale yellow plane of ethereal vaporous land with a pale yellow glowing mist that went on for thousands of miles in all directions appeared more vividly. There were luminous beings of a highly evolved spiritual consciousness radiating a great light. I watched as a small group of these self-realized beings with shining countenances as they gathered together in a small circle to communicate with each other.

I felt gratitude to Sat Nam and I experienced waves of shimmering light echo and continue issuing from him in pulsing waves. In those waves an ethereal sound reminded me of a singing bowl but slightly, as a flute that plays a melody without end. And as this occurred I communicated to Sat Nam again on Self Realization.

Still sitting in serene contemplation within the light, he spoke in the silent language of Soul. Sat Nam's voice, if you could call it that was so beautiful, like a heavenly melody, as though it were a voice of a young man and simultaneously an otherworldly sounding divine instrument. His telepathic impressions and voice was very sweet and had a refined sound as though it contained great harmony and wisdom, "It starts as the expanding recognition that you are not your human body, you are not your human mind and thoughts. You are not of the Earth world and your human self. You first recognize what you are not. There are layers upon layers like a cloak of illusions that shield you from a vision of your true God Self. A Soul is a happy entity weighed down by these bodies. Once you realize what you are not, you begin to realize what you ARE. You are the VARDAN."

"At Self Realization your light and sound increases as the expansion of the light of day fills the skies." As Sat Nam described this we simultaneously saw a vision of a Soul. The bubble of spiritual light expanded out and their sound expanded out. "You fill yourself with it and become purified until you are radiant with this light and sound. This is why the spiritual travelers glow so brightly. They emanate the light and sound of HURAY in greater measure."

As he said this he sat or shall I say hovered floating in the core of a huge cloud of light. He was seated upon nothing but the pure VARDAN, pure spirit like air, floating mid-air and lotus-style in his spiritual exercise.

He continued, "Just as the cloud saturated with water vapor is, you must be saturated with the VARDAN (spirit with light and sound) and the Master. Your consciousness filled with it and then you become this sound and greater light yourself."

"You are a child of the cosmic current; born of the VARDAN. In duel awareness you can be at once in the physical world and simultaneously in the Pure Positive Worlds. The Sailor keeps his eyes to the North Star. Always he steers his ship by this light, knowing it will guide him home."

"The HURAY, VARDAN, and Margatma is your North Star that you fix your inner eye on to steer your spiritual vessel and life towards it. We always fix our sights to the guiding sound and light of God's star: The Margatma, the Living VARDAN Master is also this bright North Star for the initiate that he can fix in his inner eye, guiding him to these higher spheres."

"Even if the ready one does not know what to gather his attention on to be in and see that the higher worlds fill his inner worlds, he can casually wander like a child wanders in a day dream. While in school sitting in wooden chairs and desks he is simultaneously visiting the forest, the playground, the ocean. That child travels there unknown to him."

"He bringing his attention to these places, he simultaneously dwells there as Soul. His body in school but his consciousness in part dwells in these places. And so it is with the VARDANist. Like the famous saying, "Thy feet are on Earth but thy heart is in heaven." As all the VARDAN Masters say: "The initiate is always present in the higher worlds or conscious of his inner companion the Spiritual Traveler.""

In gratitude and smiling light I communicated in turn, "It is very helpful to look upon the picture image photograph of the Living VARDAN Master to learn to remember his features and then it becomes easier to place the Margatma in the spiritual eye and keep him there consciously. This can be a preliminary step to awakening in spirit in the Pure Positive Worlds of God and keeping wakeful to these."

Sat Nam continued, "He can bring himself to the cosmic worlds, pure positive heavens if he fills himself with it, that he can subtly see himself there and know it is so and simply be.

Letting go of his doubts he has faith that it is so, and like Aladdin's lamp you see reality of what you wish to create and it comes into being."

Again I responded, "This is what Allenji and I practiced which in the book *"The Flute of God,"* Paul Twitchell called: "Mold making,"[3] seeing ourselves fixating our awareness and hearts to God, being already in the spiritual state of consciousness we desired. And then suddenly six months later the true Spiritual Traveler made himself known to us. And as the traveler said when a Soul is more drawn to God then fixated to its attachments the Traveler will appear."

Ripples of light and sound continued to issue from Sat Nam as he telepathically spoke, "There are three streams that can flow within the self: the positive, the negative and the neutral, which is the pure steam of spirit. You are a cosmic flute that God can play or that the negative or positive current can play. You are an instrument of God when you tune yourself to the celestial flute of this world in the rippling wave; the pure spirit stream of consciousness. You can realize the saint that you are and be numbered among the Godly Self Realized in this world."

And then I saw a Pegasus and the expression came, "Let the HURAY, Margatma, and VARDAN be like our muse always inspiring us on in all our expressions from the God source alone. That everything we do is of this divine muse. Not the mind, not the lower worlds, not opinion, not a social source, but only God and Holy Spirit is our muse. Always ever vigilant to its voice, always consulting it first to do God's will."

Then Sat Nam like lightning flashed a vision to me from years ago when I was a new student in VARDANKAR.

3. Paul Twitchell, *The Flute of God* (Menlo Park, CA: Illuminated Way Pub., 1969)

My small fluffy pale yellow, tennis ball shaped bird friend, a cute little canary bird sat on a perch. As I looked at her and smiled I felt guided to free her of her bird cage. I felt that she would not be frightened as I had seen so many times before with birds in childhood. Her name was Bhakti which means divine love.

I called her sweet cute pet names like love chick and angel bird as I opened the small gates to freedom. Bhakti bird hopped and coincidentally placed herself right in front of a picture of a snow white swan with long outstretched wings. Because she was the same size as the picture of the swan, she suddenly looked like a pale yellow canary with large white outstretched swan wings. I photographed her and admired the wonderful picture of a sweet canary with swan wings.

"I gave you that." said Sat Nam.
A feeling of surprise came over me, "Thank you." I felt with a smile. "I love you and I love HURAY (God).

Then Sat Nam flashed to me another image of what had occurred shortly after permanently setting Bhakti free from the bird cage; something interesting happened.

I was compelled to do this because I knew she was no longer afraid of me or this greater world outside her old cage. So I put her upon the wooden floor and she suddenly began to hop around the entire parameter of the bedroom, beside the wall's outer most edge. A cheerful little happy being of God, a lovable Soul. She made her way about the room with cute little bounces all around the entire extra-large bedroom. Because I love spaciousness to dance there was very little furniture. At one point in her hopping she came to one lonely piece of furniture, a light golden baize book shelf of spiritual books. She suddenly stopped in her tracks as though she suddenly sensed something. Then she began eyeing the books.

She was riveted by the sight and looked high up at what may have looked like from her view point a skyscraper of my VARDANKAR books. With her tiny pale yellow head she craned her head and looked far up and I was amazed to see that she was moving her tiny head side to side as though she were carefully scanning and reading the titles.

At the sight of this I said "Wow Bhakti looks as though she is reading the VARDANKAR books!" After several minutes of this wonder Bhakti who became satisfied with this experience began to hop a little further. Hop, hop, hop and stopped directly in front of a mirror I used for dancing.

She looked into the large mirror that towered above her like a sheet of glass and with happy wonder she seemed to have a realization of suddenly seeing herself began to sink in. She leaned her tiny pale yellow bird head sideways in an expression of curiosity as though to say: "Who is this? It appeared to be a sudden self-recognition that within myself I felt symbolized a degree of Self Realization.

Then Bhakti again satisfied and seeing herself in this awareness continued the spiritual journey and hopped further around the room until she suddenly abruptly stopped again but this time directly in front of me. She looked at me directly in my eyes with her own sparkling tiny spherical eyes. I felt joy and wonder at seeing her acknowledge my presence and at all she had done.

After some moments I went to the kitchen and brought out two meals, one large and one small, one for me and one for her which was vegetables. We sat on the wooden floor and shared a meal together as friends. I hadn't realized it until that moment that it was Sat Nam who spoke through her, a winged friend expressing an analogy of when a Soul becomes Self-Realized. In this expression he shared how the books were a first step in part of the process of the student moving toward Self Realization where they read the words of the VARDAN Masters.

And then upon learning these teachings Soul gazes upon itself as through a mirror in greater awareness. Then through Out-of-Body Tuza Travel like a mirror we begin to realize who we are. And Soul recognizes the VARDAN Masters to move to become like them. So delicate and loving a symbol it was that I smiled with light and felt gratitude. "Thank you again Sat Nam."

Heather addressed Sat Nam, "What of spiritual self-confidence? Again Sat Nam spoke telepathically as waves of light continued to flow from him: "The spiritual seeker he looks to the Guru, the Teacher, the Saint, the holy man as the only one who can reach God. I Sat Nam from the plane of Self Realization tell you these Gurus and Teachers many of them perpetuate the myth that only *they* can connect with God and reach the God Realization State. If your Guru or Teacher implies or acts or suggests that likely this will never happen in this lifetime for you, then you could certainly start to question if he is a real Teacher. For this is perpetuating the spiritually divine low self-esteem."

"The VARDAN Masters have taught for eons that the holy way to return to HURAY (God) is through the Out-of-Body Tuza Travel. You can be liberated in my world of Atma Lok which you may have waited long for. There are others that assume they have Self Realization simply because their Guru says they have. Not every messenger is an honest one. I Sat Nam say to you the out-of-body travel with the help of a

Spiritual Traveler will help you know what is true. What is the harm in being absolutely certain not with the mind realization but with the realization of spirit?"

"Through your countless past lives in the lower worlds I have watched you and been with you waiting for the moment you return. I could call you back. You are a worthy one, if you were not you would not be reading this. But be not disillusioned that you are not a fully realized God being. Also be not disillusioned by ego and vanity that you've gone further than you actually have. I only love you as a representative of the divine HURAY."

"When or if you might be told the spiritual states are only for the few chosen, realize that he is chosen that chooses himself. Long ago ancient people spoke of various saviors or masters and misinterpreted their Teachings to leave people in spiritual ignorance like sheep in a flock. You are not a passive spiritual sheep but a magnificent Soul. Many Gurus and the like ask the student to always remain a follower. Forever a spiritual follower and never a spiritually enlightened being."

"Or even worse you are told you are a spiritually enlightened being and yet you are shown only the highest reaches of the mental plane in the worlds of reincarnation. It is filled with radiant light which by all appearances seems the ultimate heaven, like that of Self Realization."

"I Sat Nam tell you that you can experience the ecstasy of the true Self Realization and know that it is the real. You can remember who you are. You can remember why you came here. The VARDAN books are written by the true Spiritual Travelers. They give instruction in the out-of-body travel that will help you to love yourself and heal your spiritual low self-esteem if you have it. All the great VARDAN Masters, as well as Jesus and Buddha and the others of high vibration love you."

"And to you who are Gurus, you too can be released from Samsara. You can be like the Great Milarepa who was humble and said: "Maybe I am not as grand as I wish I were. Maybe I made a mistake unknown to me.""

Milarepa humbly before God asked the Living VARDAN Master: "I am the greatest sinner, please accept me. Please forgive me for all I want is the one true God."

It is like the guru who will instead say, "I do not want my vanity of thinking I am the ultimate spiritual leader. I do not want the false things of this world, I only center in God."

Milarepa chose that path. He was very brave and very Humble Milarepa."

It occurred to me how spiritual individuals feel spiritual low self-esteem.

Sat Nam continued: "The spiritual individual often either feels at times too unworthy or too conceited which is also feeling spiritually unworthy because when he or she was a child he was shown something was not right with him. Spiritual low self-esteem makes you feel spiritually small. But maybe there is more to you then you know. And then in the other direction when you put yourself above others and see yourself as much, much greater you are also in Maya (illusion). It inhibits your being God's vehicle in this world and may even cause unseen suffering by those around you that you may not even notice. Always we can look for beginner state which is even if you are the most advanced and have been trained forever, you are humble before God. Beginner mind and beginner consciousness helps you advance."

There was once a man who was designated as a Master by another path. But he observed in his own behavior attachments and missing elements so he immediately stepped back and asked a true VARDAN Master and Spiritual Traveler to train him. When someone has humility they move further faster. Those who cannot face the truth stay where they are.

6
THE PATH OF VARDANKAR

One evening I was away from home and stayed in a room with cream colored walls and maroon curtains clipped with a clothespin of wood. Beside the bed stood a small replica of a porcelain angel holding white and golden fruit. I closed my eyes to do a spiritual exercise and through direct projection felt centered as though one beamed from a spaceship in the flash of a moment in one of the many Pure Positive God Worlds known by the Spiritual Travelers as Alakh Lok (6th Plane), a heaven of vast white light with subtle yellow that spans out seemingly forever with misty brilliant illumination.

In the distance a gentle, high pitched sound flowed through the ethers with the pure spirit melody of soft blowing winds flowing into eternity. There was a joyful feeling of lightness and freedom like floating on a kite above the ocean. The light was so fiercely radiant it encompassed all, there was no place it was not.

The sheer beauty of this pure positive God heavenly world was beyond all description. Very few have journeyed to this realm as it often requires a traveler to learn how. And soon my Soul like a tiny sphere or particle of God rested before a huge, colossal globe of light so incredibly large it felt much like a firefly swallowed up beside a glowing planet. Alakh Purusha, not God, but a manifestation of God appeared and its colossal presence filled all vision. In the Pure Positive God Worlds Soul does not require a mind but rather experiences through direct perception.

In impressions this great spiritual presence of the VARDAN, divine spirit and Alakh Purusha, a God Ruler of the Alakh Lok Plane and a manifestation of HURAY, the infinite, the divine, communicated soft impressions, "Throughout eons individuals, Souls become absorbed in the human, astral, the lower world realities and become endlessly lost. Within lifetimes Soul would often not remember its original higher spiritual purpose for eons. Because of this there has always been offered to Souls a direct route home to God."

"The Spiritual Traveler and the high path of VARDANKAR is a vast light in the dark caves of the lower universes or worlds. It is not for the masses but for the few ready to return to God. It leads one to the sound current that carries one to HURAY, God. The light which makes the invisible visible before one's spiritual inner eyes and inner ears."

"The attention you have may get absorbed into the little body reality. Human fictions are spun about like a beautiful tapestry about the body reality. Like a blind sea creature in the oceans of the lower worlds the Soul's cosmic memory is erased and it swims aimlessly. It doesn't remember its true nature as a God being that is being prepared to become a coworker with the supreme infinite one, God, HURAY."

It echoed within me from an unknown book what Yogi Bhajan once said: "When the ego is lost limit is lost..."[4] "The impressions continued, "Excess Ego is the absorption in the little self to the point of complete

4. Yogi Bhajan, Book Unknown, (Good Reads.com) 2015.

distraction. With ego put under the authority of spirit you can become a vehicle and coworker with HURAY (God), omniscient, omnipotent, and omnipresent. You can be limitless in the pure spiritual worlds."

Then in the golden white mist in an impression of spiritual seeing, I saw a flash of an image that in many different eras throughout recorded history and beyond it, many groups of individuals gathered greatly motivated towards spiritual realization and as a result found what is called VARDANKAR, the Ancient Science of Tuza Travel. These beings gathered and focused upon these aspects of returning to God. This same type of gathering has through countless ages reappeared as the meeting of God seekers through all ages and cycles. The reoccurrence of the gathering of the spiritual students of VARDANKAR under the Traveler of their day has always been.

On the inner levels I next sense an impression of the Spiritual Traveler teaching his students and on the inner heavenly planes helping students learn to leave their physical bodies or even so far as to pull his students out of their physical bodies in Soul form; helping free the individual by their own efforts to evolve spiritually in Tuza Travel through the evolution of awakening in higher heavens. And then we see this as well under other countless VARAN Masters on every world and cycle within lifting the individual by their own efforts to Jivan Mukti: spiritual freedom.

What appeared to be a flowing wave of sound or light rolled across the endless plane yet was in stillness. "Centered in God Realization, you become a beacon of light and sound. Like the sun your greater light nourishes and sustains all around you because you develop as a spiritual channel of the VARDAN (spirit)."

"Prior to this moving towards Self Realization your hidden inner spiritual vision begins to open and your spiritual ears begin to open when you practice the spiritual exercises of VARDANKAR and you see what is to others in materialism invisible, true reality of the spiritual universes of HURAY (God)."

"If we rely only on the material, our outer eyes and outer ears or the astral eyes and ears, it is like being spiritually blind and deaf. The only true, complete, and absolute reality is God."

"If we rely only on the human mind it is like living in a tiny dark box which leaves Soul spiritually disabled. You can come across a child who may be physically deaf and mentally dull but perhaps this same child on the spiritual level has spiritual awareness far beyond all of the adults around him. Appearances preoccupy the materialist. Practicing VARDANKAR can awaken the latent spiritual senses that sleep and through the practice of the spiritual exercises and instructions given by the Spiritual Traveler bring divine sight."

"Out-of-body travel through the spiritual exercises thirty minutes daily is basic and more of the essence than any other practice. In addition to this the Soul needs three things on the high path to the HURAY, these are: the Sound Current, the Margatma, and the Initiation."

"These three priorities have been the same for the eternity Soul has come to VARDANKAR. Without this sound current of God which flows through Soul like a river the Soul is caught in the currents of the downward pull as opposed to the upward pull. The holy sound spiritualizes the consciousness of the individual."

"The initiation links the chela (student) with the audible

life stream."

"The initiations of VARDANKAR bring the chela through a succession of heavenly spheres or planes each moving to still higher spiritual heavens until he reaches spiritual liberation."

"Individuals fail if they do not develop the inner spiritual faculties to follow the will of God (not the assumed will of God) and simultaneously have the detachment to listen from the God Plane to follow the will of God which may at times require letting go of cherished things such as cherished opinions and the good social graces of others. This is because so often social currents and human expectation flow in a counter direction to the ocean and currents of Holy Spirit."

Alakh Purusha's radiance was magnificent and far more immense then any physical or astral universe sun. Alakh communicated, "Tuzashottama power radiates from Soul." At this I sense a soft impression of a very white intensive radiance emanating from Soul. "The realization that Soul's divine essence is the VARDAN, divine spirit."

"God endowed Soul with a part of itself, with the divine creative spark, the Tuzashottama essence or energy." We see the Soul with the spirit essence radiance pooling within and around it.

The spirit stuff of light and sound. The sound light vapor encompassing it sometimes flashing out like a shock wave. Suddenly within the spirit stuff appears a butterfly. From the imaginative faculty with shottama energy and then a field of butterflies. It continued, "By use of the imaginative faculty and the shottama energy, draws Soul in out-of-body travel to this plane or higher planes."

I perceive a floating bubble of light that appears from a lower universe to a higher one as the impressions continue, "The spiritual traveler teaches the proper method of Soul movement."

"To try to steer and control the spiritual current is to lose it and gain the psychic plane in the lower universe. To instead surrender to the holy divine will of Divine Spirit and God and to do instead only what the power of God wills through us is the beginning of eternity and coworkership with God."

"Total reliance on the VARDAN, divine spirit of the God Worlds is similar to how in the Star Wars film "Jedi" entirely rely on the force which on the VARDAN level transcends human ego and astral senses such as clairvoyance."

"In the same way the student surrenders to the will of the VARDAN divine spirit of the God Worlds. This is not to be confused with the guiding spiritual psychic forces and entities of the Astral Plane. It is not to ego or selfish purpose but God's will become his aim and arrow. By only doing that which is God's will we avoid directing the spiritual power but letting God's will direct it through us."

"Directing the spiritual power is psychic and is called magic, black or white which violates spiritual law and pulls Soul to the lower psychic planes of reincarnation."

"The abuse of the shottama gives only the illusion of evolution, power, control and progress."

"Rushing currents of light and sound like a river flowing through Soul within the center of these currents in the divine flow of the God current. The mighty light and sound current of God can wash away all impurities. Perfection of Soul requires absolute reliance on the VARDAN or in the learning process, absolute reliance on the Master whose consciousness resides in the pure spirit regions."

Within this realm a being of light flashed before me an image of a fountain of light and sound, "You are an unlimited fountain of God; a fountain of light and sound. You have access to vast spiritual awareness and knowing of the spiritual. The lower reflective pool is the mind and its limits are the lower places of time and space, duality and limitation."

"The divine fountain of God is flowing within you. In the past you had allowed others to shut these waters. When you deny your divinity as a channel for God through which these waters flow to yourself and all life, you deny God itself."

"The beautiful light and sound gives life to all, the same way physical water gives life to physical beings and plants. The unlimited fountain of HURAY's light and sound can open in each individual as the result of his stepping under the guidance of the Living VARDAN Master who is the distributer of the HURAY. Then the fountain will flow with the greater flow."

"Within the light waters the spiritual path is likened to a lake or Ocean of sound and light. Sometimes Soul will only dip its feet in the water lightly and sense something spiritually greater there; perhaps or perhaps not."

"The mind may take to busying itself with playing with ideas and arguments while dipping feet on the surface. Then there are others who are less timid and jump right in and make a great big splash."

"When Soul disciplines itself spiritually and takes up the spiritual exercises of VARDANKAR, which consists of daily practice to explore out-of-body travel with the intent of accessing our divinity and God, we are bold and bravely jumping into all things that free Soul spiritually."

Heather added, "This reminded me of the experience of Alexander the Great when he was approached by the great Ancient VARDAN Master, the Spiritual Traveler Vita Danu. According To Paul Twitchell in, "The Spiritual Notebook," The Master Vita Danu declared that Alexander could drink of these holy waters that would have flooded him with the spiritual awareness. The Master Vita Danu held out a bag of waters to Alexander. He looked over the old man before him who appeared humble. Instead of grabbing opportunity or receiving these waters offered by the Master, Alexander became impatient and immediately critical and suspicious."[5]

"Because of this Alexander hesitated. In his moment of hesitation the moment of choosing passed him by, according to Paul Twitchell his officer cut the water bag in two pieces with the sword. After several words Alexander ordered his soldiers after the man but like a flash the VARDAN Master Vanished. Alexander had the water of the divine Holy Spirit before his feet and being too arrogant and sure of himself and his opinions he let the experience pass him by."

"Had he drank of the waters from Holy Spirit he would have experienced a great spiritual enlightenment or higher states of spiritual consciousness unknown to him of a higher pure spirit Pure Positive God Worlds. Instead the Masters parting words to Alexander were a reading of the Soul records that Alexander would die young striving mercilessly for empty materialistic dreams."

Then I felt the impressions of a merry-go-round that circled round like a time machine. It was spinning around and

5. Paul Twitchell, The Spiritual Notebook (Menlo Park, CA. 1971)

around and I knew it represented the wheel of eighty four which is also called the wheel of reincarnation.

And as it spun and circled through the ages one could see before the Soul sense a flash of different periods on Soul's journey as it circled round; The seventeen hundreds, the ancient Greeks, the ancient Romans, Lemuria, and so on.

And as it went round...the Living VARDAN Master would appear and reappear again and again. Those that stepped forward to meet him and became his students found this inner road. Those VARDANists on this wheel would like apparitions appear and then disappear, wavering as though shifting between two dimensions or worlds, that of the merry-go-round and that of the pure spirit universes the God Worlds beyond duality through out-of-body travel. And those among them who took things more seriously to learn out-of-body travel to heaven, each transcended this shimmering in and out of the merry-go-round and became fully conscious and present within the spiritual freedom of the Worlds of God.

I felt within a feeling for how the humble ordinary person longs for spiritual things but feels unworthy of the divinity within themselves, accepting it often only in a smaller portion. We can accept much more in consciousness, for our true self and the VARDAN are one and the same.

The light of this God World was intense white with subtle pale yellow. And the high pitched sound continued ceaselessly as the understanding continued, "You were once told before that there is a mythology about spiritual masters being perfect like plastic, with no human emotions or human flaws. Spiritual Masters have human imperfections in the human body but not in the spiritual body. When people in ignorance come across a spiritual master or more often even just come

114

across an advanced spiritual student they are quick to judge their human flaws as proof of lack of mastership or on the other hand make the being into a demi-god to worship as an untouchable entity. When Soul embarks on this foolishness it makes becoming like them impossible."

"Such lack of spiritual sense keeps us locked in the lower consciousness like a spiritual child. The few who are brave enough will challenge themselves to shatter the veneer that encases Soul and instead pursue Self Realization and God Realization for themselves."

Many groups teach the individual to wait until death for the enlightenment and spiritual freedom of the "afterworld." This is a trick of the negative power so that the person is tricked into taking no action while he can, for if we wait until after death for spiritual advancement we will surely be surprised to learn later it was too late. In transpiring to the afterworld what we thought of as a beautiful heaven was only another lifetime in another beautiful lower heavenly plane.

We generally have little control of it and yet the entities there such as angels, spirit guides and so forth, will tell us that we have control and more.

We go to the heaven we have earned while living in the body. Anyone who has a near death experience and sees a life review will learn in the lower heavens we don't have control, we are surprised to learn we must return to the Earth. The ultimate was not as ultimate as we assumed.

Since the astral body has a limited lifespan often people that remember their past lives frequently only remember their most recent past lives and assume that they have only lived a few thousand years on Earth, on other worlds or in the lower heavens.

When we in our blossoming wisdom suddenly feel compelled to reunite with God we call upon the way shower, the Spiritual Traveler. We do not get absorbed into God losing our individuality and bliss out as some Eastern Teachings teach. That is actually Cosmic Consciousness. The true God seeker seeks to see the face of God and experience God Consciousness.

In a sense it is the ultimate destination and not the lower heavens which are beautiful, impressive, dazzling prisons. The spiritual traveler can assist us in our own journey to go beyond superficial and spiritual appearances and instead grow into Self Realization and God Realization.

Masters will sometimes disguise themselves as homeless persons to shake up the spiritual student from their preconceptions.

But even of those who are so bold as to question the reality of all they have been taught may not all seek the deeper levels of divinity.

Among these few still fewer when they get further along on the path, let go of their attachments and stay the course to where divine spirit leads Soul.

Another common obstacle to spiritual progress is the issue of entitlement and an underestimation of what it takes to find Self and God Realization. Most people understand that learning a skill such as playing the piano or dancing requires time, effort and dedication, and yet it is amazing how many foolishly believe that when it comes to spiritual matters it will be easy.

For example someone may have the unrealistic expectation

that they are going to make five years of progress in a matter of 5 months and when they fail are quick to blame the Master instead of recognizing the difficulty of the enormous task ahead and developing the desire and commitment necessary to reach their spiritual goals no matter the cost.

Letting go of Attachments and following the middle path is essential.

The True God seeker becomes what is often called the hound of heaven for there will be many tests to see whether the individual desires God strong enough to reach the Pure Positive God Worlds or whether he cares more for the things of this world and his or her own little self or ego self.

Sometimes following the course is most unexpected such as for myself when I realized that the "Master" I once followed for years was not a God Realized Master but an astral helper in what was a spiritual stepping stone to finding the Spiritual Traveler.

Many will claim to be the Master or appear to be the Living VARDAN Master. Letting go of the attachment to that mind creation, fixation, dogma, philosophy, religion or teacher was for me letting go of attachment to all but spirit. If one can first make the leap and then stay the course we find there is much more to Soul then we preconceive.

The light of this world was brilliant, glowing with this mass of light. Alakh Purusha resumed, "The path of the traveler is the sound and the road of light that leads to the all-knowing HURAY (God)."

"The high path is stepping upon and under the care of the spiritual traveler who is the Margatma, The Living VARDAN Master. He is the gatekeeper who will help you open the gates of your spiritual consciousness. There are a series of many gates one must pass in steps and stages moving from one level to the next level like the spiritual labyrinth."

"The spiritual exercises are your compass that reveal which direction to go in this maze of spiritual confusion. Within this labyrinth some will mistakenly rely on their mind and the minds of others to chart their course. This is a mistake."

"All of your concerns, questions, and deep inner longings of the spiritual nature can be brought within the inner spiritual heavens to be like the light that guides your way."

We can transcend the mind. Soul perceives though direct perception with a 360 degree view point and through the spiritual exercises we can have this expanded awareness.

"Within the maze there is also where one attunes to the understandings given from a lower realm. These look spiritual and heavenly. These can sometimes lead to wrong turns that lead to dead ends in the psychic maze. If all else fails you can know that you can rely on your inner knowingness. The knowingness is the inner compass within the maze, a spiritual faculty of the Pure God Worlds of being."

"Where you place your attention is all important. The VARAN Master, the light and Sound, the HURAY, the force of all things spiritual."

"These are the things that give the Soul true direction and permanence in realization."

"Many of the Souls now approaching this have earned the blessings of finding these understandings and have earned the blessings of finding the high path in this lifetime."

"Through hardship and tears we've gone through much. Some have waited eons for these blessings to return to the divine IT. Many who have found the traveler are ancient and have magnetized yourselves to your final return on a long journey and now step upon the road of light that leads to a divine eternity."

This understanding came to me not in words but in impressions that had a less defined visual quality."

A wispy high pitched windy sound current filled all space of the light filled heaven. And then it continued, "The living VARDAN Master is not an idol to worship but a reality to aspire to; the reality of becoming a coworker with HURAY, God."

7
THE MUSIC OF THE SPHERES

In a moment upon closing my eyes I came by Soul movement to a white world of a soft glowing brilliance, a total concentration of pure spirit that went on and on forever to eternity.

The sound was not of this world within a soft light that seems to encompass all in this region known as the endless world because it is so infinitely endless and vast beyond description. The sense of pure serenity was absolute like birds hovering frozen over ocean breeze. This heavenly realm is known by the Spiritual Travelers as the Alaya Lok, a far region of the Pure Positive God Worlds.

Within this beautiful pure God World I was shown a Knowingness and a Seeingness of the holy white music of God, the sound current that flows from the very pure plane of God, HURAY like a current of waves composed of light and sound rippling out to all the heaven worlds below through the pure positive God Regions and through the lower realms like a fountain of pure brilliance like sound and white liquid light sustaining all.

Then within this knowing formed a vision of a sound current that was clearly visible. Light and sound that was a shimmering radiance that flowed to an individual, surrounding him like rain. Then in Soul form he flowed up upon it, like one floating upon a cloud and simultaneously it illuminated his way like a spotlight on a road. And then this flow created an opening not of the physical senses but of the more subtle inner spiritual faculties; the faculty of the inner vision as opening of the spiritual sight to a greater light and the faculty of the inner hearing to a greater divine sound.

Then a Knowingness and Seeingness of impressions came from the Alaya Purusha, who is not God but of its holy expression within this vast heavenly region of Alaya Lok. Alaya Purusha in the language of Soul made known to me that the choice of the sound within the universes that we choose is significant in the life of the spiritual student.

"It can be the sound of discord or that holy sound that spiritualizes the consciousness to the frequency of pure spirit. A sound that destroys or the sound that creates, uplifts and sustains."

Alaya Perushia continued, "The Margatma, the Living VARDAN Master connects us like a wire reconnected to a telephone to this spiritual music, the holy divine sound current. (Lesser so-called Masters connect Soul with sounds of the lower universes.) When we make our home within this sound current we are in the arms of HURAY, God's light and sound embrace."

"Sound has a vibration, a frequency like waves that reach a radio. Low vibration sound of a low level pulls us down to a lower plane of heaven. And also like a radio tuning into a higher vibration sound shifts and tunes us into higher God Plane Heaven. The sounds we choose have these effects on the spiritual bodies by choice of our self-tuning. In the musical sense, we are like an instrument like a flute that we can let God play to make spiritual harmonies."

The ethers seemed electric, "Higher vibration music is

spiritually uplifting and helps the spiritual bodies spiritually. Music of the discordant type with a course vibration, a harshness or hypnotic of beat can pull Soul to the astral heaven with influences of entities of that realm. We can if we wish choose a different sound and fix our consciousness upon the holy sound and keep it there."

"We can center on the Zikar (the repeating of the names of God) and we can center on the sound current. We can experience the word of HURAY as a state of awareness or others studying the works of the Shariyat-Ki-HURAY we can find a way of living within and having our being within this music of spheres."

The inner Knowingnesses continued to roll through me like the wind, "Submerging ourselves in the brilliant white light and harmonies of sounds of the omniscient HURAY spiritualizes our consciousness much like changing a battery. Over time our glowing light grows greater like a spark that becomes white fire."

"And our sound grows greater like a single cord that becomes an eternal symphony. When the student steps on the path his light may be dim like a poorly lit spark but years later these spiritual forces within him accumulate until his light and sound radiates around him like a radiant glowing star, an immense sun reflecting light and sound upon, all around it like a sustaining force, a vehicle of HURAY."

"The spiritual exercises of VARDANKAR build up these spiritual forces in the initiate. She or he too will have a realization of oneself as a fuller expression of the holy light and sound."

"The impressions from the all-pervasive Alaya Purusha came like waves upon the ocean, "The spiritual sound exists upon every plane and world. As you move from the higher realms to the lower with each shift the sound is stepped down or reduced in vibration and vice versa from course to pure spirit."

"A shimmering sound lingered and my attention was held to it as I continued to perceive. "Practice of the spiritual exercises helps us to deepen our relationship and understanding with this holy sound, this voice of HURAY (God). It is God, HURAY's way of reaching out to us, touching our lives spiritually."

Then within the knowingness appeared to me the impression that in being exposed to the sound we are transformed in its presence. It spiritualizes our consciousness so that our spiritual nature shines through and reveals itself.

It blooms in the way light strikes a plant and the plant suddenly is brought to greater life force within it and it thrives. In ancient times people played beautiful spiritual music and sound for plants and these plants with sound in proper measure flourished. Likewise these ancient people of advanced understanding played highly spiritual ethereal heavenly music for themselves and their spiritual natures soared. These practices were merely additions to the inner sounds they attuned to on the inner heavenly planes.

With these expressions I was then shown a flash of an impression or image of an ancient people long ago on a distant planet. The musical instruments they had upon this planet were like spiritual harmonies unknown to Earth, so beautiful beyond words of ethereal spiritual sounds. They also revealed in the experience of the sound current being beyond words. As a result their people were more advanced and wise spiritually. There is strangeness that with all the technologies on Earth today that there is little sensibility in creating such instruments that uplift the Soul and uplift the spiritual bodies and the spiritual heart.

Through this beautiful light filled world a spiritual presence cloaked in light communicated, "The VARDAN (Spirit) or what some call Holy Spirit is God's voice by which it communicates with Soul in multiple forms and levels. We are now in the early more positive pole of the dark cycle, the Dark Age or Kali Yuga. This shows why the music most preferred is so negative in word and vibrations. When Souls move deeper into the Kali Yuga there is a progression of much intolerance, harshness, coldness among people. We put ourselves into a prison of our own making and call it good. We restrict our brothers and in so doing restrict ourselves."

The knowingness continued, "We can end the endless rounds of reincarnations with both cycles of joy and cycles of suffering when we come to realize our true role in the universes as coworkers with God (HURAY). We realize the natures of ourselves are a blending with wholeness with light and sound of God. When we let ourselves experience the inner light and sound and outer spiritual sounds as an ecstasy and make these our hearts joy and delight our spiritual consciousness multiplies."

In this expression an impression or image was then shown to me of a former life in a court as a dancer in Medieval England. Even though I had no true higher outer spiritual path, I flowed and moved and had my being within the ethereal and to me spiritual sounds of music which I experienced so deeply, that I experienced a sensation of flying that felt boundless. Unknown to me at that time I was out-of-body traveling, being in two places at the same time both in the body and in the other worlds simultaneously, while dancing, embracing the sound within the little way that I knew at that occasion. When we begin with one expression

124

of sound then we grow in it and are shown the next and our efforts multiply.

In this world we choose our bliss. If we love materiality most, loving things of the lower world's most, these become our inheritance. It is like the saying, "The meek shall inherit the Earth." Only other words can be substituted for "meek." It expresses within our actions in what we place as priority above all else. If we lack the discipline to place all things spiritual as priority in proper balance with the physical, we miss the glorious sound of God, HURAY, that heals us in this endeavor to put first more spiritual loves, that free us to be more the God beings we are.

We can fall in love with this sound current which is like falling in love with God. Although it is not falling but rather rising in love with God. When we give our time, our attention, our enthusiasm to this sound and light and HURAY we build in the same way that we interact with a person. We build a relationship with IT. We become one with this sparkling white light and shimmering harmonious white music of God as the all in all.

"Even though the books are not the path, by reading of the books of VARDANKAR these are like sounds and lights translated into words that point Soul to the inner road of light. When I touch a book that contains much of VARDANKAR awareness, there is the distinct lift in spiritual vibration and on the inner levels I am there. This is because in the physical elements these help us to move into the higher octave sound and light of HURAY."

I then felt within myself the awareness, "The Zikar is like the breath of spirit that moves through the Soul. It gives Soul wings. We see an individual and around him his thoughts and emotions are dark and unpleasant. Unpleasant images and words and thought forms flash around him.

"When our thoughts grow dark, worrisome, confusing, sad, we can beam ourselves out by fastening our hopes and focus upon the Zikar, the chanting of holy names. Then these negative thought forms like so many flies will scatter to the winds and be blown away. And in their place holy spirit, the light and sound will rest upon his shoulders like a cloak of light and sound as he spiritualizes his consciousness in the music of spheres."

After a pause as I attempted to reenter the God Plane, a negative entity over and over attempted to flash a negative image of a rock band leader that I have never listened to or had any interest in. Also music of a negative vibration was also prior repeated like a broken record. Some people don't realize that there are different entities that can attach themselves to and control different types of music. Some negative vibration music has a negative astral entity that attaches to and enters the consciousness of the listener. This is why when parents have concern about their child listening to harsh and negative music they have good reason.

I have found that even when I do not listen to a song but merely pass it by, even hearing it for a few seconds the entity can enter the consciousness and hence you may hear the repetition of the negative music. These negative lower Astral entities can be likened to thugs or criminals one might meet on a dark street at night. On this occasion one such negative entity attempted to use the negative images to keep flashing the image into my consciousness.

As this occurred I filled my inner vision with Gods light and sound and the images of the ancient VARDAN Masters Rebazar Tarzs and Yaubl Sacabi. And then when I attempted to meet with these Masters the negative entity tried to interfere to discourage the practice. When the student encounters these things he can call out for help and guidance from the VARDAN Masters just as the Christian can call out for Jesus when the negative nature interferes with him.

It is important to realize that in spite of interference, obstacles and delays that we persevere and have patience with the spiritual exercises for Soul movement to heaven by which eventually we break through the interference in God's time.

The VARDAN Masters have referred to Earth as "The ash can of the universe.", meaning there is an appalling amount of negativity and ignorance of God's law here that Soul must transcend it if it is to make spiritual progress on the path.

The obstacles and difficulties are like the spiritual pressure that makes coal into a diamond. They exist because under pressure Soul can unfold more quickly when it confronts resistance in the similar way to when one travels to the moon, the lack of gravity or resistance makes his muscles weak from disuse or greater gravity or resistance can with the proper training make him spiritually stronger than he would be if he were living a life of spiritual ease.

The VARDANist fasts from the negative music of those negative entities that work to attempt to pull the Soul down to the lower astral levels. This is also why the individual is not permitted to join VARDANKAR until he gives up use of illegal drugs like marijuana as drugs attract such negative entities and it is dangerous to mix drugs with Tuza Travel in any form. He fasts from the Kal things and fills his consciousness with the light and sound of God.

Instead he learns to listen to the divine holy words and sounds such as the VARDAN sound current of Holy Spirit. These sounds lift Soul to higher heavenly planes.

The impressions continued, "Mantras of themselves that attune to the lower worlds can't do much for the Soul. The charged words of the spiritual traveler attune the individual to a higher octave of the higher spheres. The Zikar (chanting of charged words) can be about you like breath, an embrace, a fragrance. Just as we always breathe, we can breathe in and out the sound of God. The Zikar is a gift."

"No matter how imperfect or flawed we falsely assume we are there exists a spiritual perfection of God within us that is spirit waiting to be awakened to itself."

"A God being within each of us that longs for fuller realization and expression, waits to find the words, the sound and the light to bring it forth to a fuller expression."

Within this 7th plane heavenly world I noted that there is a stillness that lacks landscape like a vast sweeping expanse of pure shimmering light with a sound that is also all pervasive. There is no motion and yet a flowing-ness. The all pervasiveness of spirit is all present. It is infinite, all knowing, and all perceptive. Alaya Lok seemed to hum like the internal melody of all things. This humming was like the way a tree has an internal melody.

Then continuing, the understanding came, "Many people do not remember who they are. It is often lower world phenomena to become lost in the human personality. We think we are like a character in a play. We lose ourselves in a part. We don't waiver from the script that defines us in profession or role. The pure sound cares for none of these things. It is not contained in that kind of limitation from the mind and psychic heavens."

"When under the guidance of a spiritual traveler, the

Margatma, the Living VARAN Master and under the practice of the spiritual exercises given through him from HURAY, we grow spiritually and eventually come to Self Realization. We give life to the God self, the VARDAN within us. We can be one with this celestial VARDAN."

8
THE SPIRITUAL TRAIL BLAZERS

I withdrew from all exterior human senses, withdrawing from the outer ears and closing the outer eyes of worldly sights and sounds making everything quiet and black. And then after gathering my attention in the spiritual eye, a calm serenity with an inner pulsing light appeared in my spiritual eye expanding and contracting slowly like a soft pulsating light. Initially the light was purple in color and the sound was a high pitched current moving like a cool breeze.

I came upon the supra physical level, a plane somewhere between the Physical and Astral levels to a body of water in the distance. There was a flowing motion over the large body of water. And then I hovered over it with no vessel but the spiritual self. It was here I found myself sitting with Allen above this silvery water.

In the distance we saw white light reflecting off of what looked like a spiritual city. At the shimmering water's edge was some sort of palace like structure composed of light. This light palace, like illuminated crystal reflected illuminating the water as we rested hovering over the shimmering waters and spoke together on the wonder of Spiritual Trail Blazers.

A presence of the VARDAN gave a soft awareness and impressions, "Listen to the rhythm of God from the Anami Lok, from the Ocean of Love and Mercy, the VARDAN which flows from it. All else is conjecture, assumption. The only spiritual trail blazer is the HURAY itself. And through it the VARDAN, it's very voice as light and sound. We become Trail Blazers when we are the VARDAN, the light and sound itself, for we exude it and reflect it."

"There are some who mistakenly confuse Spiritual Trail Blazers for: Spiritual Celebrities, False Masters, and so on but most of whom haven't ventured beyond the countless mid to high Astral Plane regions or a chosen few in the Causal and Mental Plane regions in the lower heavenly realms of duality, light and dark, time and space. In such roles they have not even sought for the spiritual traveler to attain even Self Realization for themselves."

Some claim that it is noble to be in ignorant mystery about the heavens and these things until after death on the physical plane of existence.

"The HURAY (God) itself and the VARDAN which flows from it is the only true reality. And out-of-body travel is the mode with which to enter it. We become this divine reflector, this Trail Blazer when we are consciously the VARDAN at the opening of Self Realization which occurs on the Soul Plane far beyond these lower realms."

At that I see an image as an expression of a Spiritual Trail Blazer, blazing a trail lit up and the one who blazes it, himself exudes great light and sound shining brightly like a colossal sun flowing through him from the HURAY, the VARDAN expressing through him its eminence. A huge sphere of light surrounds him. Then our vision comes to rest upon a vast sea of guiding lights flickering like candle flames. When we lean on the light of the little self it is like the clinging to the light of a dimmer heaven.

If you were to look at the definition of a Spiritual Trail

Blazer it would obviously imply someone that defies timidity and conformity and is daring enough to risk going in a new more vitalized or more spiritual evolved direction of unfoldment. It blazes a trail like fiery light and higher sound. It centers in being, knowing, and seeing as a vehicle and champion of the VARDAN itself.

And then Allen with light shining in his crystal blue eyes spoke, "It reminds me of becoming a great Dancer. Say you don't know how to dance at all. The first step to become a great Dancer yourself is finding a mentor, someone who is themselves a Great Dancer."

"In a sense you surrender to that person to be a good student. At that time we follow behind rather than leaving a trail. We are learning to follow their lead and learning to surrender to their motions. This is as we are dancing with them. Over a certain period of time you follow and your skills improve and you become better at it. Then you reach a point where your skill level becomes high enough where you wouldn't have to follow their shadow."

"This is the same with VARDANKAR, the spiritual path. You are the spiritual trail blazer in the sense of accelerating your spiritual evolution. In another sense you are not the trail blazer as you need a guide when you first start, which initially is like someone to follow like a child. But eventually you get to the point where you're walking side by side."

"If your mentor were really your friend they would be happy to see you reach a point where you break away from their shadow, no longer emulating them but reach spiritual independence. If they were really your friend they would be happy that you are walking side by side and then on your own."

Then I responded, "It is true, a true spiritual friend revels and rejoices in his student walking by his side and becoming a coworker with God himself. In the past I had the shock in discovering I was in an offshoot path when I realized that my guru wanted me to forever remain a spiritual child. But this is not what I wanted, not why I joined. I became a part of his works to reach God Realization and becoming HURAY's coworker. It was then I knew and the Margatma showed himself."

"The opposite confusion of remaining the spiritual child is when individuals in vanity leap too soon to false spiritual adulthood. They confused, break from the guided dance, claiming spiritual Mastership or Teacher-ship before their time comes. This is equally as dangerous a trap of the negative to keep us trapped in the lower worlds."

Allen continues, "A good Teacher you emulate because you know it is the fastest way to learn. If a Teacher is coming out of vanity he wants the student to always be the child and control them. A true Master isn't like that at all. Initially you're following their lead and eventually side by side and then you forge ahead on your own."

"They give you freedom to be yourself rather than follow or emulate anyone. But starting without emulation is a difficult road to Mastery."

And then further contemplating upon the subject of Spiritual Trail Blazers we closed our eyes to do a spiritual exercise yet again. Then very soon we found ourselves surrounded by a gentle white light that was everywhere. And then we felt the familiar presence of Peddar Zask (Sri Paul Twitchell).[6]

6. Paul Twitchell who's spiritual name is Peddar Zask was the living VARDAN Master

from 1965 to 1971 when the teaching was known as "Eckankar".

A gentle sound permeated this world and there was a feeling of divine love and calm that surrounded us with its protection. This world was beyond time and space, a world of pure Beingness. It was a place one could have joyously stayed, almost forever.

Then very rapidly Allen was aware as Peddar Zask began sending him almost telepathic like communications. Peddar began, "Soul is ever choosing between slavery and Mastership; between expansion and contraction. It's indeed amazing that as Soul can occupy less space than a gnat one second and a million galaxies in the next. There are always choices. But it basically comes down to a simple question: Do we desire to be the effect or do we desire to be the cause?"

"If we choose to be the effect, then there are many Souls who will use our energy for their own purposes. There are countless traps we will fall into, countless pleasures to experience and countless suffering. All in all we will drift from one extreme to the other and back again, moving through the middle where things will be more balanced, through the negative or path of destruction and back through the middle and into the positive or that of creating good karma. Actually a better analogy than a pendulum would be that of a spinning vortex or wheel."

"Countless volumes of books could be written on the subject of Soul being a slave to the Kal or negative power, and in essence being the effect. However a far more exciting topic is the one you have chosen for this chapter, that of being a Spiritual Trail Blazer."

"The Spiritual Trail Blazer is like the Cliff Hanger on steroids, ever reaching new heights, he or she is never satisfied and is ever aware that there is always another step to take. Spiritual Trail Blazers without exception always practice

Out-of-Body Tuza Travel."

"This seems obvious but for some they do not believe in Tuza Travel. A simple analogy would be in order to be a Trail Blazer you have to walk on the trail. Sitting next to the trail and watching other people walk on the trail is not going to do here."

"The second principle is those who are campers. In other words, they walk a mile down the trail, pitch a tent on the side of it and remain there for inordinate lengths of time. The true Spiritual Trail Blazer has learned to deal with fear, by not dealing with fear. In other words Out-of-Body Tuza Travel allows the individual to view life from the lofty heights of the Soul plane and above, beyond time and space, beyond the mind, emotions, or anything of the lower bodies."

"So the Spiritual Trail Blazers unlike the physical trail blazer is a "non-confrontist," meaning they have learned the hard way usually that it's pointless to face a problem head on when you can simply go into a higher state of consciousness. A good analogy would be if a bicyclist encountered a very large and mean bear. He could get off his bicycle and try to fight off the bear but if he was smart he would simply outrun the bear. So it is the Spiritual Trail Blazer has found two very powerful secrets. Number one they have learned to practice Out-of-Body Tuza Travel and let the VARDAN move through them and be a part of it. And second that since they are a part of the VARDAN they must serve it."

"They have also learned that they must choose whether to serve the Kal or negative power or the VARDAN which is the middle path and the pure positive. When a Soul ceases to identify with its lower bodies, it reaches for God Realization and fully realizes that IT is the pure VARDAN and that it must serve IT because IT is IT. Then that Soul is a spiritual trail blazer because that Soul has become the path itself. Because that Soul is the VARDAN and does any of this make sense to you?"

He continued, "We can follow the traveler to the heart of God. The traveler will always be waiting for him between the sun and moon worlds. The one who follows the social currents is too busy worrying about what his neighbor is thinking of him. The trail blazer seems to swim against the social current to the heart of God. The spiritual trail blazer has his sights set higher than the lower worlds of duality. He is always outside the pack, the individualist."

"He is not surrendered to dogma, religion and opinion but to God itself. Most birds with the flock roost in a hen house, the rare bird turns face from the flock when the VARDAN calls and will even move in a completely different direction that defies all sensibility according to the flock if it means it will bring him closer to God or he'll be a vehicle of spirit. The spiritual flock on the other hand go the safe familiar route by pure physical and social instinct."

"As said before the social settler seeks for safety in numbers, but the bold, spirited individual is brave enough to venture to the God Worlds and won't take any wooden nickels. He is not attached to popular opinion of the spiritual sort. The Spiritual trail blazer follows his own inner spiritual compass which is set to spirit, Itself. He follows spirit really. God, HURAY wants conscious coworkers with IT."

"The God force, the VARDAN is stronger in the spiritual trail blazer. Again it's because he is on the trail. He is a free spirit."

"There are those who assume the things I have shared about the lower worlds and the higher worlds and the spiritual travelers are made up. The spiritual trail blazers aren't sitting on their tails assuming truth, they are travelling out-of-body experiencing these things and they know the difference. The spiritual pioneer gets his direction from spirit. The social settler gets his direction from the spiritual social forces and the lower worlds. Where we get our direction is where we go."

Within this world of light Heather then had a question. Peddar Zask seemed to know instantly as did I for this world of pure light was a world of knowing and being.

Heather asked, "Paulji, many of your students and others had the best of intentions. They wanted God Realization and strove for it. They did out-of-body travel for years but then with the passage of time something changed, individuals got caught in social currents. Many of your old students were scattered. What is your view point related to this?"

An exceedingly bright light began to enter this world. It was the presence of the great Soul Rebazar Tarzs. The three of us greeted Rebazar and we all knew that Paul had sent for him or should I say invited him to answer the question?

We could hear Rebazar Tarz's gentle laughter, "The highway to God is strewn with the skeletons of those who have failed. This is an excellent question, for vanity is the last thing to go and no Soul in the lower worlds that is, should believe that it can never fall. This is a great riddle. But I shall attempt to answer it."

"The word I choose is attachment. Talk is cheap. Men claim that they love God, when they don't even know what God is!" We could hear Rebazar laughing and it echoed throughout this entire plane almost as if God was laughing with him.

"Attachment! Our opinions! Our experiences! We hold them so dear as if, if they were destroyed we would lose ourselves! This is ridiculous! How can a Soul lose itself! And yet this is precisely the kind of mediocre thinking that causes countless Souls to fail. If you're afraid you will lose yourself if you view life from a changed consciousness then it goes without saying you will be afraid to change your consciousness! In other words Attachment! Attachment! Attachment!"

"But what are we attached to? Illusion I say!...Nothing more and nothing less. Those Souls who become the great Spiritual Travelers have learned the art and Science of Bourchakoum. They have learned in essence that they are NOTHING! And EVERYTHING! They have learned that they are GOD! Of course man can never become God, for he will always be a part of God; but never the whole. So I say unto you, as the great Peddar Zask has written, to cease to have opinions. Seek truth for the sake of truth without any ulterior motives. Do not let the ugly face of attachment cause you to ever under any circumstances shun the very truth of the VARDAN. The very light and sound that sustains all the world of God will only accept those Souls who are in total harmony with it and are IT!"

"Any Soul who places conditions upon God, any Soul who demands anything from God, any Soul who attempts to negotiate with God for their own personal gain is only praying to the Kal Niranjan."

"Souls will deny this, they will point to the virtues of the Kal. They will point to kindness, they will point to love, charity, noble actions, and world reform. They fail to realize that the Kal has two faces. The positive face and the negative face. The true seeker of God recognizes that the Kal power is

138

his worst enemy and never his friend. He or she clings to the Spiritual Traveler like a small child clings to his mother for protection."

"The wise Soul will cling to the Masters until they are strong enough to become Masters in their own right. They will NOT befriend the Kal. They will not pray to the space gods which are only aspects of the Kal. They, if necessary give up everything in order to be in harmony with the universal power: The only true power, the light and sound of God or HURAY."

"This in the nut shell is why these individuals have failed. They could not rise above duality. They could not learn detachment because they did not love truth above illusion. This is normal, as Souls must fail again and again until they are willing to give up everything in order to follow the Master into the heart of HURAY and become a Master themselves."

"Volumes of books could be written and much wisdom is to be found in the Shariyat-Ki-HURAY of the various planes. But for the purpose today this discourse will have to do." and with that Rebazar disappeared.

9
THE SPIRITUAL GOD POWER

Within I sensed the divine presence of pure Soul: the radiant VARDAN Master Rebazar Tarzs. I felt gratitude for his presence as a shining God being and looked to him intending telepathically if he wished to travel to the 9th world, the pure spirit universe that the spiritual travelers know as Agam Lok.[7] He agreed in the silent language of Soul and through direct projection, like being teleported like space travelers across galaxies, we appeared deep within the Pure Positive God Worlds in one of the higher pure spirit universes of God.

A shimmering, pulsing field of light of intense whiteness appeared and seemed to go on and on forever into eternity as it was infinite in Agam Lok.

The vast spiritual radiant bright light had such a burning, searing brilliance like pure white holy fire or being in a vortex or conglomerate of a million suns that swallowed up Soul within this lonely universe. The brilliance encompassed all in this pure spirit universe in a way that there are no words, nor senses of the lower heavens that can fathom its depths and indescribable radiance that would totally blind the physical and astral eyes if they could even enter such a place.

7. The 9th Plane (not to be confused with what some call 9th dimension) is the Agam Lok deep within the Pure Positive God Worlds.

The sound was so pure and high keen in one long endless stream, like a steam that never ends but flows through out eternity. Light was crackling almost like lightening rippling or pulsing through the ethers like some holy vibration not of this world. And in the midst of the crackling spiraling fiery white light I saw a huge, enormously gargantuan, formless light mass which was that of Agam Purusha. Agam Purusha is the divine God Ruler or manifestation of HURAY within this Pure Positive God World. I emanated gratitude toward Agam Purusha for all I have learned with Agam Purusha's divine help; things I have greatly needed to know to be useful to HURAY, God.

Without words Agam Purusha gave impressions to venture to the VARDANKAR Temple of Golden Wisdom of this pure spirit universe with a flash of ITS impression or light. Within this ethereal bright space I perceived the radiant VARDAN Master Peddar Zask. He comforted me in his presence and understanding as he communicated, "The spiritual individual needs both divine love and the spiritual holy power."

"Without the spiritual power the individual cannot reach the Pure God Worlds. There are spiritual Gurus and spiritual leaders who convince their followers that all forms of power are negative and unnecessary. This is a false premise based in the cosmic consciousness awareness. Power destructively used is negative and destroys. Power used in coordination with the HURAY's will (God's will) is spiritual and necessary and of the divine HURAY. In dogma, religions, and philosophies individuals are tricked out of their spiritual power and are convinced not to aspire to the higher things for themselves."

At that moment Agam Purusha stuck its magnificent light essence or what I liked to call head, although it was not through the essence of this temple or radiance of a ceiling if you could call it that, as if to peek inside. After thanking Paul I floated out like a balloon to greet Agam in my awareness more fully within its presence. I was filled with bliss. In this higher spiritual plane heaven the vibration of sound and light were so much more radiant white and fine then all the worlds below.

A huge crackling mass of formless, fiery light which had jagged light forms emanating in intense energy bursts, pierced all directions. From the ball of formless light issued crackling radiant forms leaping and spiraling and as said before a divine reflector of God, Agam Purusha but not God itself issued impressions in an echoing all-encompassing powerful voice or awareness that was not a voice but an impression and knowing, "Power....Without the power of God the individual is a weakling lead by the nose. A helpless follower pushed left and right by spiritual leaders and can't do much for himself."

I knew within it was true. It flashed within my consciousness former church members blindly going along with anything they were told, no matter how ridiculous or hurtful. Some were suggested to only be worthy of doing the most menial tasks in spiritual service like stocking toilet paper or cookies. Even when what was told them hurt them so deeply, they would obey for fear of punishment and loss of initiations or membership. Fear was used to keep them tightly controlled, obedient and those who proved themselves passive, compliant religious followers were rewarded with initiations, leadership positions and high opinions. And this is why those who pursue the spiritual traveler are rare and small in number because pursuing this science requires an adventurous and independent spirit that few choose to have.

The powerful impressions continued: "The Soul that has not the God power within him is the pawn and effect of the universes. He has no control of his spiritual worlds. His every thought is created for him!!" This force roared. The light of the formless mass swirled up and had so much intensity electrifying everything with pulsating white light and sound.

I addressed the large mass of radiant light: "Agam Purusha what would benefit the spiritual individual?" The brilliant crackling light in a mass of lightening and jagged light forms rose up and expanded like an explosive current in all directions in an enormous mass of light: "Often man bows down before everything but God in his ignorance."

"The way to true spiritual power in the worlds below is the sound current and the spiritual traveler. The God man can reconnect you with this sound current of God."

The initiate can draw upon the spiritual power in accordance with the will of HURAY to carry VARDANKAR passionately into the lower worlds and boldly share HURAY's love via the ultimate way to return to IT: VARDANKAR in what manner we are guided like a spiritual Knight for God.

Stepping upon the spiritual path with no purpose in spiritual service is useless like a swan that doesn't bother to use his wings or a songbird that has no song.

Being God Realized and a coworker with God in its point and essence is spiritual service as the whole as a total state of one's being. Some reach such high states and a great flow of light and sound enters them like a fluid light cosmic river, but if they do not spiritually serve in greater measure pouring this great current of light and sound out to those who need it through spiritual service in accordance with the will of HURAY, it becomes destructive. A coworker with God lives and breathes in spiritual service to HURAY because it loves HURAY and sees what HURAY wants done to release the suffering of its creatures that long to return to IT.

Like a flash of lightening an insight appeared in my consciousness of how only two years prior I moved from a community of freedom and lightness, to reside briefly beside a new age church in the Midwest. It was startling as the vibration and consciousness by contrast was heavy, controlling and even dark. It nearly felt like going back in time to the medieval or dark ages and being surrounded by many who appeared to perpetuate this great restraint of the God Power.

Instead of God, many demanded everyone shall be perpetually submitting to a lesser authority, of a social source.

And the ways of hiding one's true voice, that which flows from divine spirit, the VARDAN ITSELF was oddly seen as exemplary. It was in a sense the perpetuation of pure complacency creating the false ideal of each person as worth-less as a spiritual being, as well as help-less, being they were encouraged to help less in smaller or menial tasks, and also judgmentalness meaning a sense that none were or would ever be good enough to return to God as a God Realized being.

The river of light and sound that flowed through the individual, the VARDAN, divine spirit or spirit of independence, oddly angered many to control and harshly judge because the space for individuality in that religion was so narrow.

This once great path degenerated into an offshoot path with dying embers or sparks of truth dying and flickering out from Paul Twitchell's God Wisdom. All of these qualities above were the complete and total opposite of what the Spiritual Traveler Sri Paul Twitchell taught his students, that the student becomes not the pawn and effect of social forces but rather he is instead the individual, the individualist, the cause, pure cause or the cliff hanger who is an outsider to the sleep like state of the religionist or the masses.

When Paul Twitchell translated a man named Darwin who was not a Master but Paul's student took over. Without a Master with the God Consciousness state the path was no longer the high path or direct path to God and God Consciousness. Paul taught and retaught his students again and again of the spiritual empowerment of the individual, who is an individualist that has his consciousness in the Pure God Worlds. And that VARDANKAR as we call it now is never a religion nor belief system but rather an applied science in the divine mastery of Soul movement to the heavenly universes.

But often the Master will teach his students these things again and again and the student is only half listening or rather has selective hearing to not disturb his life. Not to mention many cannot tell a real VARDAN Spiritual Traveler or Master from a false one to save their lives, so often because it threatens familiar attachments to things of this world: social ties, dogma, buildings, personalities and so forth as man is often a creature of habit.

After this off shoot in a different direction there was too much focus upon enforcing individuals to become fearful and timid versions of themselves. This is the role of the religions that disempower the spiritual individual. God has little use in this life for those who have disowned the God Power within them and are instead filled with fear and dogma. In this way the individual remains small like a spiritual child. It is as Peddar Zask once said, "The definition of evil is that which makes something large into that which is small." [8]

8.Paul Twitchell, The Tiger's Fang (Menlo Park, CA: Illuminated Way Pub., 1967.)

That is, to trick the individual into all sweetness and light and out of their spiritual power and is, contrary to popular opinion, negative. Without the divine Love, Wisdom and God Power within him he has not the strength to return to God.

My appreciation flowed for Agam. It occurred to me the importance of these insights of how the individual begins to more deeply resemble the God Power and that power in accord with Gods will is, contrary to popular opinion, is not bad, that is to be more spiritually powerful enough to return to God.

An immense light rose and extended in a vast mass of incredibly huge white brilliance. Crackling jagged light forms streamed in all directions across the top portion and I saw an inner impression of the individual using his imaginative faculty to allow divine spirit to flow through himself, a mass of powerful light and simultaneously a sound. I could see that this force can propel him forward to embrace a more spiritually bold and powerful version of himself, yet not his false self, but his true eternal self-Soul in harmony with spirit in doing God's will.

Thousands of electrical tendrils like lightening beams filled all directions, with sharp, fiery electrical light. Then more impressions arose and the source was not clear.

"Like the cave of fire on the Astral Plane which burns away impurities of Soul like a scorching, purifying heavenly fire, so it can move into higher pure positive heavens to a much higher finer level. Soul, the individual again comes to this Agam Lok to face the Lotus of Fiery Light."

As Agam Purusha communicated I felt the intensity and power of the light and sound and it was of such intensity and burning searing brightness that it was beyond description.

"Freedom and opportunity is hidden within that fiery light in putting all of our impurities into this radiance. We can surrender this into the lotus of fiery light along with any impure thought, any judgment towards God's Souls, or any lingering doubts can meet with God's holy flame. Far beyond the magnitude of the cave of fire, the Lotus of Fiery Light brings you to the recognition that HURAY is the only power, the omniscient, the all-powerful."

An image arose of a previous version of myself at an earlier time venturing toward the cave of fire and how determined and thrilled and clamoring I felt to have spiritual impurities removed, burned away. It was a sense of how thrilled to be freed of these and likewise there is a spiritual power in being freed of the extraneous in this cave that resembled the greater awesome fiery light.

Any and all anger toward any being or any lower impulses like addiction can evaporate; vaporize in its radiance as we shift into a different state of consciousness. We can shift out of the lower impulses that bind us to the world of duality. These are things of such deep value to the spiritual individual determined on returning to God."

"Another impression arose. It has some semblance to the mythical phoenix which is a bird destroyed in fire and according to mythology it "rises" from its ashes a more spiritually powerful and renewed version of itself, freed of the lower consciousness."

"A new self is born that is divine spirit, more purified from lower impulses and under the direction of spirit in a greater purity of consciousness. An old weaker self or false self dies and its baggage is left behind in the ashes of the lotus of fiery light. One is reborn risen from the ashes a God Realized being."

In the lower worlds we go through the fires of what strikes out of us impurities until eventually we see the futility of these things. One man was given a view of so many countless lifetimes as a warlike being for countless ages of past lives. He was a war general of nations and worlds and flew space ships and caused much destruction. After many of such lives he grew deeply sick of the scourge of his own brutal actions which through the law of karma caused himself much suffering.

The spiritual power under control of divine VARDAN in proper measure brings us as a vehicle of spirit to its creatures. One being aimed for this high point, aiming high but missed the mark. When we misuse spiritual power and attempt to direct it or place ourselves above others, not to guide them to God but to put ourselves over them to dominate we miss the spiritual mark. If we pretend our anger does not exist it slips into the unconscious mind and controls us like a marionette.

Denial and the five passions which are anger, vanity, lust, greed and attachment, these things that pull us below our spiritual potential can in an instant, like a flash of lightening be surrendered like all lower impulses into the colossal radiance of the lotus of fiery light. And surrendered to God. And in its radiance we can purify ourselves of hindrance. We then come to realize the past is dead and a new present is born.

One could see a sheer white searing intense white light, fierce and fiery. There was a sound not of this world. I see the white light of Agam Lok and yet also an intensity of other levels simultaneously.

Before our cup can be filled with greater spiritual purity

and be released of the spiritual impurities that grow like mold, these are purged, scorched, burned out, released and surrendered to Spirit.

Spiritual purity in God is the spiritual power to do God's will throughout all eternity, perpetual, like a ring of light. It is as Allenji has said that Soul is only a pure channel for God. The power to be a vehicle of HURAY's, or God's will can be like a gift returned. When Soul is ruled by its base or carnal desires: anger, vanity, greed, and other passions of the mind and has less control of itself within a cycle of a lifetime as a result it has less of its spiritual power flowing though it for the whole. The cave of fire and the lotus of fiery light in a progression of lower to higher are the purification of Soul and the reclaiming of spiritual purity.

But without moving into the pure positive God worlds of VARDAN, Soul cannot be this pure channel for God. Soul must bathe in the pure audible life stream and surrender to IT. Without this we can be pure in heart but spiritually poor from lack of Awareness and the higher Realizations and consciousness that will use us as ITS channel if we live, move and have our being inside of IT. Moral purity is all but useless if we do not have this Audible Life Stream consciously flowing through us until we are IT and IT is us! Then we retain our individuality but are conscious channels for IT and are spiritually free to move throughout the many heavenly worlds at will!

We may feel we have less control when the five passions or perversions of the mind rear their ugly heads in our worlds like negative thinking or addiction or blaming. But we in the instant of a moment can shift to a different state of consciousness and have more control then we realize. Instead of being the psychic effect we can, "Seek first the kingdom of God and all else will be added unto you." That is to become divine cause. We become less the created effect of the limited consciousness or negative habits. We are purified into the realm of cause in surrendering to spirit the VARDAN and within it making our eternal home in those higher Pure Positive God Worlds of being. And in this way listening to spirit, confiding in spirit, consulting with spirit and when contemplating spiritual understanding is sometimes given.

We surrender all things to IT. If we feel we lack the ability to overcome the lower impulses and things that keep one chained to the lower worlds and are overwhelmed with spiritual problems, Soul can surrender all to the VARDAN (spirit) and then to the Margatma, the Living VARDAN Master. We can ask for help with spiritual intentions and surrender all to God. In this we know we cannot change ourselves but instead shift from one state of consciousness to another.

Souls will read something or are told something spiritually or of some dogmatic belief of the nature of spiritual reality is given and Soul will hypnotize itself into this reality too deeply. It becomes our world. The hidden danger comes when we hypnotize ourselves so strongly into a religious belief that even the spirit of God itself cannot convince us otherwise. And it must package itself according to our limited beliefs. Doors open to the next greater spiritual level of heaven and Soul firmly closes the door in front of it.

Steadfast persistence on a spiritual path is admirable until it solidifies so firmly that even spirit can scarcely enter it. This is the sticky web of Maya that keeps Souls paralyzed like insects snared in a spider's web.

When we put ourselves above others or judge others in that moment we become blinded by vanity and can scarcely be of use to God. The spiritual power can arise within us through surrender to the VARDAN divine spirit and the will of God, the HURAY. HURAY can free us of these things. Each Soul is destined to return to God. And each will reclaim its spiritual power to become a coworker with God, a divine vehicle of God though out eternity.

Then unexpectedly, a second funny sort of awareness came related to a film directed by Richard Donner that I saw as a child of a hero who flies: "Superman." An image of him gathering himself in his "fortress of solitude"[9] appears.

And it came to me that the spiritual student, his fortress of solitude is his or her inner temple where one travels to the spiritual worlds, the heavens. And in his spiritual fortress it is here that he knows. He is not interested in the material knowledge of the universal mind power but instead in the spiritual things. His knowingness with practice becomes vast as he centers in the silence and pure sound by which his divine power flows through him. His spiritual vision is vast and his hearing is not limited to the world of the senses but is beyond material to higher sounds. And he loves the sound and he loves the will of God more than his own needs. This more divine "rescue" is not physical defense but the spiritual sort. It is the individual rescuing himself from the clutches of his own lower impulses and the lower worlds.

This is the sort of "Superman" that God guides each of us to find and then guides us to aspire to. For eventually we find within ourselves the power of God is everywhere like an all-encompassing wave of echoing omnipresent sound.

The false treasures and fool's gold of the lower worlds dazzle the physical and Astral senses until we look for a far

9. Dir. Richard Donner, Original Superman Film (US, UK: Warner Bros. Pictures, 1978)

greater treasure, a door into the other spiritual worlds beyond time and space. Light shines from these worlds with unearthly melodies of sound. In shifting rooms or states of consciousness we then release ourselves from attachments and problems. Vaster planes of consciousness open. In this way we become more selfless because we don't identify ourselves with our lower natures or mentally perceived higher natures because we know these are only rooms of consciousness. We are not our accomplishments, we are not our spiritual attainments, we are not our past lives and we are not our rooms of consciousness because identification and vanity lives in these places.

When we do a spiritual service, speak a spiritual truth, write a spiritual book, give some kindness, or share a spiritual gift, if our intentions are pure and done for God, in the name of God without ever thinking of reward; we know these things are not of the ego but come from Spirit. And being Spirit ourselves we become more ourselves, our true self Soul.

Then I was in this inner world shown an impression of a former version of myself in a moment I was overwhelmed by some problem. I was on the phone with two people. On the inner planes the VARDAN had me lifted up through initiation into another plane. Immediately in this new state of consciousness I said: "Oh, I am fine now." I was suddenly above the problem. Surrendering to the VARDAN and a readiness to shift with the winds of divine Spirit to other states of spiritual consciousness opens doors to pure positive higher states. This eternal spiritual power that flows through us is best when we surrender to divine spirit and the VARDAN Masters. It best flows when the current is under the VARDAN, divine spirits omniscient direction.

And again I am aware that this fiery fierce white light extends on and on forever. An old weaker version of self expires and in its place something greater rises. Its worldly baggage is left in dust and ashes within the sheer brilliance of the lotus of fiery light. And then beyond this plane within the Anami Lok in this vast stretch of light, one is reborn risen from the ashes, a God Realized being.

10
THE ANAMI LOK

In an instantaneous beam of light like a teleportation through space, yet beyond time and space; I appeared like a flash of light beamed from the striking blaze of the 9th plane heaven and into to the Anami Lok on the 10th plane. A beautiful, all pervasive, endless soft white light spanned out in all directions and went on and on like a breathtaking glowing white universe.

It was the most beautiful, deserted, desolate stretch of glowing soft white light and shimmering otherworldly sound that made me want to listen for all eternity to its Love, Power and Wisdom.

This is the indescribable, sheerly breathtaking realm of pure spirit. It is the realm of God Realization. The realm of Knowingness, Seeingness, and Beingness. It is the heavenly, Pure Positive God World unencumbered by matter and time, and I felt as though I were in a world suspended like frozen stillness, eternal and silent.

The sound of this world was like the sound of a sucking wind, sucking water or air much like a whirlpool like sound in a long unbroken continuous note that went on and on without end.

Within the stretch of soft glowing light was this whirlpool like spinning whirling sound. I shifted back and forth between two images, one of what appeared to be an infinitely vast, gentle, soft and yet brilliant white concentration of light, so concentrated like that of an enormous glowing white sun that shone through the whiteness.

Here within this world I sensed Rebazar Tarzs, the great VARDAN Master's presence in my awareness. The mass of swirling light was spinning like a vast whirlpool that almost resembled a spiraling galaxy.

It was a mass of swirling light essence, like a whirlpool of spiraling light going out endlessly in all directions. As we've described before it was the sheer opposite of a black hole like a spiraling light hole. Perhaps almost like that of a whirlpool. It was filled with a sound also like a whirlpool were water is sucked as it flows in a circular motion in perpetual spin.

In one sense it reminded me of a majestic light filled galaxy...and yet I struggle to form words for this was a place beyond description yet I feel strangely compelled to try...Perhaps it is so some of you may recognize, if only for a moment your true home lay far beyond time and space.

The light and sound echoed in waves through all worlds like impressions of the VARDAN, divine spirit with flowing light and sound simultaneously everywhere. It also reminded me of a shockwave of light that flows out in all directions like a cosmic boom. And yet all is still and infinite.

A soft almost defused light spread out everywhere and went endlessly out in a sort of lonely emptiness in all directions into eternity. I communicated with love and reverence to both Anami Purusha whom appeared as a radiant light, a manifestation of God. And simultaneously I also communicated to HURAY, God, "I love HURAY forever. There is nothing else in the universes but loving you

HURAY."

What I experienced is that HURAY is the only reality, God is the only reality. It is the essences of the universe, the one true God. It is far beyond human estimation, approximation and verbal or written articulation. No rituals, meditation, religion, titles, dogma can approach it. Only when we come in our pure spirit essence, the true self, Soul, in Out-of-Body Tuza Travel with the help of the spiritual traveler to experience HURAY that we realize that HURAY IS.

We experience God; not by bringing God into our lives but by bringing our consciousness into the very heart of God, in the Ocean of Love and Mercy.

This has and always will be the only way for man to become the God man; to reclaim his divinity. No reading or study or thought can do this for him; only experience in the higher God Worlds of VARDAN (spirit).

Rituals and opinions are set matter like stones on hills and mountains that seem to reach so high that they appear to almost touch the heavens. But they do not touch the heavens, the pure formless substance of the Pure Positive God Worlds which are the realms of the HURAY.

Instead Earthbound practices and Earthbound gurus keep us bound in the lower bodies and lower worlds. We can through Out-of-Body Tuza Travel increase our vibrations and concentration of Spirit until we experience the Pure Positive God Worlds ourselves. Not through
hearsay of religious texts but through direct contact with the infinite power ITSELF.

All else is conjecture. Only the experience of God can unite Soul with God.

Only the experience can unite Soul with its purpose, its mission, its essence, its divinity; and with the wonder of HURAY.

All else is weaving and spinning of Earth and Astral hinged spin offs, unless under the direction of the Living VARDAN Master, a God Realized being who is selected not by human committee but by the HURAY, God ITSELF to return its children to IT.

Through the infinite wisdom of HURAY, the Living VARDAN Master guides the individual through the outer works and inner works to reach the goals of Self Realization, God Realization, and VARDAN Mastership; where upon which the individual flows in partnership and coworkership with the infinite one.

Returning to this experience, Anami Purusha's sound was again like a spiral like whirling sound and seemed to be everywhere at once. Wordlessly I felt a knowing, "When the individual Soul reaches this God World and surrenders all, when invited that Soul has reached the level of being a spiritual VARDAN Master."

At the mention of this I saw off in the distance vast orbs of light like that of radiant Suns that are the Souls who had advanced to this spiritual plane hovering off in the distance.

Anami Purusha communicated in impressions, "When you became a new VARDAN Master your only greatest wish is to carry out the will of HURAY, God. In each and every action you humbly consult with HURAY, God to be in accord with IT's will and that IT's will be carried out into the worlds. Being in partnership, a coworker with God, HURAY is the Soul's greatest driving force."

Heather shared, "There are some who had become new VARDAN Masters in times past and in their inexperience or youthfulness they focused too much on the needs of the human-self which began to limit their service to all life as HURAY's vehicle."

"A Master or higher initiate that does not outflow properly in greater measure can if not careful shift into being a negative channel as when much spiritual current of light and sound comes in, it must be released with the same force like a waterfall of light and sound flowing out."

Anami Purusha was all pervasive, there was no place it was not as it continued, "At every level of the spiritual planes, even as a VARDAN Master it is vital to be vigilant that you are humble and do not put yourself above others." It is as Paul Twitchell has said, "The moment you put the self above another you became almost useless to God."[11]

"Some of the advanced ones who make it here stumble on this and then humbly return. When you are truly humble you see the God-self in all Souls and you support and celebrate their full spiritual empowerment as though it were your own."

Through the glowing white cloud Anami Purusha continued: "Persistence, the persistence that focuses on the goal like a laser is what helps the individual return to God."

"In much consistent practice of the spiritual exercises the Soul bit by bit refines the consciousness so that it is spiritualized light and sound and can always know the will of HURAY (God) at any given moment and in every situation. It develops the sense called Knowingness that knows all things to carry out the will of God."

11. Twitchell, Paul. *Eckankar Key to Secret Worlds*, Illuminated Way, Menlo Park, CA. 1969.

"If the seeker is called to God in his heart, than he can follow his heart. The VARDAN speaks to the seeker and the initiate through the heart center. When your heart yearns for returning to God put aside distractions and listen. You can follow this call back to God."

In that moment it came to me this impression of a new initiate. He explained that he had an inner experience of seeing himself go through millions upon millions of lifetimes and a sort of ache he felt at feeling utterly lost.

He asked: "Why was I shown this?" He was shown this to experience for a deepened sense of gratitude for how vital and how blessed he is to find the high path in this lifetime to move towards God.

When we know this we are less likely to carelessly waste time excessively in distractions or be more careful to be vigilant on the path in the Spiritual Exercises of VARDAN so as not to potentially lose an opportunity as often happened in lifetimes prior. And being so blessed, when Soul truly enthusiastically knows how rare and special an opportunity it is, IT will stop at nothing to ensure IT has the motivation to move towards God to reach the goals of VARDANKAR: Self Realization, God Realization, and VARDAN Mastership.

I relate to his pain because when I was a youth I likewise felt ancient on the inner levels and had an aching for my long journey to finally end and again come to completion with God. These sorts of feelings although painful are a gift that propels us to create the momentum to do what will bring us to God or endure years or most often lifetimes of waiting.

Returning once again to my inner experience which was truly beyond words and yet I feel compelled to try to form them hoping some will gain that spark that turns into a flame or will see truth hidden that they have long been seeking.

A soft, misty white light swirled about this mammoth world. Ethereal sound and a huge mass of glowing misty light spiraled. The light was spiraling and yet seemed still. Shimmering sound lingered, as a high pitched heavenly melody of spirit. The feeling of this realm was electric and beyond magical. I felt swallowed up within it like feeling engulfed within the center of a glowing star.

And then an image was felt of a time years before becoming an initiate. I was a teenager in a dormitory room playing music in which I would leap up and spin in circles. I spun with the sensation of flying and in my mind's eye I saw Souls that looked like pure light. Each were gathered in a circle within this spinning flow, like a spiral and from this circle of Souls, glowing like clusters of glowing stars, patterning themselves in a circle formation; came from a beam of sound and light which was their great love. All their individual beams of sound and light converged into a single brilliant sound and ray of light which was their great love for God which they, like a powerful laser, beamed up to God.

When I went to my first outer gathering of spiritual people chanting God's name (HU) years later, it flashed back to this gathering sending up waves of love in a white shaft of brilliant white light and sound.

Rebazar Tarzs shared, "The more Soul's heart is ignited and followed the more you are connected to the heart of all hearts Divine Spirit. It is not emotionalism or human desires for material things or vanity. It is the current of Spirit speaking to the individual through the heart center guiding it to follow HURAY's will and the will of VARDAN (spirit)...like the common phrase "Follow your heart." Some individuals talk about the fear that if they follow their higher heart they could lose certain things or it might be too risky to follow the call of God."

Heather responded, with appreciation, "What you express is truth. People often follow what is most safe. One individual had a fear come up within him that if he followed his heart and followed the Spiritual Traveler he would lose close friends. He was at first so excited until that realization sunk in that in following his heart he could lose much of his human interests. When this idea set in he quickly changed his mind.

For that reason he didn't follow his heart because he felt he had too much to lose. Another individual hearing the same heartfelt call would follow their heart to the road of light no matter what the fear of what it could cost them in human attachments because they want God that much. The heart is an aspect of the voice of VARDAN (spirit) that HURAY speaks through.

Sometimes people instead of following the heart, follow what is most safe or what gives them the most material or social comforts. There is so much spiritual and phychic persuasion from all angles and the following of the higher heart is a simple way of breaking up confusion of all these influences that pull at our mind and distract from the true highest spiritual direction we wish to go as Soul (to the heart of hearts.)

A form of light emerged like a being yet without features, composed of only pure sparkling light and yet formless communicated, "The only way is HURAY, the one true God, the highest God. Look to the Master form. This self is directional to model and shape one's life to like a sculptor's stone. Inside the stone, which is also like the human form unlocks from within the stone (matter) a form hidden within which is the VARDAN, the God Self, the pure light and sound hidden within."

"You make your own choices and in this you are also a creator of your reality like the sculptor to his stone. In an instant you can let go of the past. You can let go of every wrong you have ever done and in this very moment live a new life."

"A life filled with the bliss of God, the HURAY. God doesn't hold against you your flaws and mistakes, it is only the human self that punishes itself through unceasing incarnations and lower experiences until it satisfies itself. In an instant you can shift from these and seek to know the Living VARDAN Master who can also in an instant help you shift step by step to a fuller expression of your God aware self by way of the sound current, the Master, and the initiation. If you are a God seeker this will help you move towards Self Realization, God Realization, and VARDAN Mastership."

"Even if you appear to be the most humble or lowly person, even if you have made foolish mistakes and see yourself the biggest fool in ways that embarrass you, you are loved by God and can surrender all the past to God. Then you can travel the road to return to God. In surrendering all to God and following the inner compass, the Knowingness, you have the way just like the Sailors who followed the stars of the heavens."

"The Margatma, The Living VARDAN Master is like the North Star set upon the Earth by the HURAY to be a guiding light. Follow this North Star to your ultimate destination. In this way you will more swiftly pass through the passage of storms and sunny days and unnumbered obstacles in the lower worlds and reach the goals of VARDANKAR. You can only recognize this North Star, not with the naked eye or the faculty of the mind but rather only through the inner spiritual perceptions that come from the Pure Positive God Planes."

"God Realization is a moment Soul is united with HURAY (God). And then even after this spiritual experience Soul can have union with God through the VARDAN and duel awareness that channels through the lower bodies in thought, word, and deed as VARDAN (divine spirit) courses through him and directs his Earthly life. He is forever centered in his pure spiritual essence, Soul in this God World while his earthly body lingers below. In God Realization Soul will realize that God IS and more than that God's presence is known, felt, and experienced. Then he carries it with him like a cape or blanket wrapped around his shoulders."

"We learn that the initiated Soul always dwells in the high worlds of God! We learn that we may dwell in the Pure God Worlds at all times and yet keep our feet on Earth and act as conscious coworkers with the Living VARDAN Master, the VARDAN (spirit) and the HURAY (God). We enter into grace and in God we live, move and have our being."

"We learn that we may die daily during our spiritual exercises and experience all of the planes of God under the watchful eye of the Spiritual Traveler: the Margatma the Living VARDAN Master…and that no harm can come to us as long as we are under the Masters protection."

"We learn that nothing can happen to us except in accord with our own awareness and state of consciousness."

"In Souls inexperience it expects the most Earth shattering, startling experience for God Realization, something like one might experience on the astral plane with all of the lower astral or physical senses."

"It can take for granted that experiences of the Pure Positive God Worlds use different spiritual faculties then the lower worlds of M.E.S.T. The once forceful faculties of duality dim, the mind body recedes and is left in the lower worlds, the lower perceptions dim and in their place we see pure spirit."

"Soul's awareness is like that of Spirit, all pervasive, having divine Knowing and Seeing and Being that is subtle and soft and omniscient."

"This journey can be so subtle that Soul in its inexperience can overlook it and not be conscious of it, acknowledge it or even feel that nothing has taken place. This is like the saying that we become aware and listen to "the still small voice within," which is of the subtle realms of the God Worlds where we begin to have the eyes to see and the ears to hear the truth, the true reality, the God knowledge."

"If we choose worship of the personality of a spiritual teacher instead of reaching or rising to the higher ecstatic states for ourselves this is idolatry. Worshiping personality instead of reuniting with God does not lead to spiritual freedom."

"False Masters will offer that they are the way to God Realization in one breath and in the next breath influence the individual to believe God Realization is an impossible dream that he could never reach in this lifetime. The individual remains forever a spiritual follower and never a spiritual Master. In the lower heavens individuals can have blissful experiences in these heavens but the lower worlds are not the worlds of spiritual freedom."

"By enthusiastic practice of the spiritual exercises of

VARDANKAR you can materialize within yourself a precise spiritual compass that will give you direction. You will know true north from what only appears to be north spiritually."

Having spiritual experiences in and of themselves proves nothing for most all religions, philosophies and paths have spiritual experiences, it is when our compass is set beyond the direction of human group mind and instead set to the compass of God itself.

Spiritual group mind itself creates heavens in the lower worlds in the likeness of the wishes of those practitioners that create them with their shared opinions. This is not the heaven the VARDANist is interested in."

"We move, love and have our being within the pure eternal sound and light, the HURAY in the eternal Pure Positive God Worlds or Heavens of HURAY."

"All else other than this is illusion set to set the Soul back on itself…Settle for nothing less than God."

11
THE HURAY WORLD

One morning sitting on an elevated sleeping space beside a maroon curtain was a porcelain angel; upon closing my eyes, in the next moment I felt a sense of appearing like a flicker through Tuza Travel into a world, an indescribable, breathtaking heavenly universe.

A vast desolate field of light extended out and felt like an endless desert of pure, brilliant, white light and sound that stretched out forever. There was a lonely stillness that hung in this world as through it were frozen. Within this light a breathy high pitched current of HURAY (God's) sound rolled through this Pure Positive God World in a way that reminded me of whale song echoing through the Ocean.

Of the many endless Pure Positive God Worlds of VARDANKAR, the 11th plane otherwise referred to as the HURAY World exists beyond energy, matter, time and space. Having no matter it is composed entirely of pure Spirit. The sheer immensity and scope is wondrous and vast beyond all description. This is the first region of the infinite one.

Nearby I sense an indefinable presence, a divine being of sheer light whom in my consciousness appears to be like a beam of light that communicated not in words but with a soft knowingness, so soft that it could be below the threshold of awareness, so subtle like a wordless whisper of wind through the celestial ethers.

"When the Soul reaches a certain level of consciousness and a certain level of heaven, it knows. It knows its spiritual purpose. It knows its spiritual mission."

I perceive a subtle shift as though the being transforms and received subtle impressions, "A Soul like a ray, a ray that splits from the greater ray that splits from radiance greater than countless suns. It evolves and amplifies the way a spark becomes a fire and a fire becomes a bonfire which grows immense like a planet and beyond a planet burns colossal, brighter than a sun."

"The holy fire may begin subtle like a flicker which builds and increases." We feed the flames with contemplation of the holy works and dwelling in the Pure God Worlds. An image forms on other levels of perception of a Soul in its various sheaths or bodies and upon seeing closely we see suddenly within that Soul a white hot flaming mass builds and then pours like rocket fire from its heart center in white hot flames shooting up like brilliant white fireworks.

"This intensity to serve HURAY, to love HURAY (God) in return; to return IT's love, is called the Holy Fire of VARDAN." Soul in its zeal is driven like a zealot, one in love with all God's universes to return love to the HURAY, God, having discovered that it has always been in God's loving arms and God's eternal embrace as realized when it awakens to the plane of total awareness in how blessed it is when welcomed home by the presence of the Margatma."

"So often in the lower worlds Souls subjects itself to lesser loves. It subjects itself to carnal loves of things of the lower worlds. The love of attachments, passions: greed, lust, vanity, attachment. The love of a materialistic heaven on Earth, worldly wealth, pride and position and spirituality fixated in the lower realms (such as utopia on Earth or the Astral Plane).

"These attachments pull Soul like a balloon loaded down with heavy sand weights so it is pulled down to the Earth and the lower realms and fixed there. When Soul drops these weights it has nothing to hold on to, nothing to keep it from rising with the help of the Margatma in Out-of- Body Tuza Travel to the Pure Positive Worlds of spiritual freedom."

"When this occurs we are no longer the same species. Soul in its many incarnations passed through the different kingdoms: mineral, plant and animal consciousness and then finally human consciousness. When the Soul aligns with the Margatma we can then through Out-of-Body Tuza Travel learn to evolve beyond human consciousness. We become almost as a different species. Instead of human we become God beings. This is not to be confused with those who falsely see themselves as Gods but more accurately instead we become realized in the wholesome and pure state of God Realization. This is rather always walking in the presence and full awareness of God and doing IT's will like the phrase, "Thy will be done.""

"In the human state of consciousness a Soul will say "My will be done." And he will say he is doing God's will, when in reality he is really doing whatever (he/ego) wants and while falsely calling it God's will. Most will deny they are doing this. But this is common like the plague was in human kind. In fact at that point Soul is often not even doing its own will but the will of the force which enslaves It. The Kal or negative power, whose purpose is to bind Soul to the lower worlds for as long as possible and delay Soul's return to the HURAY."

"This has caused people to shift into a state of delusion to harm others in the name of God throughout history of human kind. The inquisition was an example of this kind of rationalization where the individual lies to himself to justify his harmful choices and falsely make himself feel better that he is truly working for a higher cause. Although in actuality he is working for the Kal itself (the negative power). In this case his motto becomes, "My will be done," even though he might call it God's will. These carnal loves and attachments pull Soul to the lower realms and things that it loves so greatly."

"Thy will be done" is instead a shifting to often See, Know, and Be in harmony with Spirit, the VARDAN, which is often what the human self would find unappealing or difficult. Such as the spiritual leader or initiate who realizes he is not as spiritually evolved as his ego would assume."

"His human ego would find it painful to admit any weakness and hence seek out tutelage with the Margatma to finish his spiritual training for spiritual Mastership. The world is filled with the excessively proud since vanity is often one of the last attachments to go. But often personality worship is just as illusive."

"If the currents of God, light and sound were like water pouring through an individual, without spiritual service for this inflow of Spirit to outflow; these waters pouring into him would bloat him like a balloon."

"Perhaps too long this way he could practically burst beyond his capacity. He then becomes instead of being a channel of Spirit to lift those greatly in need, he becomes instead a harm to himself and to those around him. Initiation in VARDANKAR is really an opportunity to know and be and outflow to a certain level of consciousness."

"The individual may or may not be able to live up to that

level of responsibility he was blessed to receive. If he surrenders all to the VARDAN, the Margatma, and the HURAY all things spiritual are possible, but the Spiritual Travelers caution us that a foundation must be built so that we are strong enough to handle our new found Love, Wisdom, Power and Freedom!"

"Then a flash of images related to the Holy Fire appear, seeing the heart center in Soul is connected to the heart of God. Just as Soul creates cords of love between themselves and other Souls, we can create a bond with God, a connection with God, a relationship with God and be centered in IT and have our being in its presence. Then the light and sound comes through us. VARDAN Masters are centered in God and have a relationship with IT."

"Being a channel for God happens when we are in a high state of consciousness. When we are dwelling in the Higher Worlds we become and act as a conduit for the Light and Sound. When we are centered in the Higher Worlds we become a fountain of the higher power. It is not merely what we say and do. Many mistake Doingness for following God's will. It is a mistake to become human doings. When the individual goes out to do social reform he can be just going through the motions and be unconscious spiritually."

"In focusing awareness in the Pure Positive God Worlds we become conscious. The VARDAN Initiate always dwells in the Pure Positive God Worlds. If we are dwelling in the higher worlds while we are interacting with other people, we resonate the light and sound of the God Worlds."

In writing this book Allen and I spoke on this topic. We managed to record much of it and although I tried to get what Allen said as accurately as I could....there may be some errors, but the gist of the conversation is relevant and

170

important:

Allen began, "I have had many lifetimes and I am sure you have to, where I was being selfless and feeding the poor or caring for the sick, or doing something whether it was as a Missionary or Priest or Doctor or Nurse, or Nun… all of which touched people's lives on a physical level. But those lifetimes didn't do anything spiritually for me except create some good karma. Which I then used up… kind of like money. And you get good Karma. You use it up like money and then it's gone, and you're back to where you were. And that is completely different than being a Conscious Coworker with the HURAY (God)."

"Because in effect what you are doing is letting go of the little self, and you are coming from the greater self, the VARDAN. You are becoming pure Soul which ironically you always were but were asleep to. Or at least you are moving in that direction. So it's a completely different experience. Everything is centered on consciousness, on being-ness rather than doing things."

"The negative power wants us to serve our fellow man and try and make a utopia on Earth, but this is a negative ideal. The Lower worlds are not Soul's true Home. What we must do is serve the HURAY, or God, directly and through the VARDAN or Holy Spirit. If our consciousness is in the Higher Worlds we can be used as a great channel to uplift others spiritually. We find we are this light and sound, this divine VARDAN or what some call the Audible Life Stream that sustains all of life on all planes of existence. Then we become a light unto the world, sort of like a mirror that brings in the vast brightness of the sun into a cave of darkness. It is our Beingness, Isness and presence, for when we dwell consciously in the Pure Positive God Worlds, although we of ourselves do nothing, we become great channels for the God power and IT uses us rather than us using IT.

Soul contains this divine imagination that is that of the HURAY or true God. Soul is a happy and creative entity that must become conscious of its birthright as a conscious co-worker with God. If we only become actors on the stage of life reading our lines and playing our parts we end up serving our fellow man but not consciously. We may give a man a piece of bread but we know not who or what we are nor what he is. When we serve the HURAY or God on the other hand we may give him far more then something that satisfies the hunger in his stomach."

"So there is this quality of Being, basically being the light and sound or divine love. This comes through the practice of the Spiritual Exercises of VARDANKAR and through practicing the presence of the Inner Master. In a way you are practicing being God, but you're not God, but you are practicing being Spirit which is the very voice emanating from God and that sustains all of life and draws Souls back to the HURAY."

"So there is a being-ness there which you don't find when you're doing things for your fellow man. The problem with doing things for your fellow man or women or child or village or country, mankind, whatever you want to call it, all relates to the consciousness in which it is done."

"There is a difference between doing and Being. When I had past lives where I was serving man through different things, trying to make people happier, trying to help cure people of illnesses, feeding people, helping people get work and so on and so forth it only created some good Karma although at times I interfered with their goals or failed to ask permission and ended up taking on some of their burden

Thousands of Visits to Heaven and the Heart of God

or Karma."

"This is also part of the problem. Not only are we unconscious when we try and serve our fellow man but we often interfere in his Karmic affairs and actually hamper his spiritual progress because we are not directed from the VARDAN but from the Kal or negative power. Also known as the Universal Mind Power."

"If you teach somebody how to fish, they might feed their body for a life time, but it's probably not going to do much for them spiritually, on the spiritual level it may do nothing. There is nothing wrong with teaching a willing man how to fish so that he and his family may eat, but keep in mind, there is a vast difference between doing and Being."

"When I was serving through "doing" I was going through a lot of motions. I was physically taking food to the poor and distributing it to them, or whatever it was I was doing. I was trying to be a good person by serving other people; but as I was doing it, it wasn't about my state of consciousness, it wasn't about who I was, it was about what I was doing for other people so it was outside of myself. It was external. My actions did not actually lead me back to God nor did it lead them back to God."

"And therefore it was not very deep and working from a rather superficial level. I did develop some love, being selfless and going out and developing certain qualities such as some love and compassion. But it was still outside of me. When you do the spiritual exercises or when you begin doing Out-of-Body Tuza Travel and you start going into these other states of consciousness; it's like you start to become the VARDAN. The VARDAN or Spirit demands more and more of you until it has all of you! Then one day you discover that you are the VARDAN and yet you have maintained your individuality. But it is not the individuality of the ego or little false self, but that of Soul our eternal God self that is this spark or drop from the Ocean of Love and Mercy where God or HURAY dwells. This is not some abstract idea or poetic expression but a living breathing reality for those who are bold and adventurous in their daily practice of Out-of-Body Soul or Tuza Travel! It is not that there is anything wrong with helping others it's that we must serve God first and from serving God we serve all of life from that State of Soul which is Seeing, knowing and Being. We find we can consciously dwell in the higher worlds and know all things."

"We soon realize we are Spirit ITSELF. We are practicing surrender to the VARDAN. We are learning to flow from Beingness rather than be a channel for the lower power like a machine or an external thing that we are doing. This creates an entirely different dynamic. It creates a way of expressing where we are able to do things that we would never be able to do if we were working from the ego or little self or human self. Because in effect what we are doing is letting go of the little self, and we are coming from the greater self or the VARDAN."

"A lot of people do things for the good of man and mankind, which they find out later was a mistake. People do things thinking they are helping the world, only to find out later they were hurting it. So we've got that human consciousness or that negative consciousness. It's like we are trying to use the negative consciousness to decide what God wants. And so basically we are serving bodies."

"Whenever we are serving man or people we are serving bodies, and when we become a conscious coworker for the HURAY (God), we are serving IT."

"And IT knows everything and so it's going to bring us in

touch with those Souls that need spiritual help rather than bringing us in touch with a bunch of bodies that need food or they need clothing or education. There is nothing wrong with it, but it doesn't lead us very far spiritually and is exceedingly slow as a way to reach the HURAY. In that sense it is sort of a spiritual dead end. Now once one finds the higher worlds then we may serve at a much higher level even if we do end up feeding the homeless and other acts of compassion and kindness. I know this sounds confusing to some but without the direct experience of the pure Positive God worlds Soul is lost and in unfriendly territory."

"For example a man who consciously serves God or the HURAY, may indeed feed the homeless but his vibratory rate and his effect upon the world is totally different than a man who is working from the lower states trying to serve his fellow man from the Kal or negative moralistic consciousness."

"The moralistic consciousness demands that man try and make the Earth into a utopia but the lower worlds are not man's true home. We can only serve limited within our vibratory rate and consciousness. This is God's law. There are many states of Beingness and Conscious Awareness. Only by reaching beyond the Etheric Plane which contains M.E.S.T. (Matter, Energy, Space and Time) do we find eternity and truth. Truth is not found in the lower worlds or mind or the Universal Mind Power. Only partial truths. If a cup of spring water is mostly clear with only a slight amount of poison, is not the water still poison? So too, the false gurus who preach the message of the Kal are only delaying Soul's advancement into the Pure Positive God Worlds!"

"My experience has been that a lot of the lifetimes seemed like repeats, different masks of the same life. The Shakespearean actor that plays the same part over and over and over again. And so I have had many times in different parts, different roles. And after a while I had to ask myself: How many times can you be a Soldier? How many times can you be a Scientist? Of course the technology when you're a Scientist changes. Sometimes I was a Scientist from another planet where the technology was very advanced. Sometimes I was a Scientist on a planet where the technology was not so advanced. But it was the same basic ideals in many respects of trying to put the world together through observing things that were happening. It was external. "

"I think this is one of the points that is really important to understand. For the most part most people's whole world is based on external reality. Philosophy, Religion, Science, Politics, they are all based upon these false artificial realities almost like photographs or holograms. These false images that people have of reality that are outside of us, that have nothing to do with Soul but are just pictures that we create. Roles that people want us to play. The people that try to control these pictures, like Religious Leaders use them to try and control people, usually for their own benefit and not the benefit of the individuals in the group. They try to get them to be the way they want them to be and so they teach us all these things, to try to program us to be this certain way. They try and plant picture files in our minds and emotional Engrams so we act a certain way, so we can be predictable. But it is all based on what is outside of us, it is all based on external illusion or the Maya of reality."

"We add the emotional or Astral component and the same thing is true. These Astral forces are also mechanical and consist of feelings, emotions, desires, and fears. Again they have nothing to do with our eternal God self-Soul, but are only lower bodies resonating and reacting within the lower worlds of time and space. Again these mostly consist of picture files stored on the Causal Plane and below as well as impressions made on the Astral and physical bodies. To a lesser degree the Mental Body."

"With VARDANKAR we find that all of this is for the most part just empty. All these external illusions, there is a sense of reality to them. It is not like you just ignore them. But at the same time it's sort of like the heart of the seed, it's like when you have the tree. Contained in the very center of the seed is the blueprint for the entire oak tree. And then you've got all this around it, and the shell and all this stuff around it all."

"But when you get to the center, the core, contained in the core is the essence. The essence of the whole thing, it's like Soul. In order to find that essence we have to practice the VARDAN Spiritual Exercises and get back to who we really are, that eternal being. To do this we must leave the physical body via the Audible Life Stream or Sound and Light. As we said beforehand there is a sustaining wave that moves out from the Heart of the HURAY or God and then this wave returns back in an ascending wave. We must follow the ascending or returning wave and the Inner Master who is the true Spiritual Traveler and way shower to help Souls return back to their God source."

"Now it is really important to find Self Realization and God Realization before attempting to be a full coworker. Because the key word is conscious coworker."

Heather shares, "It is sort of a great, great blessing when a Soul after eons of incarnations finally reaches a level of maturity where it starts to feel this longing inside, like you start to feel really ancient and you start to feel like something is really missing from your life, no matter how many hobbies you pursue; be it arts, sciences, exploring technology, business; things like this. No matter how many things you do;

177

eventually when you achieve all these goals in countless lifetimes and reach the point where you've done nearly everything, eventually you just feel like everything in human consciousness feels empty. Something feels missing. Something doesn't feel right. A lot of people call it the mid-life crisis. But I suppose in this case it would be an end-lives crisis."

"But it's at that point where Soul reaches a level of maturity where it suddenly says: "I am tired of all this," "I am tired of living selfishly, I am tired of living my life around superficial things that never go anywhere." "Like I can make lots of money in business, but what does that really do for me?" "It gives me a temporary heaven on Earth and then that all fades away when I come into the next life. Or I can be a magnificent Artist and make amazing paintings and then I die and then I go to another world."

"Soul eventually after countless years or lives reaches the point of maturity where it wants to move on; it wants to do something more meaningful, it wants to reconnect with God and give back to the whole, and at that point when it is ready to become a coworker, it will naturally gravitate to the Margatma, the living VARDAN Master."

Allen shares, "Many move on but only to the Astral Plane or the Causal Plane, but this is not even close to our true destination and still in the area of Reincarnation and Karma. It takes a great desire to find God, only the bold, cunning, courageous and adventurous will find IT."

"It is very easy to get into that savior mode or do-gooder mode where you're just out there trying to save the world or help people. Many find the Astral Plane and try and help others reach it but the Astral is only the second plane and not even close to the Pure Positive God Worlds!"

"The unselfishness that many exhibit is fine and can at times help develop love, but it can be a distraction if you're not careful. Generally we don't want to be selfish or introverted where everything is about us. You don't want to be introverted and just focus on yourself: me, me, me, me. There's a goodness and a wholesomeness to serving people. But you really don't want to be serving people. Like I said before this is serving the Human or negative consciousness of man! Serving the social consciousness; serving the Kal or negative power. We want to be serving the VARDAN (Spirit), serving the Margatma, serving the HURAY (God), rather than serving people we are serving HURAY, God."

"Through this we may facilitate acts of kindness and compassion, but it is because the VARDAN or spirit directs it for ITS purpose. But most of all we can carry the Light and Sound of God or the Holy Spirit by consciously dwelling in the Pure Positive God Worlds of VARDAN. Then we can do all in accord with the will of God on a conscious basis! We do without doing. We truly realize that we of ourselves can do nothing it is only Spirit that moves us. Not the lower world forces but the pure VARDAN at a very high expression. Unlike the universal Mind Power that is duel in nature, meaning positive and negative and within the world of opposites."

"You become a true light unto the world rather than a social reformer and do-gooder."

"The Kal power which pretty much runs the Astral and physical worlds has two faces. The positive and negative. The negative is often known as evil or darkness. It is generally easy to see when someone, for example murders or hurts someone's lower bodies out of Anger that they are being negative. The other face of the Kal is kindness, personal or human love, goodness, morality, etc. This is the part of the Kal that many worship falsely, believing it is the way or proper way to live their life. They do not understand that while goodness of the social sort is "Good" it is not the way back to the God Head but only a way to remain in these lower worlds or reincarnation and perhaps create some good Karma that has to be worked out later in other lifetimes in the lower worlds. Some incarnate in one of the Many lower world heavens and falsely think they have arrived in "Heaven" but this is only an illusion and these lower planes, although some can be very, very wonderful compared to the physical world, are not Soul's true home nor has soul found even Self Realization."

"If one truly desires God, it is important to do the spiritual exercises and especially to travel through Out-of-Body Tuza Travel, to go to the other worlds to meet with the Inner Master and to meet the different Masters.   To go to the Golden Wisdom Temples of the different planes. Each plane has a Golden Wisdom Temple where we can study the Shariyat-Ki-HURAY, the holy book of VARDANKAR and gain the divine Wisdom under the tutelage of a True Spiritual Traveler.   It's a process. It takes time. But yet it doesn't; it is beyond time and space"

"It is really remembering who we are. It is not so much a process of growth, although it is, but it's a process of remembering. It's a process of Spiritual unfoldment. We find out that we have already done this before.

It is kind of a funny realization that we've already been there. So it is like we are remembering who we are and then we start experiencing or remembering these different planes, especially the higher planes, the higher worlds; the Soul Plane, the 6th plane, and above that. And then we become not one with Spirit or VARDAN but we become the VARDAN. It's sort of like the Ocean, each drop of water is part of the Ocean, it is like we're flowing as part of this river of light and sound, this pure Love, Wisdom, Power and Freedom, the VARDAN, the Holy Spirit. And yet we retain our individuality as Soul, in other words we are the individualized conscious expression of the VARDAN, or Spirit but also we have Beingness and Isness.

It is difficult to explain and this is why we need to have our own personal experience via out-of-body travel under the instruction of the true Spiritual Travelers. This is a path of personal experience rather than philosophy, religion or metaphysics where you are told to just believe what you read and have faith."

"The word VARDAN is very charged, with a very positive energy, because it's a charged word."

"It's like coming from that place or source of all of life known as the Ocean of Love and Mercy where dwells God, or the HURAY. Beyond the Universal Mind Power and beyond all Karma and causation; beyond all time, space, matter and energy; rather than coming from the human consciousness where you're interested in social reform such as, I am going to help stop this drunk from drinking, I am going help this guy get a better job, I am going to help this child eat food. Those things are noble and fine, but as we pointed out before, in the end, the Soul that you feed food to or you teach them how to do a trade, or whatever it is you are doing to help them physically, maybe even mentally or emotionally, isn't going to last long and they are going to end up in the same position they were in before you helped them, in the same place. It's a cycle."

"Most don't understand this because some of the cycles can be hundreds or even thousands of years long."

"It is a very slow way of working. I think that's the key. VARDANKAR isn't the only path back to God but it's the most direct path back to God. Helping other people, helping people as a goal is an extremely slow way of reaching spiritual perfection, because you are working in the social consciousness, in the lower consciousness. The lower consciousness and the higher consciousness don't meet. They are different. They are two polar opposites and this is why some have a violent reaction to VARDANKAR. It flies in the face of conventional teachings because of this."

"So trying to reach God by being a do-gooder, if it did work, and I suppose eventually it would work, but it's extremely slow. The same holds for trying to perfect our actions, thoughts, emotions and physical body. The same holds true for fasting from all vices. All of these methods or even combining them all together, does not bring Soul back to the God Head. But if it did we could be talking about millions of Incarnations in the lower worlds of time and space, and this is the trap of being told that if we are good and kind and sweet we will find God. We may reach one of the lower world rulers but not the HURAY ITSELF!"

"It is much, much faster and more efficient to practice Out-of-Body Tuza Travel, to practice the Spiritual Exercises of VARDAN, because now we are tapping into that light and sound which is the direct link back to God. It's like the essence also known as the Audible Life Stream that which sustains all of life and this ascending wave returns back to the actual God Head. And we are going to get results, as opposed to spending life time, after lifetime, after lifetime trying to be a good person."

"One of the problems with trying to be a good person and helping people is we may have a lifetime where we really do get to help people a lot. But then the problem is we tend to forget and then we come back down to Earth or some other planet and we reincarnate again. Of course we may earn some good karma from helping people, depending on whether we are really helping them or whether we just think we are helping them but are hurting them or interfering with their lives without invitation."

"Let's say we actually do something positive for them, the problem is we tend to forget. Or we may end up incarnating in one of the other lower worlds such as the Astral for a temporary stay there. And then we come back down to Earth again but we are not in a position to help anybody. Maybe we're the ones that need to be helped. Maybe we're the retarded child or the one who is starving to death and needs food. It's really just a game we are playing. Reincarnation roulette or the wheel of 84 as it is called, it often goes on for millions of lifetimes. Soul is eternal so this can go on and on a long time until finally Soul gets tired and longs to return to its true home where dwells the HURAY or God in the Pure Positive God Worlds of VARDAN."

"One of the secrets which the VARDAN Masters are aware of is the illusion of time and space. And what it means is Soul has these qualities of Seeing, Knowing, and Being. And Being is probably the greatest. The Beingness, rather than the Seeing and the Knowing. Knowing is great. Seeing is obviously great. Because Beingness is the same quality that the HURAY has, Being, existing in that consciousness. And this is really important because Beingness exists in the present moment, it does not exist in the past and it doesn't exist in the future. It exists now in the Hereness, in the Isness."

"So when you are dealing with the higher worlds you are going beyond time, and you're dealing with Isness and Beingness. And the reason this is really important, because I know this sounds kind of highfalutin and complicated or like I am doing mental gymnastics. . .But I am really not; the reason this is important is because Soul exists now within the Heart of God."

In VARDANKAR we say the true VARDAN Initiate always dwells in the Pure Positive God worlds and this is true! There is another saying that bears repeating here. "In God I live, move and have my being."

"Now I want to talk a bit about Sri Paul Twitchell who was a true VARDAN Master when the teachings of VARDANKAR were briefly known as 'Eckankar' from 1965 to 1971."

"Paulji used to speak very eloquently about these qualities of Beingness, Isness, and Hereness and he used to say that the True VARDAN Initiate always dwells in the Pure Positive God Worlds. He didn't say the Higher Initiate, the 5th Initiate, or the 8th Initiate, or the initiate that's been in for ten years, or the initiate that's practiced the spiritual exercises for a minimum of five thousand hours, or the initiate whose read all of my books five times each. He said the true VARDAN initiate always dwells in the Pure Positive God Worlds. And Paulji talked a lot about this and quite frankly so do all the VARDAN Masters."

"Paulji also talked about duel awareness. And dual awareness is one of my favorite topics. I like the topic a lot, because I think a lot of people miss the whole point because they think they can only be in one place at a time."

"And so what will happen sometimes is somebody will sit down to do an exercise whether it is meditation or a spiritual exercise of VARDAN and they sit down and they're aware of their breathing. And their mind is thinking thoughts. Like they are thinking 'oh no, did I feed the cat?' 'Why am I thinking about the cat, you shouldn't think about the cat. You're doing your spiritual exercise and should think about God. Did I pay the bill?... Oh my God, the electric bill, It's too much money.' And then they are breathing and they are aware of their breathing. And you say "Well how did it go?" And they say "It went really badly. All I did was, I was in my physical body. And I was aware of my breathing and I was aware of this pain in my leg. My leg hurt for a second. Then my back hurt and then my elbow felt kind of weird."

"And it's like they get caught up in this idea that they can only be one place at a time. And they say it's a complete failure. Didn't get anything out of it. But the thing is this: there's dual awareness. You can be in two places at the same time."

"And that's usually what it is, that's usually exactly what we are doing. Actually we can be in as many places as we want to be at the same time. It's not limited to two. But to keeping it simple for explanation purposes, let's say you close your eyes and are doing a spiritual exercise. And you are aware of your breathing. And maybe you are also aware of a feeling, an emotional feeling like maybe you are a little bit scared about your boss, you're meeting your boss tomorrow. And then maybe there is a little bit of a pain in your knee. Or whatever it is. And so those things are competing for your attention."

"But if you know about dual awareness, you'll know that ok, that's fine, don't worry about that. So then your consciousness begins to see that something else is going on in addition to your knee hurting, and you start to forget about your boss, and you can still have an experience, while you are still aware of your breathing. The point is that part of your attention is now focused in this other plane."

"The reason that this happens is because Soul always

dwells in the higher worlds. We are not moving anywhere. What we are doing is we are moving our attention. It is kind of weird we call it travel, Tuza Travel, but really once you get into the higher worlds you're not really traveling, it is really putting your attention, or learning how to place your attention on different states of consciousness. But it's so confusing to say that, so we call it Tuza Travel so people can understand the concept. Otherwise it would be totally confusing to the newcomer. Someone who's learning it might be confused."

"Most have not consciously reached the higher worlds anyway and so the term Tuza Travel works well, but the final point is this...once we reach into the higher worlds with the help of the Living VARDAN Master we begin to practice what is known as Direct Projection, where we simply place our attention somewhere and we are instantly there!"

"So again to sum it up, we're already there and the thing that is amazing about this...well please allow me to illustrate. In the tree analogy, you've got this tree, it's a Sequoia tree, and everybody knows Sequoias are thousands of years old. I think some of them are around 45 hundred years old. And it takes a long, long time to grow a Sequoia tree so it's really big. So a lot of people might be thinking oh I am just like a little seed, it might take me thousands of years to grow into a spiritual giant or a hundred years or ten thousand years or whatever it is, because they are thinking in terms of time, matter energy and space. Mostly time. It does take some time. Paul used to say from the time someone joins VARDANKAR to the time they become a Master it's about 27 years. Some people do it faster and some people do it slower."

"The reason it is possible for somebody to do that so quickly, relatively quickly, it's because it's almost like: Imagine you have a seed. You plant the seed and then all of the sudden a few days later you go over and there's a little sprout coming out and you're looking and thinking it's really tiny. But then all of the sudden you put water on it and it turns into a 400 year old tree."

"All the sudden it's really big. And you're amazed and thinking wow it just grew four hundred years in five seconds! That's impossible! That can't happen, you can't do that! You can't get 400 years of growth in 5 seconds! And yet you saw that with your own eyes!"

"But it is possible with the high path and that's what's so amazing and exciting about Tuza Travel and about the high path; Is that you can experience thousands, if not, actually you can experience millions of years of growth in the course of almost no time at all. But, you know you have to be careful. And the Master has to make sure that you don't go so fast that you go totally out of balance and get derailed."

"On the other side of this coin some people get cocky and think they have a higher state of consciousness than they really do. Humility is important. It is like coming to an oasis for clear water to fill your canteen when you have dirty stagnant water already in it. You have to empty your cup or canteen in order to receive the new pure water. In this case it is not water but the Audible Life Stream from the heart of God that contains all Love, Wisdom, Power, Freedom and beyond; Some cannot receive this at a very high level due to vanity and attachment to their old or current state of consciousness."

"They over estimate their spiritual consciousness and confuse the lower worlds consciousness for the higher worlds."

Allen continued, "Dual awareness can be a huge advantage

in the field of service. If you're talking to somebody and they are asking you a spiritual question or any question or you're just talking to somebody and you want to be of service to God; It is very awkward to have to close your eyes, sit in the chair and say "Excuse me, can you give me five minutes."

"And then you sit there, you silently sit there and they're wondering what you are doing. "Excuse me what are you doing?" "I'm doing a spiritual exercise." "please don't bother me right now, just give me another 4 minutes, I am going into a higher state of consciousness. I am trying to help you. Please don't say anything, I have to concentrate."

It's far better to continue the conversation while being able to Tuza Travel. We can also do this for anything whether it's writing a book or article at work, on the telephone or anytime. Eventually we realize we can have our feet on earth and our consciousness in the pure positive God worlds! But even before we reach this stage it's very useful for example to converse with a VARDAN Master or look inwardly from the Astral or Casual Plane at a situation."

Heather responded, "I agree, many times with dual awareness I'll be at work typing at a computer and simultaneously my attention will be in the higher worlds, in the Pure Positive God Worlds. And that's one of the things that the VARADN Masters teach as you said, that you can have your heart in heaven and your feet on Earth as they say."

Allen continues, "Exactly, this is very practical, most people at first learn Tuza Travel during their spiritual Exercises but soon discover this dual awareness and find they can put it to use in their daily lives in ways they could not have imagined. But it is not something that should be abused or misused."

"The wonderful thing about dual awareness as we are both saying is one can learn to be writing or can be standing there talking to somebody, and actually listening to what they are saying and at the same time can be placing their attention on another plane in the higher worlds, or a lower plane or maybe two at the same time or three at the same time. And I know it sounds complicated but it really isn't complicated."

"If you ever day dreamed when you were a child, you know you are sitting there in school and you hear the teacher saying, "Five times six is…" And meanwhile you are riding a dragon and the dragon's got giant wings and you're throwing lightning bolts at monsters. It's like, so how did you do that? Well its dual awareness."

"It's a fancy way of saying the same thing. We do it all the time. Whenever you drive a car. Most people when they drive a car they find themselves automatically stopping at stop signs and traffic lights, and meanwhile they are thinking about something else. And they are not putting a hundred percent attention on driving the car, usually. Especially if they have done the trip a thousand times. We do it all the time. We are always splitting our attention."

"It is a fancy way of saying something we have already done. The only difference is when you start using it to go into the higher worlds it can become very exciting; very, very exciting!"

"And that is where the VARDAN books and the discourses and the tapes come in, because it begins to put a spotlight on these other planes that have existed forever. These are our natural homes. Being with the HURAY in the higher worlds is Soul's true home."

"Now keep in mind I am not talking about the lower

worlds. These are also quite an experience and can be very enlivening. Visiting parts of the Astral, studying with the VARDAN Masters on the super physical and Astral...all of this can be done with Tuza Travel and is an important stage of spiritual growth. Even the Causal Plane, the Mental Plane and the Etheric Plane have great wisdom as we move upward, but we must not forget the true planes that we seek are above the Etheric world and start in the Soul Plane or Atma Lok, the 5th region or first of the Pure Positive God Worlds."

"These true Pure Positive God Worlds above the Etheric Plane are the homes Soul misses, these are the places we long to return to, and we have spent so many incarnations being distracted in the lower worlds and so it is very exciting to be given the opportunity to serve here and at the same time to be able to put our attention in the higher worlds. In a way we get to see the best of both worlds. But we do have to put up with a lot here. It is a difficult place to live, because it's not a free lunch; I mean we have to go through the health problems and the financial things and all the bodies. It's not easy and it is wonderful that you can have these heavenly experiences while still being here and serving God. It's a wonderful gift and opportunity we are given to be able to do that."

"I think in closing you know it's really funny because we really encourage people who have joined VARDANKAR, to begin service as soon as they feel they want to. We don't force people and go around saying "Are you serving, are you serving?" Because it is none of our business. Paulji used to say, "What a man receives in contemplation he must give out to the world."[14] And it's this amazing gift, this light and sound. When the VARDAN is flowing though you as this sound and light, this divine consciousness it's got to go somewhere."

14. Twitchell, Paul. Shariyat-Ki-SUGMAD Book II, Illuminated Press. Las Vegas, Nevada. 1971.

"You can't just keep taking it in, taking it in. If so, you're going to explode...Just kidding."

"But at some point there is this tremendous desire on the part of Soul to return that. And what I want people to know is you don't have to be a Master to give. You don't have to be a Fifth Initiate on the Soul Plane or a VARDAN Master or the Living VARDAN Master, or a great author, or a great poet or great musician. You don't have to be any of that to serve."

"In fact that is one of the beautiful things about the way the lower worlds and the higher worlds are set up, that is that every Soul is a spark, every soul is a drop from the Ocean of Love and Mercy. Every soul is a drop from God; a spark of God, from the HURAY. And so we are all sparks of God. And so we are all qualified to serve."

"Soul has this divine imagination or ability to dream and the power of creation. Now in the lower worlds creation is finished and we manifest that which already remains hidden on the inner, but in the higher Pure Positive God World's creation is not finished. Soul has this tremendous creativity and this tremendous Love, Wisdom, Power and Freedom but of course I am not speaking about the ego or mind or lower self. That is a dim reflection of a dim reflection of a dim reflection of truth and is not our true eternal God self, but like a series of dirty windows that impedes the light and Sound."

"Regarding Service in VARDANKAR there is a certain requirement if you want to teach a class for example. You need to learn the basics mentally, you'd have to do some reading and studying. You need to have a foundation. We find that a background in other paths does not really help because VARDANKAR is completely different and yet out of it, all other teachings arise, but they are not complete. This is because the VARDAN ITSELF is Spirit and the teachings contain the answers to all the questions anyone could ask."

"Most of this is on the Inner planes but much is also on the outer in the form of books and discourses and audio's. Once someone has a foundation in the VARDAN teachings, there are many ways to serve. Once we are doing our spiritual exercises and partaking of the Audible Life Stream it is said; what a man receives during contemplation he must give out to the world in selfless acts of Love and Service."

"Some become VARDAN Vahana's (like missionary's) who spread the word of VARDAN. Some have discussion classes or write about subjects related to VARDANKAR. Somebody might enjoy reading to the blind or helping the sick or elderly. Some serve their family selflessly. Others are Arahatas and teach VARDAN Satsang classes to study the Discourses and books of VARDANKAR. The main point is that Immortality begins with the selfless act of giving without ever thinking of reward. We do all our service in the name of the HURAY (God), the VARDAN (Spirit) and the Margatma (Inner Master or Spiritual Traveler)."

"The point is you are doing it for God rather than doing for human beings or for the little self. A selfless giving to God. And if you are doing it for God, in the name of God or in the Name of the Living VARDAN Master or in the name of the VARDAN. If you are doing that in the name of spirit, then what ever you're giving is pure, whether it is food for your family or reading to a blind person or helping a homeless person or working at your job it does not matter, for you see God and the VARDAN in everything."

"You become a humble channel for God that serves God without ever thinking of reward. Again this is the beginning of immorality. But we must become conscious of this. This is why we need the Initiations and we need to practice Out-of-Body Tuza Travel. What does it profit a man to gain the world if he loses his Soul? Of course we don't lose our Soul for we are Soul but if we are not Self-Realized and establish ourselves on the Soul Plane or 5th region or above we are not truly conscious. We are still asleep although we may be more awake then others around us, we are nonetheless asleep."

Heather added, "When we do all for God, as well as more directly serve God through reaching Souls with the message of VARDANKAR, the most direct path to God, we give them an opportunity to find Jivan Mukti or Spiritual Liberation upon reaching the Soul plane which is the first of the true Pure Positive God Worlds!"

"We may focus on sharing the high path, stepping out giving a talk or sharing flyers out in the street or in a newspaper or even on the radio. As you mentioned this is known in VARDANKAR as being a VAHANA. Different forms of sharing the VARDAN may become something that touches someone's life and changes them forever. It can change them forever, like the first time I or others touched our first VARDANKAR book. It changed my life as well as the lives of others. And it made such a huge difference to me."

"VARDANKAR is not a religion, philosophy or belief system but the Ancient Science of Tuza or Soul Travel meaning it's the path of actual experience rather than belief and faith."

"Maybe that Soul has waited so long for this moment where Spirit is going to reach out into the lower worlds and lift Soul up. And you can step forward as a coworker with God and the VARDAN and share the high path with the individual who yearns to expand his consciousness. It's life changing. And taking up the mantel of Vahana or Arahata, spiritual teacher in spiritual service, you are being a coworker with the Margatma the Living VARDAN Master which is the learning process of being a coworker with God and being a coworker with Spirit."

"The spiritual travelers return love to God being a conscious coworker with God, knowing and doing ITS will."

"There are some who have near death experiences and will often explain how they, though they were living a good religious life until they felt, with the sudden impact of the near death experience that they suddenly woke up. They woke up to realizing that there are aspects of God's true reality and will that they were once asleep to. This is like waking up just a little bit. We can benefit from not only waking up on the Astral Plane heaven, but with the help of the Traveler waking up on the Causal heaven, and then waking up on the Mental heaven, and then with the help of a True Spiritual Traveler waking up on the Soul Plane to experience Self Realization. Awakening just once is not enough."

"In fact we eventually find that anything short of Self Realization on the Soul Plane is an illusion. Most Souls in VARDANKAR will in time clamor to return to the Ocean of Love and Mercy where dwells the HURAY or one true God above all the worlds of duality, time, space, matter and energy. This is where we can become a VARDAN Master or Spiritual Traveler ourselves and this can be our goal if we are willing to be bold and adventurous!"

"We discover that what we think is the end is really the beginning. With each successive heaven is a level of awakening to God's will. When we give up our opinions and instead always dwell in the Pure Positive God Worlds and have our knowingness there, we listen and surrender to HURAY (God). We awaken the Holy Fire of VARDAN or Spirit. This will burn up all that stands between us and God, but it is not an easy thing. It will demand and consume more and more of the little self and can make us spiritually great if we are sincere!"

"Many humans are so strongly attached to opinion, putting opinion between themselves and God. With the holy fire there is only God, HURAY. The Voice of God or the VARDAN of ITSELF is all encompassing Spirit. To see oneself in the core of a flaming cloud of light. It extends out larger than any planet."

"HURAY (God) cares nothing for human custom or opinion or what Soul passes through on Earth. It cares nothing for human reform which is centered in the lower worlds. IT only wants Soul to return to IT. Soul sometimes appears as in a flaming robe of white light."

"We need to surrender to God over and over and over again. We need to chant the holy names of God such as HU. It means putting aside all expectation and perceiving God's presence through the Margatma and the VARDAN (Spirit)."

"We are Spirit, the Light and Sound, so when we surrender to Spirit (the VARDAN) we are not surrendering to something outside ourselves. What we are surrendering to is the highest aspect of our own being. It is like a drop of water surrendering to the Ocean. Yet as we surrender we remain the drop of water and retain our individuality becoming a conscious coworker. We do not lose ourselves but rather we work with God in partnership as a conscious coworker with HURAY, God."

"Then on other levels one can see an image of people pursuing every sort of endeavor and occupation with gusto. The ballerina practicing for hours and years to perfection, with clears, spins, and leaps. A man working late into the night, traveling far, putting forth his very best. The performer on stage memorizing countless scripts."

"And then we see how after we achieve the perfections in the spirit of human consciousness, these recede as afterthoughts and another desire appears and we seek instead perfection of the Soul. We finally seek the destiny of our very Soul throughout eternity. And then we seek it in perfection of the same relentless, persistent, zealous pursuit of God's will (aside from human responsibilities to family). Human endeavors or consciousness then recedes as afterthoughts and instead we come to a place where most all our time, talents, resourcefulness, and all we are is poured forth for God, in service to IT as ITS coworker without having to give up job or family. It is like the phrase to do all things in the name of God."

The same effort we once put in some Science, Art or some Business or talent as the all-consuming purpose for our being is in balance and unfolds into a new purpose of being a conscious pure channel of divine spirit ITSELF (Such as our Spiritual Mission). And at that we are inflamed in the Holy Fire of VARDAN. We strive to become first a coworker with the Margatma and then we strive to become a conscious coworker with HURAY or God. Spiritual service to God can, if we desire it become our world, our occupation, our business, our reason for being, our art, our universe; which we do all we can to master, perfect, refine, and express Spirit's perfection in the lower universes to the best of our ability and become God's conscious Coworker.

All are worthy of this because it is not about outward

appearance, or how much talent you possess, how smart you are or how perfect you are in personality or lower body perfection. Instead it is about Consciousness, Beingness and Total Awareness. We cannot judge ourselves or our natures from the human perspective for as Soul we are all Great beings of light and sound! All are perfect as Soul. We only need a great desire to be humble and allow God to use us without fear and without the lower self stopping us from serving as Conscious Co-workers.

Then we become that which we were all along but did not Realize, Conscious drops from the Ocean of Love and Mercy where dwells the great HURAY.

12
THE OCEAN OF LOVE AND MERCY

Of the many endless Pure Positive God Worlds of VARDANKAR, the 12th plane otherwise known as the Ocean of Love and Mercy or the Akaha plane is wondrous, breathtaking, indescribable, beyond all lower heavens and is sheerly magnificent because it is the very home of God, HURAY. In all the endless universes, galaxies, planes, and heavens the HURAY is the central of all centrals, the source of all sources, the essences of the universes. And while stationed here HURAY is simultaneously not stationed here but all pervasive, all knowing, all powerful, Omnipresent, Omniscient, Omnipotent.

Although there are many lower manifestations of IT's design administrating the different planes and universes, none of these are God itself but stepped down manifestations of ITSELF or the VARDAN, divine spirit. HURAY, whose home is the Ocean of Love and Mercy is the highest God, the only God. The VARDAN Masters have experienced that God does not look like a human with a beard or have human like attributes, consciousness, and wants as many will attribute to IT.

This is an idea that was created in the human mind by those who experienced the powerful but lower intermediary of the astral or mental plane heavens which are impressive and powerful administrators, but not of the highest God. They quivered at its booming voice, its great light and often said, "Surely this is God."

Yet according to the spiritual travelers God cannot be found in the third heaven, nor in the fourth but far beyond the lower heavens of time and space in the regions of pure spirit. HURAY, God resides in the Ocean of Love and Mercy.

And so begins Allen's experience of this higher Pure Positive God World beyond Worlds. "One morning upon closing my eyes the HU surrounded me, I appeared in a flash in a world of brilliant white dazzling light as if each particle of light is a fine, white mist."

"I was drawn like a moth to a flame and found myself approaching the center of an enormous white light which seemed to be everywhere yet in the core seemed brighter. In this world there was no up or down, time or space."

"Then I could perceive a vortex spinning slowly, it was like an immense whirlpool made of light and sound. I clamored to go to the next plane and then I suddenly knew that I had entered the center of the vortex and it would take me into the 11th plane."

"Without fear I flew into the center of this beautiful whirlpool of light and sound. And with great joy I found myself emerging into an even greater plane, the HURAY world. There was a tremendous calm and wisdom and all-knowing presence. And I felt I could stay here for eons. While the tenth plane was amazing and indescribable, the 11th had a freedom and a wisdom and a feeling of expansiveness that far exceeded the 10th plane.[12] Although words seem useless to try to compare."

12. The 10th Plane or Anami Lok is completely different and not to be confused with what some groups call the 10th dimension·

Then Rebazar Tarzs appeared as a dot or a ball of consciousness, as Pure Soul Awareness. And I knew within an instant that I had to move into the 12th Plane.

"This plane" Rebazar began, "is beyond wonder. And Soul can dwell in it for eons. However the plane above this one is far greater, for it is a source of creation in a way that the 11th plane is not."

"It is impossible to describe the differences, except to say that eventually Soul wishes to be more active in its participation with the universe and it is compelled to move from the 11th plane to the 12th in order to gain the wisdom of creation and manifestation."

"With that I found myself moving, if I can use the word moving because it wasn't really moving. I found myself moving into the 12th plane, which was far greater than the 11th."

"And as Rebazar Tarzs pointed out, there was a feeling or an awareness of activity or desire to create in an active way which was partly missing from the 11th plane."

"Then Rebazar began his discourse as we slowly moved toward the center of the white light which he explained was a Golden Wisdom Temple. "Behold." He said. "The Golden Wisdom Temple of the 12th plane." And with that we entered a place of brilliant, white light, filled with beings who I was aware were VARDAN Masters."

"Rebazar Tarzs sincerely began, "The light and sound that pours forth from this plane is truly immense, incomprehensible, unimaginable, and all Souls who come here face a great difficulty at one time or another." "They must return to Earth, a most dark place and they must somehow come to a reconciliation of how to distribute this great power in a world designed to fight against the pure positive light and sound of HURAY."

"And so it is they must surrender to the will of HURAY and come to terms with the fact that they are in a warring universe and that they are the enemy of the Kal Niranjan and shall be spit upon and cursed and far worse things."

"They cannot expect any reward in the lower worlds. For their love of the HURAY must be completely selfless. Otherwise they will not survive the tests they must face against the Kal who will mercilessly attempt to destroy any channel that comes from the Ocean of Love and Mercy."

"I do not wish to frighten you but you know very well that what I am saying is true and although a Master may enjoy a certain amount of latitude, they are completely detached. For any day could bring an end to their physical comforts or even to their very lives in the physical world. And yet I say to you they are happy and delighted to have the opportunity to give back even a tiny part of what they have received in way of Wisdom, Power, Divine Love and Freedom."

"They are compelled, actually it would be beyond compelled, but I do not have a word to describe this total dedication to bringing this light and sound into physical manifestation. So I use the word compelled. They expect no rewards other than the joy of being the VARDAN itself in pure expression, in this world of darkness, where so many Souls cry out in pain for relief."

"The HURAY sends messengers, spiritual life rafts. But these messengers must have physical bodies and so countless Souls make the journey into the heart of the Ocean of Love and Mercy and then return to the physical world simply because it is in their nature to love and that love alone drives them."

"No one will ever understand what I have said until they have been touched by the pure light of God. No one will ever understand what I have said until they resonate and have been touched by the pure sound of God. Some of you today will choose to return out of a sense of love for your love is the love of HURAY for its own creation, Soul."

"Some of you will serve in other worlds. Your love is no less than those who come down to the physical. It is love that sustains this world but it is not the love of man. It is the love of God."

The impressions of Rebazar's discourse changed, but much after this happened that was again, beyond mere words, emotions, thoughts or even impressions! I must say that when we attempt to share such things as this…we can only bring so much down to this Earth world. When having such experiences beyond the lower worlds of matter, energy, time, space and duality, one quickly learns that sharing such experiences is all but impossible. Words cannot express them but we try so that perhaps others can have their own unique experiences and more importantly become transformed by the Holy Spirit or VARDAN.

Sometimes it is only the vibratory rate of the words that can to some humble degree convey a small part of the way back to the God Head. The way is hard for those who pick and choose. We must be willing to let go of every preconceived notion about truth in order to find truth. Otherwise there is little if any hope we will see the true face of God! In the end it is only by moving out of our own body and making the journey ourselves with the aid of the Spiritual Travelers do we find Truth and never in books, discourses and so forth.

Heather had her own unique experience within the 12th plane, "My awareness deepened of this higher Pure Positive God World beyond worlds. In Tuza Travel one morning I appeared in a flash in a breathtaking world of brilliant white light and beautiful shimmering sound."

"I had direct projected in a flash to the 12th plane. For endless thousands and thousands of miles in all directions and yet paradoxically there was no time and space in this world. I felt the endless vast, still, yet flowing light pervading all my Beingness, like a vast other worldly ethereal presence like that of ocean shimmering. Like ocean composed of light and yet not like an ocean, all pervading in all universes. Just being in a state of reverence and wonder and centeredness in HURAY, knowing HURAY is the only reality."

"Within is only a feeling of God, HURAY, the only reality in eternity. HURAY is all. What else is there but HURAY and only God exists. Light and sound permeates all. God is formless without human mechanics and God is the formed in the vastness of all in spirit as pure light and sound. God is omnipresence as all pervasive through all places, worlds and universes. God is omnipotence all powerful, silent, moving will. And God is omniscience as in true reality and true realities all knowing. This 12th plane is not describable and only here are given impressions."

Out from the center of this endless light came a floating expression like a liquid light, it was also a sound and it flowed down through the heavenly worlds appearing to almost look like the arm of God's love reaching out to its creation or a tunnel or beam of light and then it flowed down to a lower heaven and then another and another and it soon encompassed and contained what appeared to be a gathering of people who were in a flow of love for God chanting God's holy name HU. (Pronounced HUE).

"They were encompassed by it, contained within it this all pervasive light and sound that flowed from HURAY as VARDAN (divine spirit). It was a sort of big globe of light and sound that had no shape. Among them was a man and levels of his being were in waves of sound current.

And in this moment of these impressions the HURAY in divine spirit, the VARDAN, communicated in pure consciousness, "Fill your life and moments with the sound.

In return I reverberated back, "I love you HURAY." Awareness of different aspect forms within which here are translated into words: HURAY wants those ready Souls to return to IT. "You must never waiver or give up if your goal is to return to God. The entire purpose of life in these worlds is to become a conscious coworker with the infinite one and return to HURAY of the Ocean of Love and Mercy.

In order to begin passage back to the highest God, the God seeker needs the VARDAN Master, the Initiation, and the Sound Current. And not just any Master but particularly HURAY's representative at that moment: The Margatma, The Living VARDAN Master. There are many who will falsely claim to be this Master selected by God. The way of knowing is to shift into a state of Knowingness, Seeingness, and Beingness which comes from these Pure Positive God Worlds. The Margatma is always a God Conscious being who has become a VARDAN Master who is capable of bringing Soul to this Realization of God.

In this breathtaking Akaha or HURAY plane there is form and formless. HURAY is all knowing, all powerful, and all present but mostly beyond all description. Therefore, as

Peddar once said if one is seeking God he loses God by not realizing God in the present presence of the ultimate one.

Within the center of the radiance we can be, always be dwelling within HURAY's domain. We can always be dwelling in the pure positive God Worlds in our waking life.

As one unfolds higher and higher through first the psychic and then the God planes, the white light becomes more blazingly radiant and the sound more pure and beautiful like the white music of spheres echoing and vast and increasing in its concentration of spirit with each ascending heaven. The lower planes are denser and as the planes ascend the vibration becomes higher and more pure and more encompassed by VARDAN (spirit). The higher planes are the stuff of pure light and sound, Spirit.

Regarding the 12th plane HURAY world, Peddar Zask had shared that it cannot be called a plane, being beyond description. However, the only purpose of attempting it here is to share direction within the universes of God so that we can become aware that it is possible to reach these heavenly planes of HURAY for oneself. It is not impossible as religionists claim. By hearing the experience of another individual, one can begin to grasp the possibility that it exists for oneself. This is the mission of the Living VARDAN Master, by his very presence he is a living expression of this reality demonstrating the state that one can achieve.

When a path to God no longer offers the individual progress to the states of true God Realization it is no longer the high path but an offshoot that splinters off in another direction. This is what happened throughout history to VARDANKAR, in Ancient Egypt, in Ancient China. Therefore it is helpful to attune to the pure positive God Worlds alone and consult with the highest God, the HURAY, the VARDAN, and true Margatma for guidance in all things spiritual to be in harmony with the will of HURAY (God).

Many are blown by the spiritual experiences of the lower worlds and by forces that are not God even if Soul assumes that they are. It is very helpful to know that we don't need to ask outside ourselves to find answers to our deepest spiritual questions. We merely can go directly to the VARDAN in the God Worlds for every direction in life.

God loves Soul and awaits as many of us have waited eons to find a moment such as this that you could collect yourself to return to IT.

Impressions came, "Soul foolishly exalts some so high, a folly in not moving oneself through the God Worlds. God, HURAY is in this moment and not some distant future, some unreachable way one could never know."

It flowed through me love for HURAY as impressions continued: "Contained in the one grain of sand is the entire ocean. You are like the grain of sand. You identify so strongly with your human life, the human self and it's through creations, like shells that shield you from realizing God. Within the echoing waves of sound and light reduce these shells. Be encompassed by my light and sound, let it flow through you with the highest sound."

The sound came in layers or levels of sound simultaneously. Then it flashed in my awareness a vision of a moment when I did the mold making method. I was a student of an offshoot not yet having found the high path, sitting on a sandy colored carpet reading books. At that time I asked myself: "If I fully realized and fully loved God right now, what would that look like?" Every night for my spiritual exercise I envisioned being fully present in that reality as though that reality were fully realized. It was an effort to answer the question: "How would I live if my life were in full realization and harmony in God" And so followed an effort in creating a mold and living within the mold until the goal is realized.

Peddar Zask's words echoed within and had inspired this mold making effort as he illustrated in a lower world example: If your aim and hope was to be an Architect you would within yourself make an impression or a mold like a plastic impression filled with plaster, seeing yourself as already being the Architect you desire to be; thinking like an Architect, studying and preparing yourself like an Architect, taking actions to make it so. You form the mold so completely as if it were already in present reality and eventually it becomes that you are the Architect. Likewise in the spiritual your aim is to embrace God with all your being; you become God's pure atom and coworker.

You embrace that mold of self fully realized now and not some distant future. Then the goal is emulated in action and pursued in zeal. Often the human self is too busy embracing fractured lower realities, rays and versions of itself. When the atom instead shifts and embraces God it is whole and complete.

The compulsion to look down upon others or attack others or dwell upon faults and mistakes of self and others is a waste of time when one could otherwise be dwelling in God and seeking the true freedom.

As this was written, far below on the lower astral plane I saw those leaders of my former path looking in on me on the inner planes and observing what I was doing. At first this startled me.

To them I shared telepathically, "Your time is best spent on perfecting yourself in God via out-of-body travel via the Audible Life Stream and not on focusing on me or anyone else for trivia but the very freedom of you as Soul, your eternal God self! Every Soul is a God being and in an instant can return if we have the humility to say: "I am tired of the games, all I want is God.""

And then another impression came: It was one occasion I was told that my husband was chosen as the next Living VARDAN Master. The only thing that passed through was it did not matter what human form the VARDAN or God force comes so long as the lovable Souls who have been waiting for thousands of years and have such a painful longing to return to God, have the opportunity. One could feel their pain, their longing, reaching out and finding only pieces and fragments like broken shards of glass.

Then after the next day of hearing this news of my husband becoming the next Living VARDAN Master a feeling of shock and deep insecurity rose in my heart. I felt within myself: He is everything to God and I am nothing to God. I felt like he is within an empowered role as a pure vehicle in helping Soul return and all I am is his little helper. At that moment I felt like a tiny useless minnow fish swimming beside a great intelligent whale. In the midst of insecurities bubbling forth I felt useless to God. I felt that I was of less usefulness to God. That I was less competent so maybe God didn't want me. I shared this insecurity with Allen and tears came. At that Allen comforted me and said: "Don't believe that."

The impression that expressed itself this way is important because sometimes people on the spiritual path when they see another spiritual being put into a position of being a vehicle of some divine mission they suddenly feel insecure and small.

No matter who we are or how extensive or insignificant you feel your role might be: you are needed by God perhaps much more then you consciously know if one is willing to let go of ego and surrender to God's will. You are vital to God when you realize it and come into the realization that all Souls are.

It is a realization of fully realizing Soul's God self, letting go of feeling that it is we in the human self that does greatness but rather that divine spirit does greatness through each of us.

There are those who would read the works of VARDAN Masters like Peddar Zask and feel incompetent, angry or jealous. If he thinks what is written is written by a personality then he is a fool. He is seeing with the physical eyes and not with the spiritual. It is the VARDAN itself and to be a more pure channel we must get out of the way.

For any individual who feels this painful insecurity I recommend reading of the life of Milarepa. He felt he was the most lowly of low being and a sinner, a black magician and not in God's favor and yet he admitted his mistakes humbly and moved on through delays, suffering, dry spells and errors to becoming an amazing God Conscious Soul and an amazing VARDAN Master.

The HURAY loves Soul so much because we are each divine sparks of ITS great body and contain the divine gift of divine Imagination.

We are not a thing nor a human doing but viewpoint much like God in the sense that we are cut out of this divine consciousness and have total consciousness, total awareness, total freedom, total love, total wisdom and total power and yet we are not limited to any of these for we exist simply because of God's great love for us as Soul! We can rest in the knowledge that we shall always have a plus factor and that Soul expands in awareness and finds greater and greater worlds and greater and greater forms of expression and expansion in the body of God for Soul is a conscious part of this body we loosely call the Ocean of Love and Mercy.

In this world beyond description, The Ocean of Love and Mercy, the formed and formless came the awareness, "Clear any sound around you that has a harshness or sharp clanging edge or unholy vibration. Protect your spirit from these sounds like one shields himself from acid rain."

"When your mind like a cup fills with worries, negativity, unsolvable troubles, problems, and the like; in an instant you can quickly drop these and focus on my light and sound. You can in a moment see these worries and concerns in a globule and then surrender these into the holy spiritual current. When you release and let go of your worried worldly problems and then surrender Soul to God, you release them. You can surrender to the Margatma. You then listen to the depths of yourself and you will be shown spiritual awareness and you will be shown the VARDAN. Even if the images are so very subtle or soft or blazing and large, you can listen and know… I AM."

"You can go directly to the spirit of God through the Spiritual Traveler, the VARDAN, for every step and direction in life. Simply know from the VARDAN of the Pure Positive Worlds and listen. God loves Souls and waits as many of you have waited countless eons to find a moment such as this that you could collect yourself to return." I felt an echo of love for HURAY.

"When other atoms attempt to deter you to make you doubt the spiritual…When they write hateful words to tear down your confidence or tear down my chosen vehicles for giving you the spiritual message, the God man or the VARDAN Masters I send you, know…When those atoms attempt to weave words that make God beings appear small or make you feel spiritually small don't be a fool and listen to fools, except if you wish to become a fool yourself!"

"How does this happen? This happens when you do not learn to get your answers from within; from only the highest God and the ancient VARDAN Masters."

"Often Soul clings to social opinion. An image of Peddar Zask appeared who is a God being and spiritual Master of VARDANKAR. [13] We saw atoms create mind forms focused on this Master's human flaws and mistakes and proceeded to blow these flaws so large like sky scrapers as to lose sight of the inner spiritual universes."

"Humans who become Masters have human flaws as most in the body have flaws. Obsessing over trivia leads to a life filled with trivia. You can find your answers within, even if they appear so subtle you barely hear the whisperings that flow to you from God's very heart."

"You can Block out the blaring loud voices of discord of those in the lower worlds who wish you to focus upon the endless trivia, the endless mind perplexities, the excess states of matter human reality. If you are a wise initiate you will shield yourself from these influences with this holy light and sound."

13. Peddar Zask is the spiritual name of Sri Paul Twitchell who served as the Living VARDAN Master from 1965 to 1971.

The flowing sound and flowing light was all pervading, glowing, sparkling.

"You don't need to hold onto confusion but instead know that all direction is there within your divine knowingness. When you sense or know, trust that knowingness. This dwells in the higher God Worlds, a Knowingness is all pervasive and strengthens as you embrace it. The knowingness will tell you when the old is done and the new is ready to be born. When the Master steps forward if he is the Living VARDAN Master you will know."

The impressions continued, "Soul in its confusion often needs a Living Teacher who will take Soul by the hand and assist Soul in the right direction and steps. When you do the spiritual exercises with the VARDAN Master these worlds open up to you and the Master as a God being knows exactly what you need as an individual spark to move to the higher echelons spiritually."

At that moment I saw an image of water being poured through the ears. "Open the spiritual ears."

And then a moment later I saw impressions of liquid light water flowing through the eyes. "Open the spiritual eyes." "The inner eye." "This is the protection from illusion and gives you the inner compass to return to me. When changes appear or when one Master leaves and another Master comes or something of confusion happens in your life... Are you abandoned or confused when you have your inner compass? You will just Know in all situations to keep your eyes set on the star of God."

Within the light shimmers and the sound current shimmers as well in all directions. Then an image surfaced if you can call it that, of within the endless light came a flowing form like

212

pure spirit that flowed down into the worlds and encompassed a gathering of individuals chanting God's holy name. The light and sound permeated all. The Omniscient presence reverberated impressions: "Fill your life with the divine sound and holy light."

13
THE SPIRITUAL EXERCISES OF VARDANKAR

Part 1- A Class With The Ancient VARDAN Masters

When we came to writing a chapter about the Spiritual Exercises we realized the great importance of the subject and that many readers would greatly desire to understand just how to practice them so they could begin benefiting. We found that previous training in meditation and other methods was generally not helpful to most people and that a new approach was needed in order to begin to understand the path of VARDANKAR and Out-of-Body Tuza Travel or Soul Flight.

We found ourselves in an inner class with the Ancient VARDAN Masters who addressed the subject then asked us to continue on in step by step instructions. Since this is such an important topic we have broken it up into two parts.

Part one begins with a few words from Allen followed quickly by his experience with the Ancient VARDAN Masters in this inner class on the topic of the Spiritual Exercises. Part two of this chapter we go into some specific Spiritual Exercises you can practice at home in about 30 minutes per day.

Keep in mind that VARDAN Masters flow with Spirit and Spirit is often random and does not take the road of the mind. It's important to listen and flow rather than try and judge through the mind or emotions of the lower senses. The VARDAN Masters address Soul, our eternal God self rather than our minds. So it's best to withhold judgment and simply listen. There is always time latter for questions and contemplation upon the meaning of their words.

As the VARDAN Masters like to say, there will be plenty of time latter to decide the validity of one's own personal experiences, impressions and the words of the VARDAN Masters. But we must have the eyes to see and the ears to hear. Otherwise we are like the deaf man at the symphony. We must test the words of these great spiritual Masters and not reject them at first glance. Otherwise there is no hope that we will find truth in this lifetime and if there is no hope of this then there is little hope in the next.

Allen begins: "It is important not to judge one self. We may acquire right discrimination but we should under no circumstances put ourselves down or judge ourselves simply if for no other reason than our false education in things like religion, metaphysics and philosophy has given us a very distorted view of truth and of who we truly are. A sort of false truth. Therefore we are not qualified to judge ourselves let alone become Judge, Jury and Executioner. Nor should we place ourselves on a high horse and assume we know truth simply because we have read a lot of books or had some spiritual experiences and assumed they were of the highest order.

Some who don't think they have what it takes to find God are the most humble and because of their love for God and their love for truth they have an opportunity if they can simply believe in God enough to know that even the greatest sinner can find God if he or she is willing to surrender.

The homeless beggar may be chosen by the HURAY to return to IT even though his clothing is dirty and he lay in the gutter penniless, while the merchant or priest wears the finest clothing and appears great before the eyes of their fellow man. God you see does not care about appearances or even mental equity, so-called worldly intelligence or anything of this sort. In order to find the high path or most direct path back to the HURAY one must be free of dogma, superstition and their own cherished beliefs. These and not immorality are the things that prevent one from taking the journey back to the God Head.

"We must set aside all judgments of ourselves whether its putting ourselves on a high horse or in the gutter and recognize we must find a true VARDAN Master who will instruct us on how to find the God head and not just read about it in some book!"

It was in this effort to acquire the Wisdom, Power and Freedom beyond mere mortal men that brought us to the feet of three spiritual giants: Yaubl Sacabi, Kata Daki, and Rebazar Tarzs.

Three masters who have ventured into the high God Worlds far past the 12th plane, and who have ventured repeatedly into the very heart of God or HURAY the Ocean of Love and Mercy. It is here we begin our journey; our journey Back to the God Head and to then serve as conscious coworkers with God.

I want now to share on record this experience, so that you too can gain the wisdom of these great VARDAN Masters. For this is what they desire at this time in spiritual history on this Earth world.

Closing my eyes in contemplation a scene quickly opened up before me. Rebazar Tarzs, Yaubl Sacabi, Kata Daki, and Heather stood before me in a circle we had formed in the most beautiful wooded area with medium short grass and

216

under the shade of a large oak tree perhaps 10 feet in diameter. The 5 of us sat down and Rebazar began. I quickly realized this was an inner Satsang class: A meeting or union with the Master.

No sooner had we sat down and gotten comfortable than Rebazar closed his eyes and all five of us began to chant HU. I could feel myself moving out of my body very rapidly.

I was aware that I was already out of my body and knew that I was simply moving higher from the high physical where the 5 of us had met into the High Astral.

There was a light airy feeling about this whole meeting. The kind of feeling a small child might get from being surrounded by those who love him more than he can comprehend.

It was a lightness, an airy feeling of freedom, warmth, and love. A knowingness that all was being taken care of and was in its rightful place.

But it was more than this. It was a feeling or state of Beingness...yes a state of Beingness was more accurate to describe it. A state of expanded awareness and expanded consciousness. A feeling of total freedom and liberation and love and acceptance. It was the presence of God. The presence of the Holy Spirit of VARDAN that permeates all things and had manifest in this scene and within the vibrations of this moment before me.

Then the HU chant ended and I opened my eyes to the voice of Rebazar, "Today's subject is the spiritual exercises of VARDANKAR."

"For the benefit of those Souls listening who cannot fully remember their spiritual roots I speak to them on this beautiful afternoon."

"Why is this a beautiful afternoon? Because Souls have come from all around the Earth world to listen in on this class. All that we say today is being recorded and made available to thousands of Souls. Many of them spiritually mature enough to desire God more than their petty egos or the deserts and meaningless games of the lower worlds or states of consciousness."

"It is to these Souls who desire Spiritual Freedom; It is to these Souls who desire to find God not in some future time but find God in this lifetime BEFORE they leave this world forever. It is to them that we speak."

Yaubl Sacabi nodded and then began, "The loneliness that Soul experiences during its separation from God can be a terrible pain. The compassion that God or HURAY has for man is beyond comprehension and yet God may appear cruel in that it lets man suffer by his own devices."

"Countless Souls torture themselves through the creation of karma, the game of Cause and Effect and suffer needlessly on the wheel of 84 undergoing then millions of incarnations."

"In some incarnations they play and frolic and enjoy the dark comforts of their amusements and in other incarnations they cry out in pain for they begin to realize that this world is not and will never be the true home of Soul. That part of man that is his eternal God self. That part of man that possesses Seeing, Knowing and Being and is the atom from the Ocean of Love and Mercy, the drop of God. The great consciousness we call the living breathing HURAY that is eternal, unchanging and beyond description."

"Soul is identical in substance to this great being known as

HURAY and will at some point return to IT, not to become absorbed, but to become a conscious coworker with IT."

Kata Daki began, "All of this is true...and Soul's love for God or HURAY is not to be questioned but the subject at hand is the spiritual exercises of VARDANKAR and I would like to say a few words if I may?"

"Of course." Rebazar nodded. It was clear Rebazar was the Arahata or Teacher of the class although any one of the 3 Masters: Rebazar, Yaubl or Kata Daki could have easily lead it.

Kata Daki continued, "When the heart of man or woman is ignited with divine love and a desire for God then all is possible! It is this burning desire no matter how small it may be that is like an ember or flame that burns in the heart of man and woman."

"Sometimes it may appear almost gone. And millions of years may go by before it's rekindled. But usually Soul does not have to wait that long!"

"It is the cry of the child for its mother's love. It is the tears of sadness for the husband who lost his wife or the wife who lost her husband and beloved."

"It is the tears of joy from a mother for the birth of her child or the tears of sorrow for his early death."

"It is the longing that Soul feels to return back to its source and all Souls have this longing buried deep inside their very Beingness."

"When this longing is awakened by the Living VARDAN Master then Soul begins to seek out the Master and desires to return."

"The outer man or woman may be unaware of this desire. But the inner is now seeking Spiritual Liberation or what is known in VARDANKAR as Jivan Mukti."

"At some point the seeker finds the Margatma, the Living VARDAN Master and seeks to return via the path of VARDANKAR, The Ancient Science of Out-of-Body Tuza Travel."

"It is here that the spiritual exercises become the path, the way, the door from where Soul steps through into the other worlds."

"If a Soul's desire for God is greater than IT's desire for illusion and Maya then Soul shall find spiritual liberation in this lifetime provided Soul is willing to surrender to the inner Master and follow the path of VARDANKAR."

"Most Souls find the pull of illusion greater than their desire for God, and succumb to one of the five passions of the mind; lust, anger, greed, attachment, or vanity."

"They become vain and egotistical and give up on God in order to pursue mental, emotional and physical pleasures. They enjoy their philosophies and religions, their emotional extravaganzas and material taste for money, power, sex, food and prestige."

Yaubl nodded, "But eventually the games begin to end for Soul, for like you stated so eloquently Sra Daki, Soul can no longer wait and clamors to return to the HURAY."

"Yes." Kata continued, "And it is through the practice of the spiritual exercises that Soul makes contact with the light and sound of VARDAN. The wave of creation. The very primal spirit of VARDAN emanates out of the heart of HURAY and can be seen as light and heard as Sound."

"IT sings to Soul and contains all Wisdom, Power and Freedom!"

"IT is the sum total of all Wisdom, Power, and Freedom and only IT can lead Soul back home."

"This wave of pure VARDAN, light and sound flows out from the center of God ITSELF and moves into each respective plane below. It passes into the lower worlds where it divides into positive and negative streams of consciousness. Up until it hits the lower worlds IT was pure positive."

"This wave or VARDAN, or light and Sound now flows into the last of these lower worlds the physical and then moves back up in a returning wave."

"It is the returning wave that Soul rides during Out-of-Body Tuza Travel that brings Soul back into the heart of God or HURAY."

Rebazar smiled broadly then took over, "Yes, so we see that the Margatma links the Soul to this returning wave through the initiations and through his spiritual instructions via the outer but mostly the inner channels. Especially during the dream state."

"The wise and ready Soul learns to leave its body and travel via the inner channels and rides this returning wave. Upon this wave as Kata stated is the sum total of all Love, Wisdom, Power and Freedom as it is expressed at that plane of existence."

"We simply move higher and higher through the various levels."

"However the Inner Master is there to guide us and protect us on this journey."

"This is where the spiritual exercises come in. They are the modus operandi or method by which the Soul grabs hold of this returning wave and moves or travels into the various worlds. A brief overview of the God Worlds of VARDAN Chart will tell us where we are and where we are going."

Yaubl then took over. I noticed a smoothness about the dialog as if there was a hidden inner communication that coordinated what was being said among the 3 Masters. There was none of the awkwardness that usually occurs when one person talks and then the other continues on.

Yaubl said, "One of the great points being made here is that Soul must have the proper desire for God and Soul must join forces with this returning wave of the VARDAN or light and Sound, Holy Spirit, call it what you may."

"But Soul must have 4 things in order to find spiritual liberation.
They are:
1. The Master.
2. The VARDAN or Holy Spirit
3. The initiations or the link up with the VARDAN's returning wave.
4. God or the HURAY."

"Actually the path of VARDANKAR is simple if one looks only to the basic tenants and stops asking countless questions about unimportant details."

"So the spiritual exercises are simply there to practice these 4 tenants of VARDANKAR!"

Heather interjected a question at this point, "Sri Sacabi...if it's that simple, why do some Souls struggle with them and find difficulty in using their imaginations or leaving their bodies?"

Yaubl paused, "Tuza Travel is a skill just like any other skill. You would not expect to become an expert Violinist or Dancer or Painter unless you practiced the correct method. It is mostly the correct use of imagination."

"One must have faith in the Master, God, the VARDAN, and themselves."

"They must recognize that they are just like any other Soul who has become a spiritual giant in the past. They are no better, nor worse!"

"See this is my point. Souls determine their level of development based mostly on two things: Their experiences and their beliefs."

"The two can become a vicious loop. If you don't believe you are worthy of traveling into other worlds during your spiritual exercises or you don't believe that you're capable of such things then you are not conscious of the experiences. One reinforces the other and it is self-defeating to believe you are imprisoned."

"The individual has a choice. If they will have faith in the Margatma the Living VARDAN Master then they will try the exercises with a gentle expectation."

"Heather...have you ever been grateful for something

before you actually received it because you knew in your heart of hearts the gift had already been given? It simply needed to be manifested out into the physical plane of existence."

"Of course you have. It is like the baby girl who is grateful for her mother taking her into her arms and giving her love. Ever notice that the gratitude often starts before the mother actually picks up the child. If there is a strong and loving bond between mother and child then the child instinctively knows and there is love and trust before any actions occur on the mother's part. There is a feeling of total trust, unconditional love between the parent and child."

"This is the kind of love that the Inner Master can have with the student."

"Not that the student is a baby but that the student is loving and grateful even before the gift is given on the outer."

"For it is true that the Initiate always dwells in the higher worlds and so the great secret is Soul always dwells in the higher worlds, therefore the wise Soul is grateful and gives the Inner Master his love and devotion and faith knowing that it will manifest on the outer soon enough."

Rebazar continued where Yaubl left off, "However…it also has to be said that sometimes the aspirant is skeptical and this is perfectly fine." "He may have doubts and ask the Master to prove the validity of VARDANKAR to him."

"This is perfectly normal. And the Master will usually turn it around and ask the student to prove it for himself through the practice of the spiritual exercises whether he truly is the Master and whether VARDANKAR is real."

Allen put his finger on his chin, "Seems like a bit of a

paradox. I agree with what Yaubl said about gentle expectation and having faith in the Master and I also agree with what Rebazar said. And yet it seems there is a bit of a contradiction between the two?"

Both Rebazar and Yaubl laughed.

Rebazar began, "It is not faith we are after really…but Knowingness. Beingness and Seeingness. Behold the qualities of God!!! But of course qualities are not God! They are only qualities."

Then Yaubl added, "The mind can never know truth. Only Soul. It is through one's own experience that he develops spiritually…never through the reading of scriptures or the experiences of others."

"These can be helpful but it is through personal experience that we go from being human to the next phase of our evolutionary journey which is of a consciousness far beyond what most men reach."

"Yes it is true that man has an opportunity through VARDANKAR and through the Spiritual Exercises of VARDANKAR to reach the next evolutionary stage of development."

"But this must be done on an individual basis and not as a mass group."

However if enough of the group undergoes a transformation into the God man, then it will have a profound effect on the Earth world. One new God Realized Master who brings the light and sound into this world is far more transformative than a million world reformers and do-gooders."

Kata Daki smiled, "How are we doing on the time Rebazar?"

"Ah time." Rebazar smiled, "We never did get into individual techniques, so we shall have to leave that to Heather and Allen to include some Spiritual exercises. We need to close this class and so I say Baraka Bashad. May the Blessings Be."

And with that I was back in my body.

* * * * *

Latter in preparation for this book to be written the Ancient VARDAN Masters where kind enough to appear to me again to give a spiritual exercise and some more wisdom on the topic.

Rebazar began, "We have returned to add more instructions regarding the Spiritual exercises of VARDAN. We hope you do not mind?

I smiled broadly, "No, I am most grateful that you have come back to continue where you left off."

Rebazar Continued,
"Well then let's get down to brass tacks, One example of an exercise is the Zikar. This is where the Spiritual Aspirant finds a quiet place and sits down perhaps in a chair or on the ground. He then takes five deep breaths counting each one and places his attention ever so minutely upon the Third Eye also known as the Spiritual Eye or Tisra Til. For those not familiar, the Tisra Til is located about in inch inside the skull

and between the eye browns. When gazing into this third eye we must realize this is our inner faculty of vision in the psychic worlds. Later when we go higher we will see from the much more expansive viewpoint of Soul which has a 360 degree viewpoint and has direct perception, meaning it does not require the lower psychic bodies such as the astral, physical, or mental."

"We will be looking for the light of God. This light may be white, golden or any number of other colors depending on the vibratory rate."

"We must not look directly into the third eye but obliquely and gently and minutely. This is a gentle gaze and indirect meaning we look to one side or the other and not directly into the light or third eye."

"If we look directly into the light it generally will disappear."

"After we have taken and counted our five deep breaths we begin to chant the Zikar or holy name of God. For the beginner this is generally the word HU pronounced HUE. We can chant this word in a long drawn out form such as HUUUUUUUUU or we can say the letter "H" and then draw out the "U" as in "H" "UUUUUUUUU." The second method is preferable at this time."

"So we are chanting the Zikar and looking for the light. We never push this but do it with a childlike expectation and trust in the great spirit of VARDAN. Once we have chanted for a few minutes we may stop and listen for the Audible life stream or Sound Current."

"We may hear any number of sounds such as the gentle note of a flute, the sound of bagpipes, the chirp of crickets (where there are no crickets, the buzzing of bees), there are many sounds. The sound may be subtle."

"Next we wait for the Master to appear in the spiritual eye. This can be subtle. The presence of the Master can be often seen as a blue light. Gentle, it often comes like a lantern with gentle glowing edges."

"The light of God may be much softer and more subtle than expected. It may appear as a gentle point of light like a star, or in some cases it may almost blind the individual. The sound may be very soft or louder."

"There are many experiences that come."

"There are also many words that can be chanted. Zikar means holy names. There are many that can be chanted. We generally chant those of a higher vibratory rate. If we examine the God worlds chart in this book we will see the different names and sounds."

"HU is one of the highest that can be vocally expressed as sound on the outer. HURAY is another. Aum, contrary to common belief is only around the Causal Plane in consciousness or the mental at its very highest. It is not a word that brings about spiritual liberation."

"One can also chant the spiritual name of the Master. Such as the current Master Nye-Dah-Zah. Or they can chant my name. Rebazar Tarzs or they can chant Yaubl Sacabi."

Kata Daki interjected, "This is one of the most important techniques for it tunes one into the great cosmic sound current and the great light. The light illuminates the way back to God and the Sound draws Soul back. Of the two the

Sound is the most important, but the light also shows the pitfalls along the path."

"The Inner Master will work with the aspirant and guide him or her and protect the student from the rocks and shoals of the Kal or negative power that wishes to prevent any Soul from finding spiritual liberation."

"Without the spiritual traveler there is little if any hope of finding God Realization."

Then Yaubl Sacabi continued, "Imagination is one of the greatest tools Soul has on its journey. Although most misaligned people forget that imagination molds spirit and without it man is little more than an animal by nature. "

"The very fabric of imagination responds to and is made out of spirit. What we strive for is to use the Audible life stream and the VARDAN and become born anew rather then become the effect of our own fears and ignorance."

"Although the Metaphysicians, Philosophers and Religionists talk and talk about imagination, visualization and setting goals, they fail to understand that without the VARDAN Audible life stream or Spirit and without the true VARDAN Master or God man, all they are doing is perpetuating reincarnation and Karma. They are simply reworking and reformatting Karma and engrams or picture files. None of this leads to freedom only slavery."

Rebazar Tarzs nodded, "The topic of the spiritual exercises runs very deep but without a good foundation in the VARDAN teachings results will be haphazard. This is why the student must be patient and set for himself the noble goals of Self and God Realization rather than simply seeking cheap thrills and psychic phenomena. Psychic phenomena is cheap and common among man, but of little value since it fails to bring one to the God head and can be dangerous because man does not understand the great Astral forces that he is playing with. Again this is one very important reason why a spiritual traveler is necessary to reach God unless one wants to place a great amount of wear and tear upon their lower bodies and reduce their likelihood of success to almost zero."

"We shall leave it at this for now and allow Allen and Heather to write part two. Perhaps some of the readers will understand. As it is said, most do not have the eyes to see or the ears to hear truth...but those few who do simply know and it is them that we best address rather than those who are simply not ready for truth in their respective lifetime. "

And with that the Ancient Masters let us ponder their instructions and words of wisdom.

In closing this first part I would like to say that VARDAN is not taught but caught! And once we catch it we are indeed changed forever. The intellectual, the mildly curious, the lukewarm for God will never find truth. They are too busy trying to find materiality and expand their little ego self to find God. For them their God is like a genie who serves them and perhaps their family and others, or they are so caught up in dogma and belief systems that nothing the Masters say will convince them that truth is any closer than their faith in their material Space God who gives them vague promises of everlasting happiness at some future date and place. In the end their desire is for materiality and to turn the lower worlds into a sort of false paradise.

On the other hand those who sincerely do the spiritual exercises and love God and love truth shall in time find truth not in the distant future but in the here and in the now.

Truth is not what the Philosophers, Religionists and Metaphysicians claim it is. No, it is far greater.

In the next part of this chapter we shall explore some more spiritual Exercises and how to apply them to "Catch truth rather than opinions and faith."

Opinions are a dime a dozen, it is only through personal experience with the Audible Life Stream the VARDAN, the Sound and Light that emanates from God and returns to IT that we find truth in the journey and destination upon the Anami Lok or 10th and eventually the 12th plane where dwells the HURAY and the Ocean of Love and Mercy.

Upon reaching the 10th plane we of ourselves are invited to join the order of the Bourchakoun and become VARDAN Masters so that we too can help Souls find the Pure Positive God Worlds above all time and space.

13
THE SPIRITUAL EXERCISES OF VARDANKAR

Part 2- More Instructions on Proper Methods

"In silence listening to an inner melody during a spiritual exercise I hear a heavenly, ethereal shimmering sound that in some ways resembles singing bowls, other worldly ethereal sounds rise up. Simultaneously I hear a high pitched melody like the music of spheres that spins out a breathtakingly beautiful high pitched sound. In the midst a soft lovely light rises with it. There is a stillness and expression so vast it is beyond description."

"In the midst of this sound an image flashed before me from spirit, a soft knowing, a reminder of the sacred blessing that the spiritual exercises open up to the individual beyond their wildest dreams."

Heather

When we first begin the spiritual exercises of VARDANKAR, which are quite different in method and results from meditation and prayer, we find we may keep them simple such as the Zikar exercise given in the last chapter by Rebazar Tarzs. The light and sound or what is known as the Audible life stream or VARDAN is the foundation of the Spiritual Exercises of VARDANKAR.

The exercises can be simple or more complex, but what matters is that we approach them with an open heart and with a sincere desire for God and for Truth.

Sometimes the most effective methods are the simplest, for the VARDAN or Spirit is not concerned with the mental apparatus but only with Soul our true God self!

Prayer, meditation, reading of books, or the words of Earth bound gurus, none of these can free Soul from the bounds and shackles of its human shell which blinds Soul from its ability to soar through the heavens to return to the essences of the universes (God).

The directions given out by the Margatma, the Living VARDAN Master in spiritual exercises however do precisely that which frees the individual to return to God through the progression of the expansion of the individual's awareness through a succession of higher and higher levels of spiritual planes he unfolds through. This is the path of Total Awareness through Out-of-Body Tuza Travel!

Each plane in turn corresponds to a level of initiation where the individual makes his spiritual home on that heavenly plane until comes the time the individual graduates to the next heaven.

It is virtually unknown by many philosophies and beliefs that we can progress to higher heavens and therefore unknowingly most individuals end up focused on the physical world under the belief that once they die they will go to heaven. This ends up being a trap and most either incarnate back on Earth or spend some time in one of the lower heavens such as the Astral Plane.

Some can travel within a few of the lower worlds and falsely believe they have reached a high state of consciousness when in fact they are only able to operate somewhere in one of the astral sub planes or perhaps somewhere within the Casual world.

Those who believe they just need to be "good" and will go to heaven later on have fallen for the oldest trick of the negative power to trap them in the lower worlds. Generally, it is only when living in the human body that we can make progress to the higher heavens and become a conscious coworker with God.

Some may balk at this and say why not simply serve God without a very high state of consciousness. Who needs Total Awareness or God Realization when we can serve our fellow man here on Earth.

This is a great trap. In order to be a channel for the God power we must become conscious. Anyone who is asleep will be of little use to the HURAY or God, and will only serve the Brahm or some other lower ruler such as Kal Niranjan, lord of the Astral Plane.

No amount of Good deeds will bring spiritual liberation to Soul. Only the journey back can do this, and this can only be accomplished through Out-of-Body Tuza Travel and not Astral projection, meditation, prayer or any other methods that require the God force to lower its vibration down to the body consciousness which of course is impossible. The two can never meet but only a tiny part may express itself in this world. A golden thread so fine as to be invisible and yet so strong as to be unbreakable. This thread is the VARDAN or Spirit. But it must be taken and followed as the Audible Life Stream otherwise there is no spiritual liberation for Soul.

Out-of-Body Tuza Travel to heavens is not the adventure sought by the timid or closed minded but only those Souls who are brave enough, bold enough, and driven enough to wholeheartedly push past obstacles that stand in their path to progress into the God Realms. Results in out-of-body travel are not always immediate like the sorts of instant gratifications offered in the modern worlds.

But these come with enthusiasm, not pushing too hard and daily discipline. The mind itself is trained to deny the reality of the spiritual inner worlds.

Both subtle and direct spiritual experiences seem like nonsense to the mental apparatus, so initially when we first take a leap into the unknown and experience these for ourselves we may at first over look our subtle experiences or even fear them because of our unsound spiritual training. Things like fear or pushing too hard make such experiences recede.

In the following pages we have listed several spiritual exercises designed for Out-of-Body Tuza Travel to the spiritual worlds. It is helpful to create a momentum by experimenting and then selecting one for continued use over the course of one or more weeks or even months before experimenting with additional exercises.

Over time additional exercises can be alternated as desired as the VARDAN (spirit) will often guide us through which lights up for us as which exercise we are ready for next. Doing spiritual exercises for thirty minutes daily is recommended to spiritualize one's consciousness, open one's spiritual faculties, explore Tuza Travel, and open spiritual growth to higher levels.

Just as a child learning to play the flute improves and becomes more and more skilled with ongoing practice over weeks, months, and years of practicing the correct methods, so it is with the spiritual exercises.

Gentle expectation combined with enthusiasm, while refraining from pushing too hard for results tends to improve the ability to out-of-body travel. Patience is most helpful for those who don't experience immediate results as this can vary depending on the individual.

The experience of seeing light and hearing sound is also a spiritual experience on the inner planes.

Some individuals find it helpful to set a time daily to practice. Additional spiritual exercises can be found in other VARDANKAR books and Member only Discourses.

In practicing the VARDAN Spiritual Exercises some may see some similarities with meditation, however spiritual exercises in spite of some superficial similarities are for the most part completely different. In meditation the individual may focus on some chakra like the navel or Solar Plexus and chant a word and empties their mind in a passive state. No purpose or destination is usually chosen and the individual generally stays in their body or the Astral Plane. This accounts for why so-called Gurus and holy men often have little if any knowledge of the heavenly worlds, and what little experience they have is generally on the Astral and Causal plane of consciousness.

We were surprised how many have barely touched the super physical (Only slightly higher in vibratory rate then the physical) and yet consider it the highest!

Meditation has been a dismal failure as far as finding Self Realization and God Realization. Upon further examination we find that all truly great spiritual Giants throughout history have used Bi-Location also known as Tuza or Soul Travel as their means of obtaining whatever enlightenment they have achieved. Few will talk about this for so few know the truth…and also many have died at the hands of the priest craft who does not want the common people leaving their body and getting answers on their own. It is difficult if not impossible to control a person who has the ability to Soul or Tuza Travel and such individuals are often considered dangerous to the Orthodox teachings and Dogmatic Religions and philosophies of the times.

Spiritual exercises are also different than prayer which may be petitioning God for needs, but the individual is still grounded in the physical plane and may be contacting spiritual entities in the lower worlds. Spiritual exercises are different than meditation in that the individual by placing attention on the inner VARDAN Master, is linking up with the light and sound current which are God's voice, the returning wave of the audible life stream. Soul travels upon this returning wave that uplifts Soul drawing Soul closer to Self and finally God Realization via Tuza Travel.

By the individual's efforts they may be able to float above their head as a 360 degree viewpoint of Soul and experience Seeing, Knowing and Being through the direct perception of the Soul body which is far beyond the Astral and mental senses bound by time and space.

The works of the Living VARDAN Master is like a matrix since the Master is centered in the God Worlds and therefore the individual can get much further with this link than on his own.

There is a saying in VARDANKAR: a Master can only take you to whatever heavenly plane and its corresponding state of consciousness he has established himself at. This is the great secret of all the VARDAN Masters. They dwell in the body but as Soul they are in the true God Worlds and are aware of the actual presence of God for they are not limited like other men to time and space.

They preach that we too can achieve this end if we are dedicated!

In spiritual exercises we can select a purpose and sometimes destination. The individual may wish to learn about some spiritual topic and he can choose a destination or VARDAN Master to meet in any of the spiritual planes he feels he will best accomplish the spiritual purpose he chose for himself. Spiritual exercises can be adapted to our spiritual purposes and needs.

However we must learn to be detached and random. In other words if we set the goal of visiting the Soul plane and the Master comes to us to take us into a VARDAN golden temple such as Agam Des here on Earth, we should not be disappointed but delighted and go with the Master in our Soul body to receive the inner instructions!

I must say that it is essential that one gain the help of a true Spiritual Traveler for the purpose of protection and to help in the journey and guide one away from the Rocks and shoals that can trap us in the eddies and sub currents of the Kal traps that await any Soul who is bold and adventurous enough to attempt to find God in a single life time! As said before, a Master or teacher can only take you as far as he himself has gone and no further than this. Therefore from our experience, only the True VARDAN Masters have actually gone into the very heart of God and are qualified to lead Souls into the higher worlds above M.E.S.T. (matter, energy, space and time).

Truth is not for the faint of heart and as Paul Twitchell has said in the Shariyat-Ki-HURAY that the path back to God

"...is strewn with the corpses of those who have tried and failed."[14] The reasons for failure are many. Mostly it is vanity or one of the other five passions of the mind such as lust, greed, anger or attachment.

There is of course also dogma, superstition, cherished beliefs and other goodies that await us if we are foolish enough to refuse to let go and let God.

Belief systems are a strange thing. One can believe almost anything and make it true in their universe. The trouble is that Truth waits for no man or woman. If we refuse truth because we desire to hold onto lies then truth will not go away...it will simply wait for us to desire it more fully. The world is full of those who do not desire truth. Truth is God and God is truth. There is no other reality that is real other than the HURAY and Soul. All else is illusion. Half-truths are like lies and lies are like half-truths. Some argue that there is truth in everything but it is the highest truth...God, that we must seek unless we want to be made into fools. No lie or half-truth has ever brought Soul Spiritual Liberation. It is only through the grace of the Audible Life Stream and the God Man that truth is found in its entirety.

Truth again cannot be found in books. It must be experienced and in the highest way possible. That of Tuza or Soul Travel and returning back to the God head in this lifetime!

The following are just a sample of some of the more common spiritual exercises that are useful to the beginning student.

14. Twitchell, Paul. Shariyat-Ki-SUGMAD Book I, Illuminated Way Press, Las Vegas, Nevada. 1971.

In this first exercise we place our attention upon the Tisra Til or third eye located between the eye brows about an inch inside the scull.

This is a simple exercise involving the Sound current or VARDAN the Holy Spirit also known as the Audible Life Stream. As we spoke of earlier it has two waves, the ascending wave and the returning wave. We use the returning wave to move as Soul, back home to God or HURAY.

In this exercise we simply sit in an easy chair and again place our attention on the Tisra Til. We try and do this in a quiet and darkened room as to not disturb the eyes or ears with outer clutter. We try and find a place where we will have 30 minutes of undisturbed time to practice.

After having placed our attention lightly and minutely or obliquely on the Tisra Til we take five slow deep breaths counting each and every one. Then we begin to chant the word HU pronounced as in the color HUE. We do this in a long drown out sound. "HUUUUUUU."

The word HU is an ancient name for God but it is also the word on the 10th plane, the Anami Lok (see God Worlds Chart). HU has a very high vibratory rate. Please note that the word Ohm is on the Mental plane or 4th plane.

The best way to chant the HU is to pronounce the H first. As in the letter "H." and then chant the U in a long drawn out voice. The "U" is pronounced as in the letter "U." Note we do not sing this but chant it.

Listen carefully to your own inner rhythm and that of the HU. What we are doing is tuning into the inner sound current and resonating with it as Soul. This HU will move throughout all our inner bodies but we are not concerned with that so much as Soul taking hold of this sound and moving into another plane.

As we place our attention upon the Tisra Till we look for the inner light. This light may be any number of colors corresponding with the various planes. We may see blue, white, gold, orange, green or any number of colors. It is again important to look obliquely and minutely at the Tisra Til. We do not stare directly at this area.

If we see a light it may be a pin point or it may radiate an entire area of our inner vision. It may appear as a gentle globe or be brighter.

It may be blindingly bright or barely noticeable or anything in-between. This light is the light of God steeped down to whatever state of consciousness you are turned into at the time.

Physical tends to be green, Astral pink, Causal orange, Mental blue or purple, Soul Plane yellow, higher worlds white, but these are simply general guidelines. Others will see visions and there is no need to judge the experience but simply let it be what it is.

Be grateful if you see this inner light and don't worry how bright it is or what color it is. It is a sign that you are spiritually open to the light of God!

However if no results come be patient. Often it takes time. We also listen for the Sound Current. We may inwardly hear the sound of thunder, the chirp of crickets, a high pitched ringing sound, the sound of violins, the single note of a flute. If you have studied the God Worlds Chart, you will have a sense for what sounds and colors correlate with each plane but the main point is to listen for any sound no matter how faint or loud.

Please keep in mind we are speaking here of the inner hearing and inner sight. These inner faculties are more subtle and require less effort and strain and a childlike expectancy and love for Spirit and God. Sincerity is the key here. How sincere are we in finding truth in the here and now?

Some hear the sound of the rushing of the wind, others the sound of bag pipes, the buzzing of bees or the sound of violins. There are many celestial sounds. A rushing wind, the sound of woodwinds and many others. We may also meet the Master or any one of many Spiritual Travelers.

Contrary to popular opinion Jesus was not the highest master but studied under a VARDAN Master. He is now on the mental or fourth plane and much misinformation has been written about him. Many attempt to follow him not understanding that just as an infant cannot get nourishment from a departed mother man cannot follow a departed Master and find Spiritual Liberation on the Soul or fifth plane. I know many will disagree with this statement but if you look at history you will see this to be so. One also cannot find spiritual liberation from a book no matter how great it may be. Nor looking to an angel or saint bring one into the heart of God. One may reach the Astral world perhaps but generally no higher than this.

We can chant the HU for a few minutes then fall silent and listen for this inner sound current. Then go back and chant again. Please follow your inner guidance or sense of knowing. Many discover that they have been hearing the inner sound current and seeing the inner light for years. Many children see the light and hear the sound. Later in life they also remember seeing the VARDAN Masters as children. The HURAY always gives Soul an opportunity to return home, but most do not take it. Some must wait a long time when they refuse the opportunity but it always eventually comes around again and again for them to choose whether to wait for another distant lifetime or take the chance now to find Enlightenment.

Many will study with past VARDAN Masters when VARDANKAR had a different name. Some quit the path only to return again thousands of years later. Often if we look at pictures of the VARDAN Masters we may see one or two that look strangely familiar. Often we have worked with them in the past and in the dream state and so we are beginning to make the outer connection once again. Of course we may choose to forgo this opportunity, but it is a sacred moment when Soul chooses to return no matter the cost.

The second exercise involves visiting a Temple of Golden Wisdom in a particular level of heaven: Here we can select a level of heaven to visit the Golden Wisdom Temple there, (as all levels of heaven have a VARDAN Golden Wisdom Temple) such as on the Astral plane the Temple of Askleposis to meet with the Ancient VARDAN Master Gopal Das. We can start by choosing our destination and then looking into the Tisra Til (spiritual eye). Next we chant some holy word such as "HU" which is a name for God. In our imagination we can feel a strong desire to leave our physical body and imagine that we are traveling to this heaven with its Temple of Golden Wisdom.

Even if we do not know what it looks like we can make approximations and see ourselves there. It is like Paul Twitchell once said, "Where thought goes, the body must follow."[14]

14. Twitchell, Paul. Illuminated Way Press, Eckankar Dictionary, San Diego, CA. 1973.

It is the same with the spiritual bodies for we can draw ourselves to the heavens of our choosing to visit what some call the "afterworld" or "heaven" while still living. Here when we make this visit we can learn for ourselves vital information for our spiritual lives.

We may for example chant Gopal Das.....and or Askleposis...Alternating with the chanting of HU...this often will be enough to draw us to the temple if we have faith or a childlike expectation and love for God.

The third exercise is if we wish to meet with the VARDAN Master to be accompanied on the inner worlds. This is often very effective since the inner Master carries a very high vibratory rate, that of the VARDAN.

To begin we can focus on the spiritual eye (between and slightly above our physical eyes) or we can focus on the crown chakra (the top of the head). These are openings that Soul can leave the physical body through. We must realize that we are not seeking to do astral projection but Soul or Tuza Travel. Next we can begin chanting some holy word or chant the Masters title: Mar-gat-ma. We might see images appear on our inner screen or thoughts appear but we can let these pass through like water through a stream. Eventually this inner screen becomes blank. At this point the VARDAN Master may appear to bring us beyond this matter world to one of the many heavens. Some may do this exercise and use their imaginative faculty to visualize the Masters face or form which also can bring him to appear and bring us to some level of the heavenly worlds.

The following VARDAN Masters will work for this exercise although there are many others not mentioned.

Nye-Dah-Zah also known as Sri Allen Feldman is currently (As of August 2015), the Margatma, the Living VARDAN Master. There is also Rebazar Tarzs who has a closely cropped black beard, is about 5 foot 11, and wears a maroon robe and sandals. He appears to be perhaps in his 30's although he is well over 550 years old. You can find paintings on the VARDANKAR.com web site if you wish. Yaubl Sacabi is another Master who you can meet with. Yaubl Sacabi is bald with a bright shiny complexion and appears perhaps 30 although he is thousands of years old. His age is unbelievable. This being has eyes that are deep and penetrating and gazing into them is like gazing into the Ocean of Love and Mercy. The compassion he has is almost beyond measure and he is always ready to help the sincere seeker find God.

You can chant the Masters name or a word such as HU as in the 1st exercise. There are many spiritual exercises and you can make up your own exercises once you get the hang of it. Some will ask how do they know if they are merely imagining things or their experiences are real?

This is something you must determine for yourself but remember to be careful. While having these experiences if you doubt them while they are happening then the exercise may not work because you are sabotaging it. Much like throwing a monkey wrench into an auto engine while it is running! It is best to wait and suspend all doubt and judgment and belief systems while doing these exercises. Otherwise we become like the man who kills the bird before it can take wings and fly.

There will be plenty of time after the experience is over to contemplate upon it and decide for ourselves if it is real or illusionary. But I will say this. Spirit, or the VARDAN, will work with whatever state of consciousness and belief structure we possess...therefore if we only believe in Jesus then we may see Jesus. If we believe that heaven can only be one thing such as angels playing harps up in cloud filled cities then this is all we will allow ourselves to see.

Spirit is plastic in nature meaning it will mold itself to whatever expectations we have. This is why the True Spiritual Traveler and the returning wave of the Light and Sound are so essential. Then we can know with discernment what heavenly world or lower world we are in at the moment and see things from a more even keel.

It is Soul our true God self that views all of this from a 360 degree viewpoint and deals directly with Seeing, Knowing, and Being.

It is only the mind and lower bodies of man that doubt and have trouble adjusting and this is mostly due to fear.

We can let go of fear and have a childlike expectation or have the attitude of a child who knows beyond knowing that life is good, that spirit is good, that God is good and that no one is enslaved unless they agree.

When we refuse to agree with the negative power and seek out the Master then we now have a chance, for God chooses those who are ready to return...but as the saying goes, many are picked but few are chosen.

In our positions as VARDAN Masters we see many make the same mistakes lifetime after lifetime. We do not ask anyone to have faith nor to believe everything we write and say. All we request from those who are sincerely interested in God is that they keep an open mind and follow the instructions given without tainting it with Dogma, Superstition, and cherished beliefs about what is truth and what is not.

We are often amazed at how far Dogma can reach.

Dogma, superstition, and cherished beliefs can be like poison. As if a man has a canteen that is half full of stagnant disgusting water that is tainted. Until he empties his canteen of this tainted water any attempt to fill his canteen with the pure love, wisdom, power and freedom of God will be ruined by the very poisons that he holds so dear via attachment!

One time when we were still in training, we knew someone who could not have success during his spiritual exercises despite doing them every day. When asked what the trouble was he stated that every time he began to see Rebazar Tarzs or have any sort of spiritual experience he would stop it saying that he was afraid it might only be his imagination therefore he did not want to have that experience.

Although this makes no sense he was so fervent about his ideas that they effectively prevented him from any success and he quit about 6 months into it.

The paradox is an integral part of these lower worlds. If we insist on seeing life in terms of true and false, black and white we will be disappointed in life. The paradox has to do with opposites. Where there are mountains there must be valleys. Where there is love there must be hate. As long as we are in the lower worlds of opposites, matter, energy, time, space and the worlds of the Universal Mind Power we shall have to deal with paradoxes. If our mind cannot accept them then we may leave the path before we even begin.

This is a great test. Do we love God enough, do we love ourselves as Soul enough, do we love Spirit or the VARDAN enough, to put up with these paradoxes that seem to put the mind and emotions into a state of confusion?

This is why all our past study of philosophy, metaphysics, religion and so forth is all but useless in VARDANKAR and Tuza Travel. Because VARDANKAR has little or nothing to do with them. Through these Spiritual Exercises and the secret methods of VARDANKAR we soon find that all we learned from the past was nothing compared to the great wisdom, power, freedom and love that emanates out of the Ocean of Love and Mercy where dwells God or the HURAY ITSELF.

All paths are offshoots of VARDANKAR and contain threads of truth but not the whole of Truth. All that we thought we knew was simply a dim and imperfect reflection of a dim and imperfect reflection of a dim and imperfect reflection of truth but not actually truth. But in all of this, is often found that still small voice inside of Soul our true God self that upon hearing the message of VARDANKAR, knows that it is truth and the way back home to the God head!

Truth cannot be taught, but must be caught. We cannot find truth in the reading of Books, in the reciting of prayer the singing of hymns nor in any other human endeavor. We must become the Living Breathing truth of God and the spiritual exercises bring one into the field of the VARDAN Masters and eventually into the very heart of the God worlds where truth is like an endless wellspring.

Behold the great River of God, or what we call the HURAY, the Source of All Love, Wisdom, Power and Freedom! To God Soul we must return. Spiritual Greatness is our destiny as all Souls are great lights into this world and the Higher Worlds.

Many volumes can be written about VARDANKAR and there are many on Earth as well as in the other worlds. But

IT is in the experience that we know truth and life. It is in submerging ourselves within the Great River of God and becoming an active and conscious part of the whole rather than sitting passive in the sidelines. We must simply BE! We are Spiritually great no matter what, but we unfold into this realization and become aware of what we already are. Gods among other Gods. But always in humble service to the HURAY.

14
THE MARGATMA,
THE LIVING VARDAN MASTER

The Margatma, The Living VARDAN Master, is a spiritual Master who has reached the spiritually exalted states of Self Realization, God Realization, and VARDAN Mastership. In every age and every cycle throughout history in this world and beyond, a Living VARDAN Master is chosen by HURAY, God, for the purpose of establishing ITSELF through the vehicle of the Margatma, the Living VARDAN Master to help Souls return to IT. By finding a primary vehicle in a human embodiment HURAY makes ITSELF and ITS ways understandable to Soul.

This form of role and guidance was created because man himself was found nearly incapable of transcending the wheel of eighty-four and returning to God without this highly personalized form of assistance. The Margatma does not merely teach his spiritual students through books and lectures. In his inner Soul form he, as an expression of divine spirit is with them guiding and mentoring them to return to God in this lifetime or shortly thereafter which is monumental when you consider that Soul can transverse countless lifetimes.

On our many journeys with the Margatma, Allen and I traveled to heavens that step by step freed us spiritually. It was our zeal for HURAY which brought Its presence into our lives beyond our wildest dreams. Prior to this miracle, after having studied a new age religion nearly thirty years for Allen and nearly twenty years for myself, we discovered the leader claimed to be a Master and yet no matter how successfully and zealously we practiced out-of-body travel we still both felt trapped in the lower heavens of reincarnation, the prisons of the lower worlds. I loved my Teacher dearly yet realized that putting God first before all else was the call of my heart. It beckoned me to God and in doing so my world was shaken apart as this required me to let go of every safe thing in my life, attachments to my old Teacher (personality worship), dogma, religion, fixated idea, social approval, and the good opinions of my friends and spiritual elders.

This is what the VARDAN Masters speak of when they say that Soul becomes attached to the things of this world so much so that one will put these human things between oneself and God.

Finally after decades we let go of attachments and followed the pull of the higher levels of divine spirit and felt deeply blessed to find and work under the guidance of the great VARDAN Master Rebazar Tarzs who, at the time of the writing of most of this book, was the Margatma, The Living VARDAN Master. Then on October 22nd 2013 he passed the rod of power to Sri Allen Feldman who's spiritual name is Nye-Dah-Zah. As of August 2015 Allen is the current Living VARDAN Master. Our journeys in opening awareness to the Margatma was a profound leap in consciousness.

Allen shares this experience, "On a cool evening we began contemplating. On the super physical level Heather and I stood on the rocky, gnarly ground where the great VARDAN Master Rebazar Tarzs stood before us with a beaming smile upon his face. Without saying a word he swept his hand down pointing to the ground signaling the three of us sit down overlooking a view of distant mountains against the gnarly rocks and gray Earth.

Rebazar assumed the contemplative position, closed his eyes and waited. Heather and I did the same and all three of us went into contemplation. It could have been one minute later or it could have been several but Rebazar Tarzs' deep brown eyes gently opened and there was a mystical quality about them, as if he had gone on a long deep journey and was reporting back to us what he had seen and then began to speak, "There is a great misunderstanding over the nature and qualities of the Margatma, the Living VARDAN Master. Even among the VARDAN Chelas, few comprehend the depth of this subject nor the great love, the unfathomable love that the inner Master has for each and every chela. This misunderstanding arises mostly due to the failure of the chela or aspirant to fully surrender to the inner master. However this failure is easily corrected, if the chela or aspirant will but follow the Master's instructions carefully."

"One of the great mysteries of life is why so few Chelas take the words and speech of the Master seriously. Instead they take what they like from the Masters words and for the most part ignore the remainder."

"They also will feel that any criticisms from the Master do not apply to them. That they are beyond reproach and that mistakes apply to some other group that the Master is speaking of."

"The outer Master and the inner Master are one of the greatest paradoxes of all life and those who worship personality find they are at a crippling disadvantage."

"The Universal primal Margatma consciousness is identical to that of the consciousness of the HURAY. And yet IT is not. IT has the ability to completely liberate Souls from bondage and yet IT does not."

"The key to this riddle is that each Soul must make its own journey to the HURAY and that no outside power or force acting outside of Soul can give Soul Jivan Mukti (spiritual freedom), however those Souls foolish enough to think that they can make the journey to God Realization without the help of the inner and outer Master generally will find themselves hopelessly lost on the wheel of eighty-four."

"So I tell you this, the great paradox is that without the Margatma, Soul shall never return home, however Soul must become active and merciless in its desire to find Spiritual Liberation, truth, and it's true purpose in life. Until Soul becomes active and practices Tuza Travel under the guidance of the Living VARDAN Master, Soul will fail to fulfill its true purpose in life."

"I now wish to speak about the great secret that is generally forbidden to be discussed among Chelas. This secret is that the teachings of VARDANKAR are for the most part hidden on the inner planes and invisible to those who are not ready for them. Therefore the outer Master who has a physical body, eats, breaths, lives in the physical world is in a sense a doorway and Soul finds that it must surrender over and over and over again as it moves from initiation to initiation, from plane to plane, from Golden Wisdom Temple to Golden Wisdom Temple and moves closer and closer to the true worlds of HURAY."

"Look to the ideal of the HURAY, of the primal Margatma consciousness, of the light and sound of VARDAN, of the pure Golden Wisdom Temples in the higher planes. Look to the ideal of the ancient Masters of VARDANKAR. Never turn your back upon them for a split second."

"For if you can keep your attention upon the highest of the highest and surrender to it Ye shall find new planes, new experiences, and opportunities to become a vehicle for the HURAY and the universal cause of the Margatma beyond your wildest imaginations. Turn your back and all may disappear like a mirage on a desert."

"For know that your imagination and attention are the very God powers within you that can make you great or make you small. That can bring you to the heights of the top of the mountains or plunge you into a bottomless sea of despair and that your attention and imagination are best focused upon the Margatma, the VARDAN, and the HURAY." And with that Rebazar fell silent and gently nodded his head as if signaling he was finished.

Since Heather also had this experience she continues: Once again we went into contemplation and appeared in a world of brilliant light. Allen and Rebazar hovered beside me in light forms. Rebazar communicated, "The Margatma is the Way Shower and shows the way to realizing your divinity."

At that moment I saw a vast light that was like a giant sun that seemed to be here and everywhere simultaneously. We are now in the world of direct perception and were no longer burdened by our lower bodies: mental body, emotional body, and physical body. Rebazar communicated to us almost telepathically although it was much higher than telepathy. We were in a world of pure Seeingness, Knowingness, and Beingness beyond M.E.S.T., matter, energy, space and time.

Vast stretches of endless sound and pure light poured out

in all directions. No sooner than Allen asked where we were, Rebazar responded: "Behold, the 14th plane."

This plane was indescribable although we are attempting to put words to an experience beyond language.

A soft, all pervasive high pitched sound permeated every atom of this world. Then, we were aware of a gentle vortex, it was as if the very fine atoms of this world were gently spinning in an upward motion, bringing lost Souls back.

We had not seen this vortex, as if it was so subtle as to be invisible, but Rebazar Tarzs now had us hovering over it and we looked down into it (If you can use words like up and down in a place that has no time and space.)

Rebazar explained that this gentle vortex was created as a door way and almost imperceptible thread of light and sound; that this was a representation of the Margatma Consciousness. That this gentle swirling vortex provided a way for lost Souls to return if they could be in harmony with the nature of this vortex which was pure unconditional Divine Love, Wisdom, Power and Freedom. But, that it was so difficult for a Soul to find its way, that the Margatma was needed to create the personal manifestation of the purely impersonal, meaning if man were left to his own devices in the lower worlds he would spin on the wheel of eighty-four undergoing almost countless reincarnations.

For man's lower nature was that of the Kal Niranjan, the King of the negative power. Therefore, man without the aid of the Spiritual Traveler and without learning the science of Tuza Travel could not be in harmony with the high, pure vibratory rate of the higher planes or heavens and would be hopelessly trapped in his own world of delusion."

Rebazar continued, "As you know being good, kind, and loving will never bring you to the heart of God. Helping your fellow man by comforting him, by feeding him, by clothing him, helping him will never bring you to the heart of God although these things are noble and admirable, they of themselves will only create good karma for you. And good karma will only buy you more conveniences in your stay in the prisons of the lower worlds."

"It is by unconditional surrender first to the inner Master, then to the HURAY (God) itself, it is through Tuza Travel. It is through these things that you have come this far and yet the more you surrender to me the more you surrender to the VARDAN and the more you surrender to the HURAY, the greater your consciousness becomes and the less your lower nature deceives thee. For I tell you in the end you find out that all but the HURAY is an illusion and that you are but a drop in the endless Ocean of Love and Mercy and yet what a drop you are!"

We could hear Rebazar laughing in the most beautiful, Soul joyous sound that echoed throughout this world. "For you and the HURAY are cut of the same cloth and are not bound by matter, energy, time nor space."

The sound current from this plane seemed to change softer, more expansive and more refined as if we had more freedom, as though Rebazar's very words changed the way of the vibration for some mysterious reason that we didn't understand.

It seemed as though the subtle almost invisible, almost inaudible sound and soft spinning light echoed through all worlds. This presence, this God force touches all things.

Rebazar Tarzs directed us to look closer at the center of

the Vortex and as we did we noticed something quite amazing. Tiny white lights like a fine mist of stars almost too small for us to see initially, were coming out of the vortex and before we could ask the question of what they were we had the answer.

These tiny lights were Souls that had returned. And the reason they looked so small was because this world was immense and beyond description. We began to hear Rebazar's laughter again, "Behold," he said in a sound that echoed throughout the entire plane. "Countless Souls returning to this world after eons."

The laughter became louder. We began to approach the center of the Vortex. And as we did we could hear the voice of billions of Souls as they emitted the sound of joy. What we had dismissed as mist were actually God Realized Souls who were not tiny specks of mist but immense balls of white light just like us. Some of them were going back down the Vortex to return to the respective planes and some were entering into this world. They began to greet Rebazar Tarzs and soon we were surrounded by other Souls who just wanted to be with Rebazar, for they could recognize his great light.

Suddenly we found ourselves back in our bodies and gently opened our eyes to see Rebazar still sitting in lotus position on the ground, eyes closed with a gentle smile upon his face. His eyes slowly opened but he said nothing.

Again before us lay the glorious mountain. We smiled at each other feeling grateful and blessed at witnessing Souls being loved so deeply by God itself. Even though we returned to our bodies, there was a part of us that still remained in the 14th plane.

15
JIVAN MUKTI

An image arose of planets of countless worlds and then arose an image of Soul. Soul is in ways like a caterpillar in a cocoon, it keeps reemerging and reincarnating uncontrollably, until one day in its maturity it suddenly of its own accord breaks through the shell of the cocoon, at the moment of spiritual breakthrough because it works with Out-of-Body Tuza Travel. And then the shell of human consciousness and the lower bodies that had imprisoned it for eons fall off. It begins to unfurl a new pair of wings, which strengthen. Like the analogy that with practice our skills in out-of-body travel to wing our way through heaven grow stronger.

Then through training we can learn to become a free spiritual agent and like the butterfly break the laws of gravity and lift ourselves to any of the heavens, worlds or universes we choose as a conscious agent of God. We reach liberation from the wheel of 84. Jivan Mukti is that state that we reach of achieving true spiritual freedom in this lifetime here and now.

It occurs upon Soul establishing itself upon the 5th world or Atma (Soul) plane where Soul meets with the great God ruler or being Sat Nam, the first true manifestation of the HURAY. It is not an intellectual or emotional experience, but one of obtaining a certain degree of spiritual perfection upon entering consciously this great world beyond time, space and the lower bodies of man.

At writing this I recall for the first time entering a large convention space with thousands of others awake to how Soul can free itself through out-of-body travel. And from the Soul level I began to cry. I stepped psychologically back from myself and asked, "But why am I crying? I don't feel at all sad."

In my knowingness I knew I was crying because as Soul I had waited thousands of years since Ancient Egypt to have another opportunity to find the Living VARDAN Master. I had a great knowingness that I had come home spiritually. And tears welled in my eyes because I was so happy from the core of my Soul self. I was in the knowingness that I was returning home to God ITSELF. All the prizes of the lower worlds are cheap trinkets, chachkas, and toys compared to the wonder of consciously working in harmony and partnership with HURAY (God) throughout ITS universes and heavens.

Being a prisoner of the lower heavens is like living as a spiritual ant which stays absorbed in its tiny world and doesn't realize the yet much greater worlds which is in many ways unknown to it. It is like passing through an unconscious existence, which is like a state of sleep. This much reminds me of those who, for the first time in a lifetime have a near death experience and feel amazingly excited and say they feel as though they lived life as though asleep and had suddenly woken up.

This is our spiritual destiny. The destiny and birthright of all Souls that we will all one day be given an opportunity to realize we have been sleeping and suddenly wake up. But simply, we don't only wake up in the lower heavens (which is the normal near death experience of heaven or the normal experience of psychic phenomenon), we through Out-of-Body Tuza Travel continue the journey under the instruction of the VARDAN Masters to wake up spiritually to the Pure Positive God Worlds in Self Realization, to wake up to who we really are. And the further we are excited to wake up to the Ocean of Love and Mercy where we wake up to HURAY (God) in God Realization.

The Earth World and lower heavens can be like a great big carnival or fun house filled with all kinds of entertainers, priests, spiritual celebrities, spiritual gurus, psychics, mystics and so on, all claiming they have the keys to salvation, nirvana, liberation, ascension, heaven, and so on.

And we find aspects and shards of wisdom. The fun house mirrors distract, distort, and stretch our vision this way under the spell of fascinating astral sights but all the talks, books, meditation, prayer, rituals, seminars, fasts, trainings, social gatherings, although they may bring cosmic energies and even euphoria they do not bring Soul beyond the gates of the lower heavens.

All the fun house workers will promise us the world and entice us in all the rewards of the lower plane prisons. It is like that well known phrase, "Talk is cheap. Action says everything." Or rather more accurately Being says everything. And it is therefore that we come to not guess, but know for ourselves of all the things expounded upon here by actual action of firsthand experience of these heavens.

And we can in the Soul body meet with Spiritual Travelers and receive discourse from them that will bring us beyond anything we have ever seen in thousands or millions of our incarnations. Nothing we can learn is easy to achieve as these understandings take discipline, effort, enthusiasm, and perseverance."

Just as if a man were studying to be Doctor. He wouldn't

expect to master being a doctor without highly skilled study and practice. It is the same in taking up the study of the Science of Out-of-Body Tuza Travel.

In this area we can seek out the foremost expert in Out-of-Body Tuza Travel, the Margatma, The Living VARDAN Master, who will on the outer provide spiritual exercises we can practice to Master Tuza Travel. And on the inner will provide inner guidance, protection, and spiritual education in how to achieve Jivan Mukti, Self, and God Realization.

The Margatma, the Living VARDAN Master however cannot provide this spiritual training unless we give him permission moment to moment on the inner planes as his students. None of the VARDAN Masters can work with us unless we give them permission or ask for their guidance or help. We sat together to begin a contemplation on this topic of Jivan Mukti.

What follows is Allen's description of the experience we had, "Heather and I closed our eyes and began to chant the word HU. All of a sudden I could hear a gentle sound that quickly grew in strength till it began to vibrate my entire body with the light that washed through me and the sound like an electrical current that washed through me and tingled. And Heather and I were aware of a strong presence that we had never noticed before."

Then we heard a voice, a loud booming voice that exclaimed, "Behold, the unknown VARDAN Master." And we found ourselves surrounded by a dazzling wave of white light and sound that seemed to contain all the Love, Wisdom, Power and Freedom of the higher worlds. We were surrounded by this light and sound and yet we were a part of IT.

We felt like balls of light and sound riding on top of a wave. Like beach balls on top of a mighty ocean surrounded by water. Only light and sound was vibrating very rapidly. The light was vibrating with the pulsing high vibration of this place or this being.

Where we were we did not know. Then suddenly no sooner than we asked the question, it began to communicate with us. We knew it was real because we felt the presence of Yaubl Sacabi and Rebazar Tarzs standing next to us. The four of us were balls of white light vibrating in this pure glistening world of white light and sound until we could barely tell the difference between our white light and the white light all around us, except that it seemed to vibrate more finely.

Through some form of telepathy Yaubl explained that this was not some ruler of a higher plane but a Secret VARDAN Master who was a most ancient one who had come to give us a discourse on the very nature of Jivan Mukti.

"Fools." A voice shot out and a sublime wave of pure white light shot out from the center of this voice and purified everything in its path. And all of a sudden all motion ceased except for the pure vibrating sound.

Gah-Shy-Zah asked Yaubl: "If this is not a Ruler, then what is it?"

But before Yaubl had a chance to answer a magnificent being began to appear from the center of the light. Its features were surprisingly unpronounced to the point that one could barely recognize it. But never the less it began to speak,

"There was a time" its voice rang out in nothing but pure waves of VARDAN. It's very voice was the VARDAN and it did not sound human.

"There was a time, a time so long ago that you cannot imagine, on a planet, in a universe that no longer exists. When I had a body and was riddled with limitations and imperfections, for back then I foolishly believed that I was enslaved by some outside force that was controlling me and putting me into a box from where I was unable to escape."

The being began to laugh and the entire universe around us was laughing.

The white light and sound were vibrating as if they were laughing and we could feel our very atoms of light and sound with this being vibrating and pulsing and jumping up and down with joy . It was a tremendous joy, a feeling of great freedom.

"Then" the being continued, "One day I discovered the truth! That no being, that no Kal, no God, that no lord of Karma, that NOTHING had the power to enslave me or produce in me any limitations other than myself!"

"Over the course of eternity I came to know that there is nothing real except the HURAY and that anything less is not worthy of my attention."

"I gained great powers, none of which I wanted. I gained great wisdom although I did not seek it. I gained great freedom although I made no effort to find freedom. I ceased struggle for I had a secret, a secret that I shall tell you. And yet you will probably not believe me."

"I discovered that I am the creator of my own universe. Not because I am great, but because I am. All souls consist only of the light and sound of HURAY. Therefore they are identical to one another. Except that Souls tend to attract to themselves meaningless opinions, postulates, agreements, assumptions, beliefs, and that those mentioned only serve as limiting factors. So I say some call me the Nameless VARDAN Master. For I ceased to identify with any of my previous incarnations."

"I am not a Ruler of a particular plane nor am I God. I come and go as I please according to the will of the HURAY. I am not a Silent One, nor a Planetary Spirit, nor a Guardian Angel! In fact I refuse to be labeled other than as the ancient Nameless VARDAN Master. That is what I am called, the Nameless VARDAN Master. And it amuses me to no end. For in my name is a clear message that Soul must cease to identify with anything except the HURAY."

"And that when this occurs and there is complete surrender, Soul will recognize that part of each Soul,' which is none other than the HURAY."

"My philosophy, if you can call it a philosophy is not to be an isolationist who ceases to care when I see another Soul. I only recognize that part which is the HURAY. All other parts are like tissue paper that is dissolving in the rain, worthless, garbage that is not a part of Soul but a part of the Kal. Some may find me cold, but my only desire is to see Souls return to the HURAY."

"This is the one quality that all VARDAN Masters must have and so I say I am the light and sound and nothing less and nothing more. I am the voice of the HURAY and nothing less and nothing more."

"I do not care about personalities, nor lower bodies and although I have tremendous freedom I do not claim in any shape or form to be the greatest Soul in all the universe." We could hear laughter again vibrating throughout his world.

"Be not impressed with me for I am nothing except a Soul. I desire that you perhaps may learn more quickly than it took me to stop trying to be something and simply be."

"You will not disappear. You will only become far greater for the less of you that exists, the more easily the HURAY will be able to use you as a channel for ITS purpose. I am like a giant ocean among other even larger oceans. I flow by the will of the HURAY."

"Do not be impressed by the volume of my light and sound for it is not my light and sound that you see before you, it is that of the universal consciousness of the Ocean of Love and Mercy of which you are a part of as am I. So I say on closing if you want freedom stop trying to figure out what you are. For you are nothing and everything. Know that as a being of the ego you are worthless to the HURAY."

"But as a being of light and sound you are the HURAY and IT is you. Practice VARDANKAR, the Ancient Science of Out-Of-Body Tuza Travel but remember the path is simply a way to realize God Realization and be of service. It was never meant to be worshiped or control Soul in any way."

And with that the unknown VARDAN Master faded away and we noticed ever so slightly for a brief second this world of white light become darker.

Yaubl Sacabi communicated the following to us, "This Master you have met is exceedingly old, compared to any of us here. At least in the embodied state. He often gets great pleasure in teaching Souls about detachment and about ceasing to identify with the lower self. I wish to make an important point. When one learns to practice detachment and begins letting go of their opinions and beliefs and limitations they must replace them with something else."

"In the lower worlds you cannot have a vacuum. Many have tried to drop their attachments but made the mistake of not replacing them with something else. So I say fill your moments with the pure light and sound. Practice the five virtues of VARDANKAR: humility, contentment, right discrimination, tolerance, and detachment. Learn to give in the name of the HURAY, the Margatma, and the VARDAN without expectation of reward. Cease to identify with negative role models and people and ideals. And replace them with one or more of the great VARDAN Masters."

Heather added, "We can also read the VARDANKAR books a lot, every single day because it brings positive energy to replace the old. We can also use right discernment in our choice of who and what we surround ourselves with: friends, music, movies, books, activities all can affect our states of consciousness."

Yaubl nodded and then continued, "Although the Nameless VARDAN Master is correct. It's far more difficult to cease identification than most people think. You must find tricks and clever ways of replacing thousands if not millions of years of Kalistic behavior with the ways of VARDANKAR."

"The inner Master will help you but you must ask and surrender but do it in a way that keeps you from going completely out of balance so that you are useful in the universal cause and God's plan."

And with that Heather and I found ourselves back in our physical bodies.

16
THE MODERN PLAGUE OF IDOLATRY

According to the Webster's Dictionary and Got Questions.org, Idol Worship is, "The worship of idols or excessive devotion to, or reverence for some person or thing. An idol is anything that replaces the one true God." This is beautifully put as these devoted Christians wonderfully explained it. If we bow down before anything other than God itself we are practicing idolatry, the worship of that which is not God; In our former new age religion the concept of the Spiritual Master as a matrix for the VARDAN (holy spirit) was distorted when many confused the (human personality) of the Master with God itself.

Many would give excessive awe and bow down before the human personality of the spiritual leader. Many would give excessively zealous standing ovations before he spoke one word and cheer, clap, and smile with blazing intensity. There was an excessive delight and awe for the worship of his human personality. This is again in opposition to the concept of the Spiritual Master as a matrix for the VARDAN (Holy Spirit). Personality worship is a common form of idolatry.

It was also common that some bowed down in excess in deep worship for the Leadership status they received as high priests, spiritual celebrities. It is not so much a healthy appreciation but rather the clinging to and placing personalities before God. Others would bow down to the comforts of safety in numbers and of close social ties and got a sort of euphoria from the euphoric high vibrational astral feeling or energies generated by large gatherings. Others put extra emphasis on money and the acquisition of things as priority before God. I came to this conclusion because when I approached many individuals about God Realization they indicated fear, disgust or disinterest and a stronger interest in these M.E.S.T things instead.

It is the cherishing of these lower world things more than God which happens for most Souls in our countless incarnations. The VARDAN Masters stand back as there is nothing they can do but allow the individual his freedom, even though the Masters know that the individual may suffer because of wrong discernment. They may assist the person now and then as permission is granted but will not interfere with the person's choice of dogma, religion, idols or personality worship, even if that person was once their student. They patiently wait. It is the moment however that Soul wakes up from this that Soul becomes free.

Idolatry is subtle and if we are not careful it can become an invisible plague that infects our spiritually pure intentions by holding high and in great esteem objects, personalities, and human pride.

VARDAN Masters themselves, before becoming Masters have at one time or another fallen into these traps because initially it can be easy to put as the center of life the things of the human consciousness and its prizes. However it was their humble recognition of it within themselves which gave them power to overcome it, rise above it, and become centered in God in the Pure Positive God Worlds instead.

It takes humility to admit to ourselves when we make these mistakes so that we can extract the tentacles of idolatry out of our consciousness and instead place God there. Practicing the inner presence of the VARDAN Master (his inner form) as a divine matrix for the VARDAN (Holy Spirit) (which is a spiritual exercise) is not to be confused with worshiping his human personality which is idolatry, pure and simple.

Allen was at home and I was away on a trip in Philadelphia when I began a spiritual exercise to bring into contemplation the spiritual   issue of idolatry and how the individual can recognize and overcome it. Allen and I on the inner planes met and began a dialog between the spirit part of ourselves on the topic.

Nye-Dah-Zah: The body is a shell. Many mistake a beautiful package, a pleasing voice and shiny trinkets and tricks for proof of spiritual merit. This is like the blind leading the blind to the prisons of the lower worlds.

Gah-Shy-Zah: Even when we chart our course for many years on the road of light and sound that leads to God, we never know when suddenly the challenge arises: Do we choose personality worship or do we choose God? Most choose personality worship because they reap many more human consciousness rewards, such as: the good opinions of others, social status, the comfort of the same safe thing, not shaking up ties with close ones friends or family, and so on. The human mind will rationalize to defend its spiritual decisions without consulting spirit by going to the higher Pure Positive God Planes to verify truth.

Nye-Dah-Zah: Personality worship is similar to the well-known analogy of shackles made of gold. People avoid the ugly steal shackles but they will gladly put the golden shackles on themselves and chain themselves to a lower heaven. These shackles are golden because they are offered as rewards as the false guru offers all the riches of the lower worlds ranging from Health, to wealth to admiration and the stimulation of the senses, body, mind and emotions. It can be hard, so hard to suddenly in a moment of detachment: drop everything. The chains clang in a metal heap on the ground along with our temporarily broken human paradise.

And then with the chains off we can lose everything and then find God. We lose the lower worlds and find spiritual freedom. This is why detachment is a virtue. It takes bravery. It takes masterful behavior to become a VARDAN Master.

(What was said above is not to imply we run away from our families or job or responsibilities. We can meet our human responsibilities however we are not attached.)

Gah-Shy-Zah: It is important to not let the personality of the Teacher blind us nor our trinkets. In ancient Egypt we had past lives as royalty. We frolicked in a heaven on Earth with our riches and high position and our religion filled with miracles and magical experiences. We were so filled with fear of leaving that life behind for surely our families would disown us and our monies would be scarce and perhaps we would be hated and seen as ridiculous and miss out on all the good parties.

So in our cowardice when the great VARDAN Master Gopal Das approached us, even though we were greatly moved by his talk of out-of-body ventures to return to God itself, we shirked in our fear and dared not venture to do more than we had always done.

We both lived to regret it and every party seemed emptier and emptier, an empty shallow nothingness that could not feed the Soul. We waited again for thousands of years before the next opportunity resurfaced and the VARDAN Master Rebazar Tarzs took us under his wing.

Nye-Dah-Zah: There is a myth and some believe it is true that long ago there were beings from other worlds (planets) who came to Earth and because of their impressive abilities people mistook them for Gods. We put too much faith in spiritual appearances. Worshiping psychically or spiritually advanced people is negative. It is just as destructive as hating them. Both cause or create a psychological distance that makes us feel that the other being is an alien or of an entirely different species, something pushed so far away from what we feel we are, that we would never realize we can be like the VARDAN Masters. Psychological distance makes the VARDAN Masters state seem unattainable to the individual. Both hate and personality worship shields him from having to face the possibility of growing up spiritually himself.

Gah-Shy-Zah: Ultimately in this life we are the creators of our own destination. Often disgruntled people will blame others and point fingers at others for faults obsessively but in the end these are only scape goats to pin uneasiness we have hidden in ourselves on something outside of us. Ultimately we put ourselves where we are. Many became obsessed with the great VARDAN Master Paul Twitchell's flaws because they couldn't go within and find the source of pain hidden within. This is foolish because it is self-punishment to obsess over criticizing others or arguing with them inside, no matter how wrong or horrible we think they are.

Obsessing over criticizing an individual or guru is also a form of personality worship as odd as that sounds. This is because the personality of the guru we criticize fills our attention instead of God and instead of reaching our spiritual dreams, we waste our lives trapped in a prison of anger that pulls us to the lower worlds. This is not freedom. This is because we have been burned by false gurus and expect more of the same. If we are wise, we develop discernment, forgive and move on to better things and seek higher vistas that inspire, uplift, and spiritually free ourselves and others. The anger band of personality worship can become a dark place.

Gah-Shy-Zah continues, "Among the many ways that rays are broken down into pieces in the lower worlds are cosmic rays of stepped down light and sound. The human body is often split into for example, two energies: male and female. The purpose of these countless incarnations alternating back and forth between the two gender energies is to produce the spiritual qualities and areas of refinement God needs Soul to develop to be a divine coworker with IT."

"In those experiences the individual will develop both spiritual power, action, creativity and so on, as well as the ability to surrender to HURAY, divine love and compassion and so on. However when Soul in its blossoming maturity reaches the first Pure Positive God World, the Soul Plane, it gathers to itself a totality of all experience and it identifies most with the spark within the self, called Soul. In this heaven all lower bodies are left in the lower worlds. Soul is no longer the divided atom of mostly masculinity or mostly femininity. The atom is put back together again from its scattered pieces like a fragmented puzzle made whole again. Here Soul is all Godly qualities irrespective of its lower bodies."

At first these were not issues we were going to bring up until we came across numerous things which would discourage those in female form from truly pursuing becoming VARDAN Masters for themselves along with their male counterparts. For thousands of years the female has been dubbed somewhat of a scapegoat, the source of all problems of mankind, told that she is not a God being and even denied mortal and spiritual education to thrive into full spiritual realization. She was made a slave and given the lowest of expectations. Is it any wonder that so few in the female form progress to VARDAN Mastership? Plato had once said that if you do not educate the fair sex properly how can you expect them to contribute meaningfully and transcend as worthwhile Souls.

It is important to transcend the negative Kalistic body tendencies of male and female that express as Kal and Kali, male being to overpower and destroy and female being to be passive, manipulate and destroy. Instead we replace these invisible demons that secretly influence Soul and instead allow the pure VARDAN (Holy Spirit) to take over Soul and flow out to the world.

The Soul overpowered with excesses in masculinity will dominate others and try to destroy their self-worth as a God being. The Soul overpowered with excesses in femininity will pull others attention off of God into social love and destructive things. The Soul who transcends extremes yet lives in harmony and acceptance of their gender form flows with the heights of all needed God qualities of spiritual power and spiritual love and surrender like blowing with the winds of God. They are adept regardless of the body they are given. In the higher worlds we are the complete atom.

If a female becomes a VARDAN Master her atoms must be reversed and spin in the male direction. If a male becomes a VARDAN Master his atoms spin the same. It is always the male form that becomes the Margatma, the Living VARDAN Master. Although an interim VARDAN Master can be in the female form. The whole point is Soul is spirit not a body although it works though a body and needs to be in mastery over it.

Nye-Dah-Zah: We are unlimited. Too many identify too strongly with the body. They think they are their body. They think their guru is his body. Too many people also identity strongly with the personality.

274

They think the guru is his personality. And again the same with the mind. People think they are their mind, the guru is his mind. These are all the things of the lower worlds. Spiritual merit is not found in these things. HURAY (God) does not access us according to human values based on materialistic worlds. We don't have to be talented, brilliant, attractive, skilled at speaking, writing or doing spiritual wonders, or existing without human flaws. God loves us unconditionally. We can return to God even if we lack what the human mind would assume makes us spiritually worthy.

We met one VARDAN Master who explained to us that "familiarity breeds contempt," Meaning some who saw him so often and know him well and noted he was an ordinary man, a flawed human who makes mistakes and not some fantastical creature they can worship, dismissed all he said spiritually. This is the sort of subconscious urge for personality worship, a cultural entrainment that makes us believe that the God Realized Masters aren't real people. That they are impossibly perfect like plastic and therefore we could never be like them, being a simple flawed human we are.

This illusion compels people to make those who they are not familiar with into spiritual deities. VARDAN Masters are not perfect in the human body but perfect in the spiritual body.

There are some cult leaders who hide all the time from their member's sight only seeing them on the rarest occasion, so as to not spoil the psychological distance. It is the same with "ascended masters" who have been dead for thousands of years creating a psychological distance. Since not knowing someone can create an air of mystery and assumption that they are a spiritually perfect creature. Then it makes it easy for individuals to worship them like demigods. And for cults and religions this personality worship helps them control their members.

Sri Paul Twitchell once had a spiritual student who noted something he did which was humanly imperfect, that he didn't with his inner vision know exactly what was going on in her Satsang class. As a result it threw her into a state of questioning whether he was a real God Realized being. How could he be a master if he made human mistakes or did not know all things? How could he be a master if he didn't know her every movement on the outer? This is foolishness of expecting the outer personality of the Master to behave like a deity, when it is not the body of the Master but the Margatma and VARDAN, pure spirit that lifts us up to God.

VARDAN Masters can have human flaws and make what do-gooders assume are human errors. This is because these individuals are not seeing from the state of Soul but seeing from the lower human consciousness. Personality worship is one of the attachments which often pull individuals away from VARDAN Masters. Some people want magic tricks from the Master instead of pursuing having their own magical inner spiritual experiences of God, in the Higher Worlds. The negative force knows this and will show the unsuspecting individual "miracles," "waking dreams," and even profound "spiritual experiences" that come from the lower worlds to keep the individual satisfied in the lower heavens. This keeps the individual contented and fixated on feeling he is headed in the right direction. All is well and confirmed by the impressive magic tricks.

One guru in India can meet his spiritual students on the inner planes and travel through these lower heavens meeting his spiritual students for spiritual experiences. His students see this as proof that he is a true spiritual Master. However most can find Gurus of every philosophy that will meet them in these lower heavens. It is said that there is one Guru in India who can pull strings of pearls and gems right out of his hands from thin air. Contrary to popular opinion these sorts of "miracles" are magic and not spirituality.

Others can do miraculous healings that keep their members captivated. Surely with such impressive magic tricks they've found the perfect guru. But in actuality these are sometimes the magic tricks of the negative force who with its intelligence knows the individual expects and desires a magic show in the form of psychic phenomena.

Gah-Shy-Zah: Allen once noted after many years of entering a spiritual church building that he used to attend in his previous path that it was not the God Worlds centered place he imagined it would be, but really it was more like a Hollywood set.

When the building was suddenly bustling and filled with the high vibrational astral or spiritual energy of visitors from all over the world the Hollywood set came to life and was in its full glory. The concentrated group energies of many Souls gathering created a euphoria. But then when all the people left, the costumes taken off and the curtains closed... the show was over. People put on fake smiles, disinterest and highly controlled interactions that seemed very plastic and so on because it was all a theatrical play. The negative force wants to trap Souls for millions of years and needs to impress the individual with big crowds, fancy Hollywood set style awe inspiring buildings and psychic-spiritual magic tricks.

Some in the new age field communicate with spiritual or psychic entities that give a great entertaining performance. They reveal enthralling psychic plane and M.E.S.T. wisdom, healing techniques, or other helpful spiritual information. Others do what the magical religions of Ancient Egypt once did, communicating with the dead (passed on relatives), conversing with entities, or fascinating tricks. But contrary to popular opinion channeling astral entities can be dangerous.

Some new age expressions focus on all sorts of miracles like psychic surgery. It can be helpful on the physical and astral levels but it does not lead to God. The lower heavens have wisdom intermixed with illusion. And in response to the more wild new age performances Allen once joked singing in a Hollywood theatrical voice, "That's entertainment."

Suddenly Gah-Shy-Zah and Nye-Dah-Zah felt an airy humorous presence. And instantly knew it was Rebazar Tarzs who had come from the cosmic worlds to pay us a visit. In reality we knew that he was always present at all times and that he simply was manifesting a visible body, as he often did when he wanted to give a lecture or make a point.

Rebazar began to speak, "What we are really speaking about is the very nature of illusion and ironically the very nature of reality. For anything that is not reality would be defined as illusion. To attempt to define illusion would require almost endless reams of paper.

So let us start defining reality. Reality could be expressed as the pure unobstructed light and sound emanating from the HURAY. The pure essence of consciousness that contains all Love, Wisdom, Power, and Freedom. Of course trying to use human words to define reality is not reality.

But we must work with the mind in these lower worlds. The mind creates images, pictures, impressions, and pure thought forms. These emanate from the universal mind power which in reality is the Kal power or that negative entity known as the Kal Niranjan, whose job is to keep Soul in the world of illusion for as long as is possible.

Soul's job is to escape and the Margatma's job is to aid and abet Souls escape into the Pure Positive God Worlds. But you know all of this, Rebazar laughed, and might be wondering why I'm telling you this again. The reason is deceivingly simple. You see, the Kal Niranjan has at its disposal the entire power of the Universal Mind. The astral worlds, the causal worlds, the etheric worlds, and the physical worlds. It is like a tiny child playing chess with the grand ancient Chess Master who will toy with the child and may even allow the child to win a game or two.

So man is the perpetual fool who thinks he can beat the Kal at its own game and so a Soul embodied in an Earth body may murder many men and pay dearly by losing many of its own bodies.

Such a Soul eventually learns to stop killing bodies and declares itself the victor that he's learned some great lesson. All the while the Kal is laughing, for there are a billion such lessons and quite frankly it has little to do with spiritual freedom.

When a Soul surrenders to the Living VARDAN Master. When Soul practices the ancient science of Out-of-Body Tuza Travel and goes with the aid of the Living VARDAN Master into the very heart of the higher worlds that Soul finds itself connected consciously with an endless wellspring of Love, Wisdom, Power, and Freedom.

Such Love, Wisdom, Power, and Freedom could not be gathered in a million years or quite frankly a billion years of playing chess with the Kal. He will try and become a noble man, a man of virtue, a man of wisdom, a man of education, a man of great solace and refinement, an inspirational man, a man who acts as a beacon for his fellow men, a man who is a social reformer, an insightful man. He will examine every possible and conceivable quality that his little mind can think of and attempt to develop it to its full capacity.

When he is tired of all these games he will attempt to unleash these games on other groups of men and women. He will write books, give lectures, promote his ideas and opinions! Promote world reform! According to his ideals which he vainly believes represent the highest most well thought out and progressive. He will create great karma, mostly bad, trying to convince others that he has all the answers to life's problems, if they will but listen to him.

Finally after countless lives attempting to reform the Earth through the brute force of his pen and tongue, he will begin to realize that he's being played as a fool. But his idolatry has not ended, not by a long shot. He will place his attention squarely upon the Brahm and surrender to it, confusing it with God.

He will gain powers of the psychic and use them to help others mostly by interfering with their karma. He may even be called a great guru, an enlightened one, perhaps at some point his body may even appear to be glowing as if on fire. But the light that he possesses is a lesser light. It is generally only the light of the astral world or perhaps the mental or Universal Mind Power.

He will endeavor to help others and his heart will open to the positive side of the Kal power, which promises heaven on Earth. He will become less selfish and be held as an example of the ideal man. Some may call him the enlightened one. And although he is a far cry from the murderer and thief that he used to be, never the less he is still practicing idolatry.

How could this be you may ask? Remember the beginning of this discourse I attempted to define truth. He has pursued everything except the HURAY or God.

And so we see in closing there is a broad spectrum of ideological worship ranging from torturer and murderer at the low end to the light and sound and love of the Brahm on the other. Perhaps the light of the Brahm is the most deadly of all. More deadly than murder? I say yes, because it's much easier for a Soul to learn that murdering a fellow being is a negative thing. It is much easier for a Soul to learn to stop such heinous behavior and after all when one strikes another down with a sword it won't be long before they have taken from them a body of their own; but when one learns to worship the Brahm with all his heart they may be in for a very long series of incarnations, for it gives the illusion that they are worshiping the ultimate God and that they have reached the pinnacle of spiritual evolution; when in fact they are still only practicing idolatry. I know how difficult this is for many to understand how one can give so much love and yet be in the throes of illusion. All I can say is that all must be given up, all attachment, and one must completely surrender without thought of reward, without fear, otherwise illusion will enslave anyone who fears the pure truth.

Truth is nothing to be laughed at for it is pure power and will ruthlessly tear every imperfection from the flesh of the lower bodies no matter how painful or disheartening it may feel. Therefore it's essential if one wants truth, real truth, not idolatry, to cling by the side of the True Spiritual Traveler, who will protect them and see to it that they are not completely overwhelmed but gradually unfolded in a safe way.

And with that Rebazar Tarzs faded away to teach some other group of Souls with his universal mission.

17
THE BOURCHAKOUN

The Bourchakoun are known today as the ancient spiritual order of VARDAN Masters who have existed through all time and beyond it. The essence of the meaning of Bourchakoun is detachment or the state of letting go of the dependence on things of these physical and psychic worlds without running from them. Instead of the passions, we reside in the virtues and dwell in the presence of HURAY (God). When we do this we maintain a level of neutrality to keep Soul and the VARDAN in the spiritual driver's seat.

We learn to seek first the kingdom of God and then all things will be given unto us. In other words we do not seek positive qualities but seek the higher realizations and then we find truth. We are already worthy of Truth, it is simply a matter of be willing to take the journey with the spiritual Travelers and not give up on seeing the very face of God or HURAY ITSELF.

Upon awakening one morning I went into contemplation and closing my eyes I looked inwardly. In the pure, all knowing, eternal light and the other worldly music of pure spirit, its voice was within everywhere. Within this light filled Pure Positive God World I came upon the Ancient VARDAN Master who was the Living VARDAN Master of Ancient Greece whom most knew as Plato.

His face was round and intelligent and he wore a white

beard yet his features were misty and lightly glowing as his radiance as Soul was glorious.

In that moment he communicated in the unspoken language that translates it's impressions to the mind, "Soul in her eternal slumber cuts from herself her own wings, like the spiritual things that lift her to God itself. And so it is with most of us if we don't correct ourselves. In my own future life, in spite of my spiritual attainments I find myself uncontrolled in lower appetites, over eating. It causes me sorrow and suffering. Soul lingers in her vices and the passions of vanity, lust, greed, anger, and attachment. And these have increases or decreases. If these passions have unfortunate increases that which is negative seeks possession of the Soul in these things. Soul in her bondage must turn her back on the vice completely. And turn instead and only look upon the face of God."[15]

"When the alcoholic takes to her drink, one sip will be her undoing. And so it is, he is wise in the way of things who will remove these things from all sight and deal with them like a tentacled creature and has completely taken it from the flesh. Not one part remains of it. It must be disposed of and never touched, fasted from and removed like a poison."

In that moment an image appeared of a man who was a former drug user. Prior to his recovery he was shown a fast of juices or waters. The fast he did over a period of time and it restored in him a feeling of release, relief, and joy. He restored his inner peace and inner self control and he remained off the drugs and changed his life for the better to focus on higher things. From my view point Addictive

---

15. Plato often poetically referred to Soul as "her" or "she" even though he was aware that Soul is an IT and has no gender.

drugs are dangerous physically and spiritually. For this reason the VARDAN Masters state that addictive drugs are not permitted by those who study the works of VARDANKAR.

Then after the image faded Plato continued, "The Adepts of the Ancient Order of Bourchakoun, the VARDAN Masters have released themselves of all worldly things and can yet live within them. The VARDAN Masters live in the state of detachment. This means nothing shackles Soul and Soul places its attention upon God. No man controlled by the lower nature or Kal power can truly work as a coworker with God until he be divinely controlled by the God force in him instead and surrendered to God willingly and consciously."

"As you have heard before, detachment is not to be cold and unkind, without love. Detachment is but being able to flow and not stay destroyed for losses. Detachment is to not hold tight to be for something nor not to hold tight to be against something. It is to not with excess, cling and cherish our beliefs and self-made opinions which tie us like irons (chains) of our own devices."

Then, I again saw an image of a highly evolved higher initiate with striking dark eyes. He unknowingly in spite of his tremendous spiritual accomplishment succumbed to the invisible presence of vanity which subtly took him over without his knowledge. He was a good person and yet he began to take great pride in his elevated spiritual position as a spiritual leader. When we put ourselves subtly or directly to feel that we tower above others and judge them as lesser instead of recognizing the God self in those that surround us, we create our own undoing. Our purpose as coworkers is to infuse the God power in each other and not belittle or look down on our spiritual brothers.

At this, I recall one spiritual guru who thought he was

clever. He found ways to remote view or spy on, control and push his students to lower spiritual levels and into ignorance. He was completely unaware that the deeper into ignorance he pushed these individuals the deeper into the lower astral plane he descended, moving deeper into ignorance himself.

Plato continued his discourse, "Even the most advanced spiritual students into the higher or highest levels can without their knowledge be susceptible to vanity's sting. It is tricky and conniving and will like a snake, slither its way into a person's consciousness. The person will rationalize and lie to himself that this is not vanity which leads him but that he is a superior spiritual being. Humility is knowing that all Souls are superior spiritual beings that haven't realized it yet or have realized it."

"When we hold people back in our dreams we awaken to find our own hands grasping at our own throats to choke ourselves; and so it is with Vanity."

I saw Plato as light and yet simultaneously I saw Plato's mature bearded face as he communicated, "Vanity is another iron (chain) we chain ourselves to the wheel of transmigration. Reincarnation and bondage is vanity's only prize. And from this iron she can free herself and set free her higher spiritual attribute. All we must do is one day decide: I have accidently let myself be vain. I am done with it. And like that it's gone. All people are worthwhile and I stand in judgment of no one. Then she is freed, like a bird that knows itself, and in its wisdom reclaims its wings."

"The VARDAN Masters are the shining lights of HURAY which like the towering beacon shows you the way. It is priceless beyond measure to be shown the way through the world of darkness. Out from the world of darkness is Truth, Wisdom, and the God force. The Soul herself can bring out the God force in herself in leaving her body and goes to her true home."

Gratitude flowed from me to him in his expressions. And his light form faded from view into the light around us.

And then after a long pause within this inner realm came Kassapa who was the Living VARDAN Master during the destruction of what some see as mythical and others see as true, land of Atlantis of the ancient time. His insights shed light.

Kassapa began, "I watched as a once great land vanished and was destroyed in fire and water Man in his foolishness destroys himself. This is the way of black magic and the defilements of Soul, eventually it destroys the user."

"Those who came with me and left their life in Atlantis for the new country managed to break free from the downward pull and stay spiritually pure in spite of enticements not to. The entire people of Atlantis, like so many sheep, in spite of their once admirable spiritual advancement were blindly lead astray by beings that were once spiritually admirable themselves. Spiritual purity requires vigilance."

"This is why the spiritual student of VARDANKAR always has the Living VARDAN Master in his spiritual eye. He will lift him out of the negative pull and free him from spiritual bondage."

"Although the negative polarity seems to give rewards, its only aim is destruction. The destruction of the self in it and those around him. The positive polarity likewise within the lower spheres aim for him to build a bigger prison, an Earthly utopia and all things positive. These things positive and negative lead to the same place."

"On the middle path we become as spirit, not of this lower world and not bound by it but beyond it."

"Detachment is the individual's armor in these worlds which he defends with vigilance. And with his armor he carries the shield of spirit that guides him in accordance with God's will."

18
GOD CONSCIOUSNESS

Allen and I did a spiritual exercise together in preparation to write this chapter together. We both often had experiences with various spiritual beings and VARDAN Masters. Such was normal in our household. What follows for this amazing chapter is expressed by Allen in his own words and those of the Great VARDAN Master Rebazar Tarzs.

"Upon hearing this chapter title my first reaction was how difficult a task it would be to write about such lofty things as God Consciousness and God Realization. Fortunately I was aware that Rebazar Tarzs wished to speak on the subject.

Rebazar began, "On the matter of God Consciousness or God Realization I'm going to speak. There is a great misunderstanding in this world regarding God Consciousness."

"What most refer to as Self Realization and God Consciousness are in reality nothing but the Astral or perhaps the Mental plane. But even here most of those who speak of God Consciousness have not even reached the upper realms of the Astral Plane and received Astral enlightenment."

"The intellectual man creates a series of words, pictures, and images along with feelings and spews them out as if they were God Consciousness. Such fools are only deluding themselves and their followers. For if you get a man in a room and ask him a series of questions eventually you will realize that he does not believe he can experience God in the form of God Consciousness."

"What he will speak of, and usually of a lofty nature, will generally be positive qualities of the mind, such as human love, compassion, kindness, charity and so forth. He will talk about penetrating the mysteries of the universe, of possessing great knowledge and the power to control situations, time, space, and physical matter."

"None of this is God Consciousness, but only aspects of the lower worlds of duality. Such fools are like men who walk around with photographs of various objects and try to pretend the photographs are real. I suppose a better analogy would be a man who walks around with a stick drawing much like a two year old would draw and tries to convince himself that the stick drawing is a real person. So we see few men and women really believe they can meet with God and experience true God Realization."

"Their incessant chatter has little or nothing to do with the subject at hand, which is going into the great Ocean of Love and Mercy where dwells the great HURAY (God) and receiving the experience of becoming that which IS. One finds the saying: "I am that I am" applies here. And there is no mental apparatus required in the true God Worlds of VARDAN."

Rebazar continued, "Let me get to the heart of the matter, oh blessed ones, for I have been beating around the bush with this discourse and I have perhaps failed to completely and utterly make my point."

In VARDANKAR we must venture into the various high worlds of God, until our spirit, the VARDAN, the great universal light and sound is completely placed upon the great Ocean of Love and Mercy. There we behold in all its splendor the mighty HURAY."

"All obstacles, resistance, and the last futile attempts of the lower self must be dropped at once, in order to see the face, the true face of the HURAY."

"Any illusion that we are composed of, our past, present, and future must be destroyed like paper in a burning furnace. The HURAY will expect total dedication, surrender and joy; for it is uniting with a part of ITSELF that we call Soul. And the HURAY is only interested in meeting and uniting with the purified essence of ITS divine imagination. We are as Soul this purified essence of divine imagination. We as Soul are this pure essence. The great creative spark that the HURAY loves us so much that it has given a part of itself that is loosely termed Soul. But make no mistake, it is the only part of ourselves that is eternal."

"And within this part known as Soul, is the Power, all the Love, Wisdom, Power and Freedom. All charity, compassion, knowledge...Any quality imaginable, Soul has access to, provided it is mature enough to be responsible for its own creations. So I say unto you, be not fearful of meeting and seeing the true face of God. Do not look as if it is an abstract concept, a generality, a colloquial expression or a poetic picture made out of words and images, for true God Consciousness is to look up on the face of HURAY and cry out with joy, "I am that I am." And to become what you always have been but were unconscious of. Being infinite, Omnipresent, Omnipotent, and Omniscient."

"The HURAY has taken part of itself, ITS divine imagination, ITS divine consciousness and it has like an ocean whose foam becomes a fine mist distributed its essence in the form of countless individual droplets that we call Soul. These droplets or Souls undergo a form of amnesia, actually this is not completely true but let us say they are not fully conscious of their own divinity. These Souls take on the lower bodies and become chained in order that they may become purified through a long series of virtually countless states of consciousness and incarnations on the various lower planes."

"The Kal desires that no Soul shall be free and that no Soul shall believe it is possible to gaze upon the face of the HURAY."

"It is up to you to decide whether you are willing to completely surrender and recognize that you are God. Not the God of the ego or the Kal, but the God Self that reunites with HURAY to become a conscious coworker throughout eternity!"

And with that Heather, Gah-Shy-Zah and I were standing in the middle of a world of white light and sound and we realized throughout the entire discourse we had never left it. It stretches for vast distances beyond time and space into eternity.

Shimmering particles of light whirled about in circular motions, spinning and spinning its cosmic light particles again like a spiraling galaxy of light and sound, for this was the Anami Lok.

A great mass of white light hung before us in the distance. And yet again through this sucking sound and swirling like we were pulled in as though pulled through a slow spinning cosmic mass of swirling light.

Again we emerged in a world of even more brilliant white light and sound, so intensely bright it was beyond description.

291

And in the distance beyond that a vast stretch of magnificent white light and sound was an Ocean. So beautiful was this Ocean that words cannot describe it. So vast and still, in timelessness as though frozen.

We began to move closer toward this ocean. And I noticed it was comprised of countless particles of light that were Souls. And yet many of them were undifferentiated Souls that flowed and moved in various directions.

A white source of light hung in an azure sky above this immense Ocean. And from this white light emanated a sound that was indescribable and I knew at once that I had to move toward this light. To my surprise as I moved toward the light I discovered that this Ocean of Love and Mercy was everywhere. There is no place where it was not.

It seemed like the closer I moved toward this light, the larger the light became and the further I had to go. I used terms like closer and further to describe an experience beyond time and space. But words cannot describe accurately. I can only attempt a description. As I moved closer to the center of the light at first the sound got louder and the light brighter. But then the reverse began to occur.

The sound began to get fainter and the light began to take on a quality of white mist, less intense than before. It seemed I was moving toward less and less light and a finer and softer sound. And the closer I got to the center, the softer the sound and the less light, then I realized I was moving into the inner part of the HURAY, the Dhunatmik. The part that could not be spoken of, that has no qualities, the part that is indefinable.

What happened next is almost impossible to describe. I found myself in what appeared to be the center where there was pure Beingness but that no quality or qualities existed. And I was suddenly aware that I was in the center of my own Beingness and that the center of my Beingness appeared to be in union with the center of the HURAY's Beingness as if they were in perfect alignment. And suddenly I had access to the part of myself and that part of the HURAY which is pure and has no qualities. This was the center of the Ocean of Love and Mercy and yet it was the center of my own consciousness. And they appeared to be one and yet the consciousness of the HURAY although it was indescribable was infinitely larger.

Then suddenly to my surprise Gah-Shy-Zah appeared not as a white light but as a Soul; and I suddenly realized that this place or this state of existence was truly beyond space and time, for in the past I had falsely believed that one has to be alone. Initially on our first entrance this may be true. But I truly understood that Soul has absolutely no limitation and that the only law in all of the universe is the law of love and that the law of love is solely based upon the pure undeniable consciousness.

Suddenly and with great joy Gah-Shy-Zah and I shot out of the center of the HURAY into shimmering worlds of golden light. Realizing that all of this was infinite, eternal and flowed from an endless wellspring of the pure inner consciousness of the HURAY. And we realized that the HURAY had no qualities to its inner side and that we had no qualities to our inner side.

That we were nothing and we were everything and that the outer side of us was the expression of the inner side and that the two were in eternal balance and the inner must express the outer in this endless wellspring of infinite potential.

19
A COWORKER WITH HURAY

Heather and I walked on a beautiful sunlit beach. We could hear the surf gently rolling across the sand. Seagulls were singing and we could smell the ocean scent of seaweed and salt water upon our nostrils. A beautiful yellow orange sun that appeared graced the horizon as it was setting against a yellow orange sky.

I looked into Heather's beautiful dark brown eyes and she smiled gently. The sound of the ocean swelled and then faded and we soon became aware of the VARDAN sound current.

A tiny song bird began to fly almost as through it came from the center of the sun and rapidly flew toward us. As it flew it began to sing the most beautiful bird song. It seemed to drown out the ocean and all the seagulls.

The tiny sparrow flew toward us without skipping a single note and flew between our shoulders. As we turned around in amazement we saw the forest trees in the background behind the ocean and the great VARDAN Master Yaubl Sacabi gently took his finger, held it up and too our amazement the tiny bird landed on it and frantically sang an even more beautiful melody and danced in a circle with its tiny feet going round and around Yaubl's finger.

The bird almost appeared drunk with happiness and began to jump on top of his finger a quarter inch up and down. In fact the bird seemed so happy to see him that Heather and I stood motionless as Yaubl Sacabi grinned from ear to ear. Then the bird headed back toward us, landed on Heather's head and began to do the same dance on her head for several seconds and then flew away across the beautiful beach.

Yaubl motioned us to come toward the forest. Soon the three of us were sitting on a fallen tree surrounded by large Cedar and maple and elm trees. Although the bird had disappeared along the waterline, his brothers and sisters were serenading us with sweet melodious sounds.

Yaubl Sacabi looked into our eyes with such compassion and love that Heather and I could not help but have great reverence for this magnificent Soul.

Then he began to speak, "The key to immortality is endless giving of oneself without thinking of reward. Does the sun clamor for compliments or recognition. Does the bird sing for applause? Does the true lover love their beloved in order to gain from him? Does the Mother love the baby so the baby will give love back to her?"

"No, I say pure love is but the pure light and sound emanating from each Soul as a sun emanates light and must be given freely without thought of reward, without fear, simply coming from the Beingness of one's Soul, the Isness of one's Soul, the Hereness and Nowness of one moment. The moment when love shines its light upon the beloved and in that moment man and women become closer to God for this is the nature of the HURAY to give its love ceaselessly, endlessly, unconditionally without expectation, without conditions."

"You will recall the story of that Police Officer who witnessed a five year old child fall from a bridge. There was no time to call a rescue squad. No time to even formulate a plan. The current was swift and the Police Officer immediately dropped his gun belt onto the floor and jumped into the river with shoes, pants, and shirt. He was lucky that day or perhaps the VARDAN protected him and the child, Yaubl laughed softly. Although he almost drowned along with the child, he managed to save the day."

"The reporters wanted to question the Officer Hero and so they asked him, "When you jumped into the freezing river weren't you afraid you were going to die?" At which he replied, "I wasn't thinking of anything except that I needed to rescue the child." "And so we must learn to discipline our thoughts and become single minded in action, thought, and deed." At which point Yaubl fell silent, touched his hand to his chin and seemed to be waiting as if for questions."

I looked to him and said, "Master, how does one know that the love they give in service is the purest, highest love and not tainted with ego or one of the five passions?"

Yaubl replied, "Just as the fiery heat of the sun will burn up all impurities around it, Soul must become lost in the fiery heart of God's light and sound. Again this is accomplished through total surrender. Yes, it is true that the lower bodies can be impure and that man can engage in selfishness. But this should never be the focus, for nothing can survive the pure light and sound that is not in harmony with its nature."

"So I say to have no fear that your love and your service will be tainted with vanity, lust, greed, or attachment, for if one can completely surrender these things, the lower nature will drop away like a mirage in the desert sun. One must however love God, the VARDAN, the inner Master and truth and of course that pure part of themselves known as Soul, more than life itself."

"One must of course learn to die daily during their spiritual exercises. One must learn to let their imagination soar freely and take responsibility for their own creations. Only a fool is afraid of his own creations."

"The second one understands that they have created something, they have gained the power of attention. We do not uncreate something. But we can take our attention off of it with the same effect. An object, problem, situation can only exist if Soul feeds it energy. When the attention is completely withdrawn, in effect it appears to disappear."

"Some call this grace but it is not grace. Grace is far greater than this. Grace is the expression of the HURAY's endless love for Soul. What I described previously is simply the mechanical workings of the lower worlds. Grace is the path of love. It is however useful to understand that mechanical nature of the mind. For it can be like a steel trap; inflexible, unyielding, and difficult to defeat. It is however well within the control of Soul who uses the divine imagination and is disciplined enough to place its attention upon the object of its desire and not upon the negative reality of the Kal Niranjan."

"Grace represents the divine blessings of the HURAY and the birthright that each and every Soul has as a drop from the Ocean of Love and Mercy. Grace requires nothing. It is not earned, nor is it a skill, nor is it something that requires any type of effort on the part of the Soul. Grace is a product of the Higher Worlds. While karma or cause and effect is a complex product of the universal mind power and is conditional, complex, and rather difficult to understand."

"The secret is that Soul is fully capable of realization through direct perception at the Soul Plane and above. Therefore no Soul is held back because its mind is not powerful enough or penetrating enough to solve the riddle of the Universal Mind Power."

"This is extremely liberating knowing that you don't think your way to spiritual freedom or cut some complicated deal with the cosmos. Never the less persistence, surrender, patience and humility are required more than any great intellectual prowess."

Yaubl then paused looking directly into the sun. The sound current lingered. In that moment Heather then spoke, "Master Yaubl, so many have confused ideas and don't know what being a coworker with HURAY is. From your knowingness what is being a God Realized coworker with HURAY?"

"The breath of God breathes life into all life with the incoming and outgoing wave. All sustaining, all pervasive, all knowing, all powerful; Omniscient, Omnipresent, Omnipotent. A VARDAN Master is a way shower. When we become a Spiritual Traveler we work in harmony with the divine IT, the HURAY, the VARDAN."

"The breath of God breathes new life into its creation. By becoming a pure channel you are like the breath of God bringing to life the spirit within."

"A coworker with God works for HURAY's universal cause in the interests and capacities unique to the Soul. The coworker listens to the voice of God and follows its will and voice like a melody."

"God is forever spinning out divine melodies, lifting Souls to IT. Being a coworker is to play these melodies of God to return its children to IT."

"The sweetest sound, like high pitched other worldly

298

sound flowed like a cosmic wave from some invisible God World. Perhaps the 10th plane or the Anami Lok or beyond it, we did not know. Flowing to us, around us, through us, in us. Forever pulsing, we felt this cosmic wave of light and sound grow brighter and brighter until the forest seemed to fade from view and all was the light and sound."

The End.

THE GOD HEAVENS/WORLDS
OF VARDANKAR

NAME OF PLANE	WORD	CLASSICAL NAME	SOUND
ABOVE 12 PLANES... HURAY REALIZATION... COVERS ALL WORLDS			
12. HURAY	UNSPOKEN WORD	HURAY - LIVING REALITY	MUSIC OF GOD OCEAN OF LOVE & MERCY
11. HURAY WORLD	UNSPOKEN WORD	HURAY LOK	MUSIC OF UNIVERSE
10. ANAMI LOK	HU	ANAMI LOK	SOUND OF A WHIRLPOOL
9. AGAM LOK	HUK	AGAM LOK	MUSIC OF THE WOODWINDS
8. HUKIKAT LOK	ALUK	HUKIKAT LOK	THOUSAND VIOLINS
7. ALAYA LOK	HUM	ALAYA LOK	DEEP HUMMING
6. ALAKH LOK	SHANTI	ALAKH LOK	HEAVY WIND
5. SOUL	HURAY	SAT LOK	SINGLE NOTE OF A FLUTE
━━━━━━━━━━━ DIVIDING LINE BETWEEN PSYCHIC ━━━ AND SPIRITUAL WORLDS━━			
ETHERIC TOP OF MENTAL	BAJU	SAGUNA-SAGUNA-BRAHM INTUITION	BUZZING OF BEES
4. MENTAL	AUM	BRAHMANDA BRAHM MIND	RUNNING WATER
3. CAUSAL	MANA	MAHA-KAL-PAR-BRAHM MEMORY	TINKLE OF BELLS
2. ASTRAL	KALA	SAT KANWAL - ANDA EMOTION	ROAR OF THE SEA
1. PHYSICAL	ALAYI	ELAM... SENSES	THUNDER

More Information

For more information on VARDANKAR you can visit www.Vardankar.com.

Other Books By the Authors

For other books by the Authors you may write: Direct Path Publishing, 1911 Douglas Blvd., 85-165, Roseville, CA 95661, or visit www.DirectPathPublishing.com

Spiritual Event Bookings

If you would like to book the Authors as Guest Speakers for an upcoming event please contact Direct Path Publishing at info@directpathpublishing.com or by postal mail at:
Direct Path Publishing, 1911 Douglas Blvd., 85-165, Roseville, CA 95661.

Media

The Authors are available for magazine and newspaper interviews or reviews as well as radio and TV appearances as experts in the field of out-of-body travel to Heavens.

Bibliography

Twitchell, Paul, *The Tigers Fang*. New York, NY: Lancer
   Books Publishing. 1969.

Eadie, Betty, and Curtis Taylor. *Embraced By The Light*. New
   York, NY: Gold Leaf Press and Bantam Books, 1994.

Brother Lawrence, *Conversations and Letters of Brother Lawrence.
   The Practice of the Presence of God*. New York, NY: One
   World Publications. 2009.

Redfield, James. *The Celestine Prophecy*. New York, NY: Time
   Warner Books, 1993.

Twitchell, Paul. *The Shariyat-Ki-SUGMAD Book I & II*.
   Illuminated Way Press. Las Vegas, Nevada. 1971.

Roddenberry, Gene, *The Original Star Trek Series*. Paramount
   Television, 1967- 1969.

Sarris, Arian. *Healing the Past*, St. Paul, MN: Llewellyn
   Publications, 1996, 1997.

Author Unknown, *Charts of Heavens*, Sant Mat, Radhasomi,
   Surat Shabda Yoga, Spiritual Awakening Radio.com,
   2010, Paul Twitchell.

Tolle, Eckhart, *The Power Of Now*, A Guide To Spiritual
   Enlightenment. Vancouver, B.C., Canada: Namaste
   Publishing. 1999, 2004.

Twitchell, Paul. *Eckanakar The Key To Secret Worlds*. San Diego,
   CA. Illuminated Way Press, 1969.

Brinkley, Dannon. *At Peace in The Light*. Harper Collins
   Publishers. New York, NY. 1995.

About The Authors

Allen Feldman and Heather Giamboi are Authors and Speakers on the subject of out-of-body travel and near death like experiences of Heaven. They teach people how to reestablish a personal contact with heaven and with God. They claim you do not have to physically die in order to visit the various Heavens but can do so through Out-of-Body Tuza (Soul) Travel if guided and instructed properly. Allen and Heather are officially recognized Spiritual Travelers in the teachings of VARDANKAR the Ancient Science of Soul movement. They instruct individuals step by step in how to journey to higher and higher levels of heaven and consciousness and to become conscious coworkers with God.

Allen is the author of an out-of-body study program that takes his students far beyond so-called Astral Travel, Prayer or Meditation and teaches them how to leave there physical bodies and reach the various planes or worlds spoken of in this book.

Perhaps what sets Heather and Allen apart most is that they emphasize the vast differences between the Pure Positive God Worlds beyond Duality, Matter, Energy, Time and Space and what is known as the lower worlds that are often confused as the true God Heavens. They teach methods only known to a few on how to leave ones physical body and safely move out of the body into the ecstatic states of consciousness and reach true Self and then God Realization. They teach a series of Spiritual Exercises and methods that are vastly different from prayer and mediation. Finally, not only do they work on the outer through the writing of books, discourses and giving talks but they work with their students on the Inner during dreams and contemplation. More information can be found at www.VARDANKAR.com

Made in the USA
Las Vegas, NV
06 January 2025

15937360R00167